LODOWICK BRYSKETT
A DISCOURSE OF CIVILL LIFE

Number 4 of the San Fernando Valley State College
Renaissance Editions

LODOWICK BRYSKETT
A DISCOURSE OF
CIVILL LIFE

Edited by

Thomas E. Wright

San Fernando Valley State College
Northridge, California
1970

TABLE OF CONTENTS

ACKNOWLEDGEMENTS

THE editor is obliged to Professors Albert Baca and Carmelo Gariano of San Fernando Valley State College for their assistance in checking the Latin and Italian passages original to Bryskett, to Mr. Andrew M. McLean of the University of North Carolina for his bibliographic help, to Mrs. Arlene Marder for her biographical research, to Mrs. Sarah Wallace, Mrs. Carol Imlay, and Mr. Robert Luzardo for their assistance in preparing the text. I am appreciative of the use of the Giraldi text in the Elmer Belt Library of Vinciana in the University of California, Los Angeles. Finally, I am most happy to acknowledge the encouragement of my wife and the scholarly contributions which the Editors of Renaissance Editions have made to the completion of my work.

T. E. W.

San Fernando Valley State College
Northridge, California

INTRODUCTION

Lodowick Bryskett was the son of Italian parents.[1] His father, Antonio Bruschetto, an affluent merchant and important, long time resident of the Italian colony in London, was naturalized in 1536. The family had some ten years earlier come from Genoa. The denization clerk, faced with the family name " Bruschetto," Englished it to Bryskett, the word closest in sound and spelling; he may have thought " brisket " (the lower part of the breast of an animal or the cut of meat) to be the English equivalent of the Italian surname. Instead of Ludovico or even Lewis, our author, born about 1546, was given the stout, English equivalent — Lodowick. As Antonio Bruschetto's third son, Lodowick in his own account in the *Discourse of Civill Life* states that his father educated him so that " before I was five yeares of age, I had gone through mine Accidence, & was sent to schoole to Tunbridge, 20 miles from London."[2] But he complains that he soon fell ill from " the quartaine ague," an " unhappie accident," and that " not onely the health and strength of my body, but my learning also met with a shrewd checke, which I could never sithens recover sufficiently."[3] His father, nevertheless, brought school-masters to their home, and by his fourteenth year Bryskett was ready for university.

The young Bryskett entered Cambridge in 1559 as a pensioner in Trinity College, but left without taking a degree, perhaps because he was needed in the family business due to some reverses in the Marian period.[4] His early adolescent years were hardly over when, around 1562, probably at the age of sixteen, he seems to have acted as a traveller for the family firm in Italy. Sometime in 1564 or 1565 he was engaged in the service of Sir Henry Sidney of Penshurst in Kent, the father of the famous poet and Queen Elizabeth's Lord-deputy in Ireland. This new direction in Bryskett's life may have come about by the arrangement of Sir William Cecil, later Lord Burghley, and a friend of Bryskett's father.[5] Lodowick Bryskett very probably saw Ireland, the principal arena for his long civil service career, for the first time late in 1565 when Sir Henry Sidney was appointed for the second time Lord-deputy of Ireland. He remained in the service of the Sidney family until he was twenty-eight years of age — certainly a formative and important decade in a young man's life. Sir Henry sent him not only to Italy in the late 1560's, but also assigned him as one of his son Philip's two companions on a grand tour of Europe (1572–1574). If Bryskett's father had not died in 1574, when family affairs demanded that Lodowick return to England, Bryskett might well have stayed on in the young Sidney's company for the rest of the tour. With Sidney, Bryskett witnessed the St. Bartholomew Day massacre in Paris, in 1572, and also visited Strasbourg, Frankfort, Vienna, and Venice. Bryskett might have recorded that eighteen year old Sidney and he had done more than scale the Alps and Apennines.[6]

In 1575, Sir Henry Sidney was appointed Lord-deputy for Ireland for the third time; he took Bryskett there as clerk to the Privy Council — a position in which Bryskett was responsible for the minutes, correspondence, and supervision of the office staff, especially the attesting to the authenticity of all documents copied. Bryskett now moved into the more public and varied years of his life, for from 1575 to about 1600, he was deeply involved in Irish politics and in close contact with the Queen and her chief ministers in a variety of roles. He spent a good deal of time in England and had a deputy in his place. Although his letters reveal Bryskett (as John Lievsay characterizes him) to be " a literate and forceful, if not always a tactful correspondent," one must not underestimate the esteem in which he was held by Hubert Languet, Sir Philip Sidney's spiritual mentor, the powerful Sir Francis Walsingham, and Lord Burghley.[7]

His public career in his thirties is marked by a series of sinecures, the most notable being those of clerk in chancery for faculties (1577) — a post in which Spenser succeeded him in 1581 (their long friendship may have started as early as 1577) — and general controller of customs in wines in Irish ports (1579). Bryskett was also the private secretary of Sir William Drury in 1578–1579, and was visiting in London in 1579 and the early part of 1580. He did not, however, get the top civil service post — secretary of state to the Irish government — in 1581 when Sir John Challoner died. Geoffrey Fenton, the assistant, and possibly a relative, succeeded to the post for which, Bryskett complained, he was better qualified after his sixteen years' experience in Irish affairs.[8] But, in the summer of 1581, Bryskett was on tour of the northern provinces in Ireland with the new deputy, Arthur, Lord Grey, and was one of the commissioners appointed to meet the rebel Turlough Lynagh at the Ulster Blackwater. Bryskett helped to persuade Turlough to co-operate with the new Lord-deputy.[9]

Then, in 1582, Lord Grey was recalled; Bryskett and Spenser, who approved of his harsh military methods, were both temporarily deflected in their careers. Spenser lost his post as Lord Grey's secretary, and Bryskett went into semi-retirement from public affairs. Meanwhile, he had married, and a son, significantly christened Philip, had been born in 1580, and he acquired border lands, formerly monastic properties, near Enniscorthy, County Wexford. Bryskett's fortunes improved somewhat when, in 1583, Lord Grey and probably Walsingham secured for him the reversion of the better paying post of clerk of the Council of Munster. Spenser became Bryskett's deputy as early as 1584 and continued to serve until 1589. Although he probably never performed the duties, Bryskett remained in this important position and drew the fees until 1600.

Approaching his fifties, Bryskett was clerk of casualties in 1595, apparently steward to Sir Henry Wallop, and Sheriff of Wexford (the equivalent at the time of a local military commander as well as a legal officer); Spenser in 1598 was Sheriff of Cork. The terrible reversals in the rebellion of 1598 forced Bryskett and his family to flee to England, but his neighboring landowner and estate manager, Spenser, was not so fortunate in escaping safely — evidence suggests that Spenser may have lost some of his family in the burning and sacking of castle Kilcolman. Spenser died in 1599, and the loss of this friendship may have been an even greater one to Bryskett than that of Sir Philip Sidney who had died in 1586. The literary legacies of friendship with Sidney and Spenser are in Spenser's sonnet 33 of the *Amoretti* addressed to Bryskett, and in Bryskett's two poems, *The Mourning Muse of Thestylis* and *A Pastorall Aeglogue upon the Death of Sir Philip Sidney, Knight*, both in memory of Sidney, published at the end of Spenser's *Astrophel* (1595). In Spenser's *Colin Clouts Come Home Againe* Bryskett may be identified as " Thestylis."[10]

Bryskett, now in his fifties, was forced to live away from his Irish properties for more than a decade. He kept busy in the secret service. In 1600, he was captured and imprisoned as a spy in the Lowlands, and was important enough to the aging Elizabeth to be ransomed in 1601 for the Jesuit Fernand Cardin and a companion, and Hortensio Spinola. During the imprisonment, a daughter named Elizabeth was born. In 1603, he tried to settle in Chelsea, west of the estate which had been Sir Thomas More's, but he ran into trouble with his neighbor, the vicious, eccentric Earl of Lincoln. His sister, Lucretia (married in 1558 to Vincent Guicciardini), died in 1608, and Bryskett followed her before the end of 1612 at about the age of 65.[11] At the end of their study, his biographers Henry R. Plomer and Tom Peete Cross give this harsh and sad appraisal of Bryskett's life:

> Why was it, we may ask, that a man of Bryskett's education and experience never rose to any higher office than clerk of the Council of Munster and ended his days in poverty and obscurity? That he was a man of indolent nature, that he was always ready to draw his salary without giving much in turn, is evident. . . . And it may be also that his tongue was unruly and he was apt to be too outspoken. His sturdy championship of Lord Grey of Wilton, was perhaps another reason why Elizabeth and her ministers refused to recognize his undoubted abilities or to take advantage of his long experience of Irish affairs.[12]

More recent research into Bryskett and his family by Deborah Jones suggests that his fortunes improved considerably before he died; he recovered his Irish properties, and he had not of course ever lost what he inherited from his prosperous father and what he had increased in England. Neither his will, however, nor his grave in Ireland has ever been found.

2

A Discourse of Civill Life : Containing the ethike part of Morall Philosophie. Fit for the instructing of a Gentleman in the course of a vertuous life[13] was printed but once, in 1606, and entered by Edward Blount in the Stationers' Registers on March 10 (STC 3958); the copyright probably was held with William Aspley, whose name appears on the title page of a duplicate issue (STC 3959). This work, however, written over twenty years earlier, was the product, as Bryskett insists, of that short period of semi-retirement enforced on him by the recall of Lord Grey in 1582. Bryskett was living in Ireland, which he calls " this barbarous countrie . . . where almost no trace of learning is to be seene "; however, he was comfortably located within the more settled Pale, near Dublin. Though he was close enough to the government to carry on some official business, Bryskett regarded this interruption as a chance for him to read and write on subjects — certainly the ethical and political parts of moral philosophy — which he had to put aside when his public career started in the early 1560's. He is explicit in the prefatory letter, " To the Gentle and Discreet Reader ": " the booke written first for my private exercise, and meant to be imparted to [Lord Grey] hath long layne by me, as not meaning (he being gone) to communicate the same to others."[14] But friends and a sense of social responsibility convinced him to publish the *Discourse*.

The *Discourse* is made up primarily of Bryskett's translation of Giambattista Giraldi's " Tre dialoghi della vita civile," the second, non-narrative part of *De gli hecatommithi* (1565).[15] Giraldi's company is fictionalized as traveling from Rome to Marseilles to escape the plague; they discuss over the course of three days the moral virtues that are needed for " Civil Life," which is seen to be the active rather than the contemplative life. In the first day the ideal education of the child is projected; in the second, the instruction of the young man from his childhood forward into his twenties; in the final, longest session, the flowering of all the active virtues in the mature man is examined thoroughly. Plomer and Cross believe this translation was completed as early as 1567, two years after Bryskett entered the service of Sir Henry Sidney; perhaps, his translation was part of his duties.[16] Bryskett, in the *Discourse*, inserts an eloquent tribute to Sir Philip Sidney and an appreciation of Sir Henry's education of his family.[17] Besides the Giraldi material, Bryskett also used the work of two other sixteenth century Italians: from Alessandro Piccolomini's *Della Institutione morale* (1560), Bryskett translated sections and inserted them in the third day's dialogue; probably from Stefano Guazzo's courtesy book, *La Civil Conversazione* (1574), Bryskett paraphrases one section on wine and inserts it into the second day's dialogue.[18]

Bryskett is even more eclectic in the making of what he calls " the first fruites " which the Muses have yielded him: he frames his translated material with a fictional device to match Giraldi's three dialogues, each of which is devoted to one day's discussion. With charming verisimilitude, Bryskett produces a group of eight friends who visit him in his cottage " somewhat more than a mile " from Dublin; each day's discussion is introduced and ended by their original conversation. The same interlocutors have the Giraldi translation reassigned to them, with Lelio — Giraldi's dominant speaker — assigned to " Bryskett " himself, while Giraldi's other speakers — the Romans Fabio and Torquato, and a nobleman of Genoa named Giovenetto — are replaced by Bryskett's eight speakers: Dr. John Long (the archbishop primate of Ardmagh); Sir Robert Dillon (chief justice of the common pleas); Master George Dormer (the Queen's solicitor); Captains Christopher Carleil, Thomas Norreiss, Warham St. Leger, and Nicholas Dawtrey; and Master Edmund Spenser.[19] The Dublin apothecary, Thomas Smith, appears only in the opening original discussion. The most famous name in the list — Spenser's — is placed below the representative of the clergy, the two legal officers, the four military officers, and precedes that of the apothecary's. Both Bryskett and Spenser were of the same rank socially.

This original material consists of a long introduction to the first of the three days' discussion, and framing discussions for the second and third days' discussions.[20] These segments are notably autobiographical; if the reader recognizes conventional attempts to win patronage in two prefaces — the original one to Arthur, Lord Grey who died in 1593, and the second one in 1606 dedicated to Robert, Lord Cecil, secretary of state in the new court of James I — there is no reason to discredit Bryskett's " Apologie " for living the contemplative life, however strong the tone of self-dramatization rings throughout the framing conversations. For Bryskett weaves a fascinating cloth of fictional and autobiographical facts in the first forty pages of the *Discourse* where he leads the reader up to the place in which the English translation of Giraldi begins.[21] An account of this opening conversation will provide most of the information needed to understand Bryskett's ethical purpose, atypical formal techniques, and synthetic use of a variety of subject-matters.

The *Discourse* proper begins with Bryskett incorporating the first prefatory letter to the late Lord Grey into his text; the transition is gradual — almost imperceptible — from the letter to the short, reported dialogue between "Bryskett," Sir Robert Dillon and the apothecary Smith, and then to the "occurring" dialogue (the conversation reported as happening in the present) between "Bryskett" and the eight speakers. The "occasion," Bryskett says, "of this discourse grew by the visitation of certaine gentlemen comming to me to my little cottage which I had newly built neare unto Dublin at such a time, as rather to prevent sickenesse, then for any present griefe, I had in the spring of the yeare begunne a course to take some physicke during a few dayes."[22] The company arrives when the apothecary, Mr. Smith, is present; Sir Robert Dillon asks him, "with a smiling counten-ance," to what intent "he with his drugs" should make Bryskett sick. The light badinage between Dillon and Smith leads to the claim that Bryskett's melancholy can be cured better by good company than by purging. Smith lets slip the rather embarrassing charge that Bryskett must have been "more then halfe mad or in a frensie" because he resigned an office "of good reputation and profit" which would lead to higher preferment.[23] Bryskett defends his retirement against Dillon's chiding that he had a good chance to enrich himself, "to rise in credite and reputa-tion." In his defense he replies at length that the office required "much writing and long standing . . . besides the extraordinary occasions . . . to travel, to sit up late, and disorder the body, had bred such an increase of rheume . . . and of infirmities" that he thought his life might be shortened.[24] So he had informed the Lord-deputy of his desire to resign, and gained his consent. Bryskett then notes that he has "found more quietnes and satis-faction in this small time" that he has lived to himself, enjoying the "conversation" of his books and husbandry; now he would not want to go back into "service about the State" for he has Lady Occasion by the foretop — he has "begunne to renew" his studies. Bryskett convinces the company, as Dillon admits, and the conversation moves to consider "what kind of studie" Bryskett is pursuing.[25]

Bryskett's answer is that he has not been studying to profit in law or divinity or medicine although "To Physicke I was by my fathers choice appointed" — he still reads "the authors of that science" but has no intention to practice medicine. Provi-dence, he says, had one time "made me of a scholer to become a servant " (when he left Cambridge ultimately to serve Sir Henry Sidney), and now providence has given him a chance to become like " a snaile into his shell " retiring to read virtuous books for the most part about " Morall Philosophie, which frameth men fittest for civil conversation, teaching them orderly what morall vertues are, and particularly what is the proper action of every one, and likewise what vice is, and how unseemly a thing, and how harmefull to a good mind the spot and contagion thereof is."[26] Master Dormer, however, finds a contradiction in Bryskett's apology: the study of moral philosophy is meant to prepare a man for action, for " such employments as the Prince or state shall lay upon him." Bryskett replies that he has not given up the active life entirely; otherwise he would not have retired so close to Dublin — he is still doing work for the Queen, the Lord-deputy and council " when occasion serveth." With auto-biographic frankness, however, Bryskett insists that one day now is more sweet than " in seven yeares before, whiles I was Clerke of the Councell." He aims " at so high a marke as humane felicitie."[27]

At this point the Lord Primate, surprised at Bryskett's statement, cautions him that man cannot in " this low and muddie world " achieve that which can only be found in heaven. Bryskett apologizes for using " the general world in stead of the par-ticular " — he meant " the active or practicke felicitie, consisting in vertuous actions " instead of the " contemplative felicitie " possible only in the future life.[28] On this distinction between matters of divinity and of moral philosophy rests most of Brys-kett's *Discourse*, especially in his use of Plato and Aristotle " in the Latine " as popularized by the Italians " *Alexander Piccolo-mini, Gio. Baptista Giraldi*, and *Guazzo*, all three having written upon the Ethick part of Morall Philosophie both exactly and perspicuously."[29] There is an interesting admission by Bryskett that wishing to " learne the shortest way to " moral philosophy, he found Plato and Aristotle " in the Greeke and Latine tongues " difficult to understand: " I confesse that I do not find that facilitie in the conceiving of their writings, as I could wish . . . For *Plato* hath couched his sense thereof so dispersedly in his dialogues, as I thinke he must be a man of great learning and exact judgement that shall picke them out, and sever them from the other parts of Philosophie . . . And *Aristotle* is not

so cleare nor so easily understood without deepe study . . ."
Here is where " the Italians, who have in their mother-tongue
late writers, that have with a singular easie method, taught all
that which *Plato* or Aristotle have confusedly or obscurely left
written." Bryskett wishes the same achievement to be made in
English " whereby our youth might without spending of so much
time, as the learning of those other languages require, speedily
enter into the right course of vertuous life."[30]

For a moment, Bryskett deflects the conversation away from
his own studies to " a gentleman in this company . . . perfect
in the Greek tongue, but also very well read in Philosophie,
both morall and naturall." He invites Master Spenser, who has
" encouraged me long sithens to follow the reading of the Greek
tongue, and offered me his helpe to make me understand it,"
to discourse on moral philosophy.[31] But Spenser asks to " be
excused at this time " for they know that " I have already undertaken a work tending to the same effect, which is in *heroical
verse*, under the title of a *Faerie Queene*, to represent all the
moral vertues, assigning to every vertue, a Knight to be the
patron and defender of the same."[32] He hopes to finish this
work which he has " already well entred into," but he does not
feel prepared with " good advisement and premeditation " to
discuss " the Ethicke part of Morall Philosophie." He suggests,
instead, that Bryskett read his translation of Giraldi's Italian
dialogue " comprehending all the Ethick part of Moral Philosophy . . . under the title of a dialogue of civil life."[33] Bryskett's
translation can even be helped in revision by the company hearing
and discussing it. The company agrees. They have " shewed an
extreme longing after his worke of the *Faerie Queene*, whereof
some parcells had bin by some of them seene . . ."[34] Now they
want Bryskett's product of his not inactive solitude which will
" greatly benefit others." Bryskett agrees when " with courteous
force they made me rise from where I sate to go fetch my
papers."[35] He complains that the translation is in " loose sheetes "
full of " blots and interlinings " and will take a long time to get
through. Dillon agrees, but presses Bryskett to try to " acquaint
us with those worthy conceits in our owne language, which you
have in the Italian found to be so delightfull."[36] He further
suggests that Bryskett need not " follow . . . exactly the forme
of the author "; Bryskett agrees finally to " omit the introduction

of the author to his dialogue, as a thing depending upon former matter and occasion, by which persons introduced by him are fitted for his purpose, & supposing this present companie to be as apt to conceive the reasons by him set downe, & to make as pertinent objections as they did, I will begin even there where he, following the course of most others that have written upon that subject, maketh entry into his discourse " which will take " three severall dayes."[37]

Bryskett, however, does not produce the kind of freewheeling critique of his translation as this fictional passage suggests: instead, Bryskett — the *persona* — starts to read his translation from Giraldi (after omitting the initial conversation), and the various speakers are reassigned to the members of Bryskett's company with an occasional inserted passage or many short deletions of the Giraldi text, usually to eliminate the interlocution in favor of a continuous oration by " Bryskett " (Lelio). In fact, Bryskett seems to view the prose dialogue form as an inferior method of discourse to that of the prose treatise which is basically an uninterrupted oration. In the prefatory letter to Lord Grey, Bryskett fully describes his purpose and method: " The course which I hold in this treatise, is by way of dialogue (which I have chosen as best pleasing to my minde) to discourse upon the morall vertues, yet not omitting the intellectuall, to the end to frame a gentleman fit for civill conversation, and to set him in the direct way that leadeth him to his civill felicitie."[38]

His model may be Giraldi's dialogue — the bulk of his text — but his use of conversation in the original introductory and closing sections to each of the three parts or days' discussions is like that of many Elizabethan prose dialogue writers. They do not imitate successfully the dialectic of the Platonic dialogue where, in the best of them, the Socratic *eiron* works to draw out the truth of a subject; instead, they follow the more easily imitated method of Cicero where a treatise or a piece of extended discourse is " interlocuted " — interrupted by fairly short questions and statements from one or more speakers who usually serve to support rather than refute a dominant speaker's exposition of the topic.[39] Bryskett's prose dialogue — the original as well as the translated dialogue of Giraldi — is atypically Elizabethan only in that he presents an interlocuted treatise on civil life with more than two speakers. Most prose dialogues in English in the sixteenth and earlier seventeenth centuries are interlocuted treatises with only two speakers, one of whom is obviously an authority, and the other speaker plays the role of a subservient " scholer " to the " master." In addition, Bryskett does not produce the usual moderated debate or the courtly disputation — those other two models of prose dialogue in renaissance English. In the moderated debate, such as John Donne's *Ignatius His Conclave* (1611), there is (as on the scholastic and academic model) a moderator or jury who pass judgment on the contending sides; Bryskett, however, makes a dialogue in which " Bryskett " is indubitably the authority. In the Elizabethan courtly disputation, such as Edmund Tilney's *Of Duties in Marriage* (1568), the whole work is structured as a debate, but the interlocutors are male and female (usually in a dinner party, country-house setting) and the subject-matter centers on *questioni d'amore*, the questions of love and/or marriage; there may not be a decision or judgment from a moderator. Bryskett, again, follows Giraldi in using only male *personae*, and avoids the subject-matter of courtly love (which John Lyly takes on in the first parts of *Euphues : the Anatomy of Wit* in 1578, and the sequel two years later, *Euphues and His England*). Perhaps Bryskett's *Discourse* is best described as an ethical discourse by way of orations (" set speeches ") and interlocution.

As such, the *Discourse* is an English compendium of moral philosophy heavily indebted to the Italian contemporary synthesizers, especially of Aristotle and Plato, but it is not without much original material, such as Bryskett's short story of the redeemed mastiffe, and his engaging dialogue framing the three days' conversations. It is no exaggeration to say that the *Discourse* is the prose dialogue equivalent of the materials presented more dramatically in Sidney's versions of *Arcadia* and Spenser's *Faerie Queene*, especially Books II, IV, V, and VI. In this sense, Bryskett's *Discourse*, a popularization of the code of *civilitas*, stands along with these great artifices which also present the ethics for the " instructing of a Gentleman in the course of a vertuous life."

NOTES TO THE INTRODUCTION

1. The most reliable biographical sources are Henry R. Plomer and Tom Peete Cross, *The Life and Correspondence of Lodowick Bryskett* (Chicago, 1927), and Deborah Jones, " Lodowick Bryskett and His Family," in *Thomas Lodge and Other Elizabethans*, edited by Charles J. Sisson (Cambridge, Mass., 1933), 243–362. Bryskett's complete correspondence is yet to be edited. The standard biographies of Sidney and Spenser also include information about Bryskett; the best, perhaps, is Alexander C. Judson, *The Life of Edmund Spenser* (Baltimore, 1945). The commentary to Spenser's prose dialogue, *A View of the Present State of Ireland*, ed. Rudolf Gottfried (Baltimore, 1949), in vol. IX, *The Prose Works*, of the *Variorum Edition*, contains some useful notes on Bryskett's career in Ireland; the earlier edition of *A View* by W. E. Renwick (London, 1934) is also useful.

2. Further page references to Bryskett's *Discourse* will be to the present edition: *Discourse*, p. 75.

3. Ibid.

4. Plomer and Cross, p. 3.

5. Plomer and Cross include an Appendix of Italian letters of Antonio Bruscheto to Cecil dating from 1560 to 1564, pp. 85–89.

6. See Bryskett's *A Pastorall Aeglogue upon the Death of Sir Philip Sidney, Knight*, and *The Mourning Muse of Thestylis*, the two poems on the death of Sidney which were printed at the end of Spenser's *Astrophel* (1595). (They were entered in the Stationers' Register in 1587.) These elegies on Sidney were paraphrasd from Bernardo Tasso's *Selva nella morte del Signor da Gonzaga*, and his first Eclogue, *Alcippo*; see W. P. Mustard, " Lodowick Bryskett and Bernardo Tasso," *American Journal of Philology*, XXXV (1914), 192–199. Deborah Jones in " Lodowick Bryskett and His Family," in *Thomas Lodge and Other Elizabethans*, ed. Sisson, finds echoes of Bryskett's commemorative poetry in Milton's *Lycidas* (245–253).

7. John Lievsay, *Stefano Guazzo and the English Renaissance (1575–1675)* (Chapel Hill, 1961), p. 84.

8. Fenton's career, incidentally, strangely parallels Bryskett's. Both translate and popularize Italian works — Fenton translated Guicciardini's *History of the Wars of Italy* (1579) — and both served in high places in Ireland and England. Another Munster official

and colonizer is Richard Beacon, who published at Oxford in 1594, *Solon His Follie, or A Politique Discourse, Touching the Reformation of Commonweales Conquered, Declined, or Corrupted*, a two speaker prose dialogue touching on Irish problems like Spenser's *View of the State Ireland* (1595). Another prose dialogue, *Axiochus*, "written by Plato . . . [and] Translated out of Greeke " by " Edw. [sic] Spenser " (according to Cuthbert Burbie's titlepage in 1592), is a Greek dialogue of unknown authorship "concerning the shortnesse and uncertainty of this life . . ."; it is edited in the *Variorum of Spenser*, vol. IX, 25–38.

9. In addition to the account of Bryskett's place in the Irish government given by Plomer and Cross, see Raymond Jenkins, " Spenser and the Clerkship in Munster," *PMLA*, XLVII (1932), 109–121. Alexander C. Judson gives more data on ten members closely associated with Bryskett and Spenser in " Spenser and the Munster Officials," *Studies in Philology*, XLIV (1947), 157–173.

10. C. S. Lewis in *English Literature in the Sixteenth Century* (Oxford, 1954) says that Thestylis (Bryskett) is one of four poets who " can be identified. After others the hunt is still up " (p. 371). Josephine W. Bennett even suggests that Bryskett, in London in the summer of 1587, may have shown around Spenser's *Faerie Queene* in MS; see *The Evolution of " The Faerie Queene "* (Chicago, 1942), p. 239. It is not improbable that Sir Walter Raleigh was also Bryskett's friend.

11. Jones, " Lodowick Bryskett and His Family," in *Thomas Lodge and Other Elizabethans*, 258–268, and 290–358 (where research on Bryskett's sister Lucrece is presented).

12. Plomer and Cross, p. 75.

13. The full title page reads: A/ DISCOVRSE/ OF CIVILL LIFE: / Containing the Ethike part/ *of Morall Philosophie./* Fit for the instructing of a Gentleman/ *in the course of a vertuous life.* BY LOD: BR./ *Virtute, summa: Cœtera Fortunâ/* LONDON,/ Printed for EDVVARD BLOVNT./ 1606. The Latin motto translates: " The greatest thing is done by virtue; the others by fortune." This motto is also printed at the end of Bryskett's " A pastorall Aeglogue " in Spenser's *Astrophel* (1595).

14. *Discourse*, pp. 5, 3.

15. Giraldi in his Latin verse called himself Cynthius; Cinzio was often added to his Italian name, and the Elizabethans knew him as Cynthio. Bryskett's large-scale use of Giraldi may be summarized in terms of numbers of pages (this edition's pagination). In the first day's dialogue, Bryskett uses 59 pages from

Giraldi and surrounds this material with 32 pages of original discussion at the beginning and about a page at the closing of the discussion. In the second day's dialogue, Bryskett uses 51 pages from Giraldi and, in the same fashion, surrounds this material with seven and one half pages of original discussion (some of this may be paraphrased from Guazzo's *La Civil Conversazione*) at the beginning and a little less than a page of original conversation at the end. In the third day's dialogue — the longest section of the *Discourse* — Bryskett complicates his text by inserting not only a large portion of Giraldi but also interrupting that material with a section of Piccolomini's *Della Institutione morale* and an original short story of the redeemed mastiffe. Bryskett begins the third day's dialogue with two and one half pages of original talk, then switches to a page of recapitulating discussion found in Giraldi, then interrupts with a half-page tribute to Sir Philip Sidney as an exemplary youth, and returns to the Giraldi text for 53 pages (with frequent very short, original insertions, viz. pp. 124–125, p. 130, p. 153). Here Bryskett explains he has "recourse to *Picolomini*" for a better description of the twelve moral virtues "appertaining to the civill life"; he explains that "I will speake particularly, following chiefly mine author [Giraldi]; but where need or occasion shall require, I wil for the cleerer understanding of the matter, supply out of *Picolomini* what I think is wanting" (Bryskett, *Discourse*, pp. 158–159). Bryskett returns to Giraldi for 20 pages of discussion of Fortitude and Temperance, then to Liberality, Magnificence and Magnanimity. Before discussing the virtue of Mansuetude, Bryskett inserts his original short story of the redeemed mastiffe as another example of magnanimity (over two pages). He uses two pages from Giraldi and nine pages from Piccolomini (with some omissions, viz. p. 178) for the rest of the virtues: Mansuetude, Desire of Honor, Veritie, Affability, and Urbanitie. He returns to the Giraldi text for about 27 pages of discussion of Justice and Prudence; he inserts an original protest that he "wants to close up this your feast" since evening is drawing on (pp. 195–6). Bryskett seems to be in a hurry to finish with the Giraldi text, for at p. 202 there is a hiatus and a short, original bridge passage (put in Master Spenser's mouth) before a brief discussion of the parts of the soul; at p. 204, there are two more hiatuses in Bryskett's use of the Giraldi text before he concludes at p. 205. There is a page of original discussion which ends the *Discourse*.

For a specimen of Bryskett's English translation and the

Giraldi original, see the Appendix. There is no reason to believe that Bryskett, raised in an Italian-English family, did not translate directly from Giraldi's 1565 text; William A. Ringler, Jr. in his edition of *The Poems of Sir Philip Sidney* (Oxford, 1962), p. xxi, says that Bryskett was Sidney's " chief servant " on the European tour, and " it was probably under his tutelage that he learned Italian during his nine-month stay in Italy " (1573–1574). However, he could have consulted the *Tre Dialoghi* as translated into French by Gabriel Chappuis in an Italian-French text, published in Paris in 1583.

16. Plomer and Cross, p. 78.

17. *Discourse*, pp. 119–120.

18. *Discourse*, pp. 158–159, where Bryskett explains his method of inserting portions of Piccolomini; and pp. 72–74 where the *vinum Cos* section is inserted. Lievsay finds Bryskett to echo Guazzo elsewhere in the *Discourse*; see *Stefano Guazzo and the English Renaissance*, pp. 78–88.

19. Historical sketches of Bryskett's *personae* are in Plomer and Cross, pp. 81–83. Bryskett's nine *dramatis personae* (including himself as " Bryskett ") are given original roles in the framing discussions, but speeches by the four Giraldi interlocutors (Lelio, Fabio, Torquato, and Giovenetto) are reassigned principally to " Bryskett " and several others. Long is the next most authoritative figure, while the two lawyers (Dillon and Dormer) and two of the four military men (Carleil and Noreiss) are about equal in their share of the original and reassigned material; Capt. Dawtrey and Spenser share the rest of the speeches while the last military man, Capt. St. Leger, and the apothecary Smith (who drops out after the first day's dialogue) are without any " set speeches " — uninterrupted discourse of more than two and one half pages. This number, of course, is arbitrary but conveniently locates in a quantitative way the prominent speakers. Note that Spenser's six " set speeches " occur only at the end of the third day's dialogue; this placement and his prominence in the exordium-like opening are curious. I can detect no pattern in the reassignment of Giraldi's *personae* besides the dominant Lelio; Bryskett in the first day's dialogue, for instance, assigns speeches by Fabio to Dillon and Dormer and assigns speeches by Giovenetto to Dillon, Carleil, and Long.

20. A. C. Judson in *The Life of Edmund Spenser* (Baltimore, 1945) says " the long introduction to the first day, appears to belong to the spring of 1582. But on the third day we learn that Grey's successor is now governor of Ireland "; " at least two years would

seem to have elapsed between the first and third days " (p. 107).

21. *Discourse,* p. 26. John Erskine's article, " The Virtue of Friendship in the *Faerie Queene,*" *PMLA,* XXX (New Series, Vol. XXIII) (1915), 831–850, is valuable mainly for a summary case against those earlier writers (such as Todd, Grosart and Jusserand) who took the conversations to be real reports; Erskine says " the fact is that except for some dramatic trimming, such as the reference to the *Faerie Queene,* except for the change of scene and persons, and except for that one passage from Piccolomini, Bryskett's book has been taken literally from Giraldi " (840).
22. *Discourse,* p. 7.
23. *Discourse,* p. 8.
24. *Discourse,* pp. 10–11.
25. *Discourse,* pp. 11–13.
26. *Discourse,* pp. 15–16. In Thomas Starkey's *Dialogue Between Pole and Lupset* (written between 1533 and 1536), Lupset corrects Pole's misinterpretation of " Civil Life ": " This is not the civil life that I mean — to live togidder in cities and towns so far out of order as it were a multitude conspiring togidder in vice . . . But this I call the civil life, contrary: living togidder in good and politic order, one ever ready to do good to another, and as it were conspiring togidder in all vertue and honesty. This is the very true and civil life " (ed. K. M. Burton, London, 1948, p. 27). I am indebted for this reference to Mr. Andrew M. McLean.
27. *Discourse,* pp. 16–18.
28. *Discourse,* pp. 18–19.
29. *Discourse,* pp. 20–21.
30. Ibid.
31. *Discourse,* p. 21.
32. *Discourse,* p. 22.
33. *Discourse,* pp. 22–23.
34. *Discourse,* p. 23.
35. *Discourse,* p. 24.
36. Ibid.
37. *Discourse,* pp. 24–25.
38. *Discourse,* p. 6. With the phrase " civil conversation " Bryskett translates Giraldi's *civile conversazione,* which means civil life or society, not talk. For a discussion of *conversazione* both as a social custom and a literary genre, see T. F. Crane, *Italian Customs of the Sixteenth Century and Their Influence on the Literatures of Europe* (New Haven, 1920), and J. W. Draper,

" Shakespeare and the *Conversazione*," *Italica*, XXIII (1946), 7–17. Crane regards Giraldi's book as a " dry and tedious philosophical disquisition, relieved at long intervals by a few classical anecdotes, and based largely on Aristotle's *Ethics* and Plato's *Republic and Laws* " (pp. 376–377), and Piccolomini's work as " based on Plato," an " elaborate treatise on education, in which the training suitable to the various ages is discussed " (p. 378). Crane also says that Guazzo's *La Civil Conversazione*, along with Castiglione's *Cortegiano* and della Casa's *Galateo*, " were the three popular handbooks of manners in Italy, and their vogue in other countries served to introduce Italian customs and manners and powerfully to mould society " (p. 396). Giraldi, of course, is better known in English literature for his collection of novels in the *Hecatommithi* which provided plots for Shakespeare in *Othello* and *Measure for Measure*, and for other Elizabethan writers.

39. The editor has in preparation a study of the techniques of prose dialogue in England, 1500–1660.

40. *Discourse*, pp. 174–176.

EDITORIAL PROCEDURE

The present volume attempts to give an accurate text of Lodowick Bryskett's *Discourse of Civil Life* in a moderately modernized printed edition based on one issue, STC 3958, for use of scholars who appreciate having a monograph sized text (instead of the microfilm roll) with a short introduction and notes. Permission to use the copy in the Folger Shakespeare Library has graciously been given.

There is no known MS. The first and only edition was in two issues in 1606: STC 3958 for Edward Blount, and STC 3959 for William Aspley. Both copies are identical; the only variant is the name change on the title-page. Bryskett's *Errata* have been silently incorporated into the present edition. Obvious typographical errors have been silently amended, viz. p. 12, l. 4, " cilmbing " changed to " climbing."

Modernization has been made of *i, j, u, v,* long *s,* and *vv.* Contractions have been expanded except for &. The original italics for proper names (except for the Lord Primate and Bryskett) have been retained to keep clear which persona is speaking. The Epistle to the Reader in italics has been set in roman type. Variations in the type of the titles has not been observed. Otherwise the intent was to reproduce a close facsimile of the original.

The notes to the text include the identification of direct quotations wherever possible. To identify the many other references would extend the size of the volume beyond the limits possible for the Series.

TO THE RIGHT HONORABLE, HIS SINGULAR GOOD LORD, ROBERT EARLE OF SALISBURY, VICOUNT CRANBORNE, LORD CECILL BARON OF ESENDEN, PRINCIPALL SECRETARIE TO HIS MAJESTIE, KNIGHT OF THE MOST NOBLE ORDER OF THE GARTER, &C.

This booke treating of the Morall vertues, being now to come under the censure of the world, doth summon me of it self to crave protection from your Lordships honorable favour, as the personage, who knowing best their worth, may best protect him from the injury of any that should attempt to carpe the same. And my private obligations for your manifold favours (among which, the great benefite of my libertie, and redeeming from a miserable captivitie ever fresh in my remembrance) doth make me hope, not onely of your Honors willingnesse to patronize both my selfe and my labour; but also that you wil be pleased therein to accept of the humble and devoted affection, wherwith most reverently I present it unto your Lordshippe. Vouchsafe therefore (my most honored good Lord) to yeeld me the comfort of so gracious an addition to your former favors and benefits: and to give to all the yong Gentlemen of England encouragement to embrace willingly that good which they may receive by reading a booke of so good a subject, the title whereof bearing in front your noble name, shall give them cause to think it worthy to be passed with the approbation of your grave judgement. Which being the most desired frute of my endevour, I will acknowledge as none of the least of your great graces, and ever rest

Your Lordships most bounden and
humbly devoted,
LOD: BRYSKETT.

1

TO THE GENTLE
AND DISCREET READER.

Right well saith the Wise man, that there is nothing new under the Sunne; and further, that there is no end of writing books. For howsoever in a generalitie the subject of any knowledge be declared; yet the particulars that may be gathered out of the same, be so many, as new matter may be produced out of the same to write thereof againe: so great is the capacitie of mans understanding able to attaine further knowledge then any reading can affoord him. And therefore *Horace* also affirmeth, that it is hard to treate of any subject that hath not bene formerly handled by some other.[1] Yet do we see dayly men seeke, partly by new additions, and partly with ornaments of stile, to out-go those that have gone before them: which haply some atchieve, but many moe rest farre behind. This hath bred the infinitenesse of bookes, which hath introduced the distinction of good from bad, used in best Commonweales, to prohibite such as corrupt manners, and to give approbation to the good. For that the simpler sort by the former drinke their bane in steed of medicine, and in lieu of truth (the proper object of mans understanding) they introduce falshood decked in truths ornaments, to delude the unheedful Reader. Whereas on the other side, the benefite which we receive by the reading of good books being exceeding great, they deserve commendation that offer their endevours to the benefiting of others with books of better matter. Which hath made me resolve to present unto thy view this discourse of Morall Philosophie, tending to the wel ordering and composing of thy mind, that through the knowledge and exercise of the vertues therein expressed, thou mayst frame thy selfe the better to attaine to that further perfection which the profession of a Christian requireth; and that everlasting felicitie, which, assisted with Gods grace (never refused to them that humbly and sincerely call for the same) thou mayst assuredly purchase. As my meaning herein is thy good chiefly: so let thy favourable censure thankfully acknowledge my labor and goodwil, which may move me to impart after unto thee another treating of the Politike part of

Morall Philosophie, which I have likewise prepared to follow this, if I shall find the favourable acceptation hereof such as may encourage me thereunto. The booke written first for my private exercise, and meant to be imparted to that honorable personage, *qui nobis haec otia fecit,*[2] hath long layne by me, as not meaning (he being gone) to communicate the same to others. But partly through the perswasion of friends, and partly by a regard not to burie that which might profit many, I have bin drawne to consent to the publishing thereof. Gather out of it what good thou canst: and whatsoever thou mayst find therein unperfect or defective, impute charitably to my insufficiencie and weaknesse; and let not small faults blemish my travell and desire to benefite thee.

But say to thy selfe with that worthy bright light
of our age *Sir Philip Sidney, Let us love men*
for the good is in them, and not
hate them for their evill.
Farewell.

A DISCOURSE, CONTAINING THE ETHICKE PART OF MORALL PHILOSOPHIE: FIT TO INSTRUCT A GENTLEMAN IN THE COURSE OF A VERTUOUS LIFE.

Written to the right Honorable Arthur *late Lord Grey of Wilton: By Lod: Bryskett.*

When it pleased you (my good Lord) upon the decease of maister *John Chaloner*, her Majesties Secretarie of this State, which you then governed as Lord Deputie of this Realme, to make choice of me to supply that place, and to recommend me by your honorable letters to that effect, I received a very sufficient testimonie of your good opinion and favourable inclination towards me. And albeit your intention and desire in that behalfe tooke not effect, whether through my unworthinesse, or by the labour and practise of others: yet because your testimonie was to me *instar multorum Judicum*;[3] and because that repulse served you as an occasion to do me after a greater favor, I have evermore sithens caried a continual desire to shew my selfe thankfull to your Lordship. For when at my humble sute, you vouchsafed to graunt me libertie without offence, to resigne the office which I had then held seven yeares, as Clerke of this Councell, and to withdraw my selfe from that thanklesse toyle to the quietnes of my intermitted studies, I must needes confesse, I held my selfe more bound unto you therefore, then for all other the benefits which you had bestowed upon me, and all the declarations of honorable affection, whereof you had given me many testimonies before. And therefore being now freed by your Lordships meane from that trouble and disquiet of mind, and enjoying from your speciall favour the sweetnesse and contentment of my Muses; I have thought it the fittest meanes I could devise, to shew my thankfulnes, to offer to you the first fruites that they have yeelded me, as due unto you, from whom onely I acknowledge so great a good. That they will be acceptable unto you, I make no doubt, were it but in regard of the true and sincere affection of the giver; who in admiring and reverencing your vertues, giveth place

4

to no man alive. Howbeit there will be other respects also (I doubt not) to move your liking and acceptance of the same. For if the travell and industrie of those men be commendable, who curiously seeke to transport from farre and forraine countries, either for the health and use of the bodie, or for the pleasing of the exterior senses, the strange grafts, plants and flowers, which excell, either for any medicinable qualitie, or for delight of the eye, the taste, or the smell: how much more will you esteeme of my endevour, and be delighted with my translation of these choice grafts and flowers, taken from the Greeke and Latine Philosophie, and ingrafted upon the stocke of our mother English-tongue? Especially being such as will not onely promise delight and pleasing to the senses, but assuredly yeeld health and comfort to the mind oppressed and diseased? Neither is it unlikely but that the receiving of so unlooked for a present out of this barbarous countrie of Ireland, will be some occasion to hold it the dearer, as a thing rare in such a place, where almost no trace of learning is to be seene, and where the documents of Philosophie are the more needfull, because they are so geason.[4] Perhaps the want of that same sweeter tast & relish, which those Clymes of *Athens* and *Rome* could give unto them, and ours here of England and Ireland cannot affoord, may make them seem unto your Lordship at the first somewhat harsh and unpleasing: But the wholsomnesse of their fruite will easily supply the desire of the pleasing taste, and satisfie you rather with that it hath, then mislike you for lacke of that it cannot have. For although our English tongue have not that copiousnesse and sweetnes that both the Greeke and the Latine have above all others: yet is it not therefore altogether so barren or so defective, but that it is capable enough of termes and phrases meete to expresse all those conceits which may be needfull for the treating and the discoursing of morall Philosophie. And the doctrine and consent of the wisest and best learned Philosophers being truly set downe and declared, though it be not done with that flowing eloquence wherewith *Plato* and *Tullie* did utter their learning, having the use of two such noble and flourishing languages: yet will not the appearing of this faire virgin-stranger in her homely weeds and attire, be any impediment (I presume) why she should not be as welcome and as willingly embraced as if she had come decked in all her gorgeous ornaments and apparell. For of her nakednes I do not feare she shall need to be ashamed, though of her pompe and garnishments shee have no cause to be proud and haughtie. That your Lordship will not reject her, but courteously entertaine her, though she be but the hand-maide of the doctrine of Grace, I do the rather assure my selfe because I have bene an admitted testimonie, how often and very willingly you were pleased to recreate your selfe with her companie, at such times as either the waightie affaires of this your governement would spare you, or that you found cause to refresh your mind by drawing it from the depth of your other studies. For if I did perswade my self that you wold, as soone as you saw her, frowne and avert your countenance from her, as some men of this our age do, and say, that, where her Ladie and mistris is, she is not onely needlesse, but also perillous; I would truly have kept her from your presence, contenting my selfe alone with her companie, and presuming that my familiaritie with her should neither inveigle me to like the lesse of her said Ladie and mistris, or to use her otherwise then as the servant and hand-maide, fit to make her Ladie the more reverenced and the more honored. To your Lordship therefore I now direct her, that under your honorable favour and patronage she may be denizened:[5] For I nothing doubt but that the example of your courteous entertaining of her, will easily draw many others to delight in her conversation, and to feele the true taste of the healthfull and delicious fruites which she hath brought with her to furnish this our English soile & clime withal. Whereby we may with the lesse labour and cost henceforth have them to delight and nourish our minds, since we shall not be constrained to fetch them from *Athens* or from *Rome*, but may find them growing at home with our selves, if our owne negligence and sloth cause us not to foreslow[6] the culturation and manuring of the same. The course which I hold in this treatise, is by way of dialogue (which I have chosen as best pleasing my minde) to discourse upon the morall vertues, yet not omitting the intellectuall, to the end to frame a gentleman fit for civill conversation, and to set him in the direct way that leadeth him to his civill felicitie. Wherein though I have (I feare me) hazarded my selfe to be reprehended by such as looke after formalitie in all things : yet because my intention is to give light as well to the meaner learned (whose judgements can be content to busie it selfe rather to learne what they know not, then to find faults) as to the learneder critiques that spend their eyes to find a haire upon an egge; I have the more boldly followed mine owne liking: making account, that if I may purchase your liking and allowance of my labour, to whose satisfaction I do most recommend it; I shall the lesse esteeme the censure of any that may hap to carpe or mislike whatsoever part of the same. For as I can be content to acknowledge my infirmitie and weaknes, and to confesse and take upon me those faults which I may have committed, when they are civilly and without malice discovered and made knowne unto me: even so shall the over-curious searcher of errors or escapes, to make them faults, very little molest me; being resolved to content mine own mind with the good that I hope wil be found in the work, rather then to dismay my selfe or be grieved because I cannot do a thing in that high degree of excellencie, that there were no fault to be found by any man in the same. The occasion of the discourse grew by the visitation of certaine gentlemen comming to me to my little cottage which I had newly built neare unto Dublin at such a time, as rather to prevent sicknesse, then for any present griefe, I had in the spring of the yeare begunne a course to take some physicke during a few dayes. Among which, Doctor *Long* Primate of *Ardmagh*, Sir *Robert Dillon* Knight, M. *Dormer* the Queenes Sollicitor, Capt. *Christopher Carleil*, Capt. *Thomas Norreis*, Capt. *Warham St. Leger*, Capt. *Nicolas Dawtrey*, & M. *Edmond Spenser* late your Lordships Secretary, & *Th. Smith* Apothecary. These coming of their curtesie to passe the time with me, and chauncing to meete there one day, when M. *Smith* the Apothecary was come to visit me also, and to understand what successe the physick he had prepared for me did take; Sir *Robert Dillon* with a smiling countenance asked of him to what intent (I being to all their judgements in health and well) he with his drugs should make me sick, and force me to keepe the house, whereby neither I could come to the citie, nor they being come to me might have my company to walke about the grounds, to take the pleasure of seeing how the workes of my hands did prosper, now that the season of the yeare filling the plants and all other living things with the naturall humor, which the sharpe cold of the winter had restrained and kept within the inwardest parts, did bud and breake forth, to give proofe and tokens of their prospering.

To which M. *Smith* answered, that he had ministred nothing to me but what my self had prescribed: and that if I was sicke

7

therewith, it was mine owne doing and not his, who by his trade and profession could not refuse to compound and minister such physick as should be required at his hands. But to tell you the truth sir (quoth he) I could find in my heart to give him a potion that should purge him of his melancholy humor, because he hath no small need thereof in my opinion.

And whereby perceive you any such humor to raigne in him, replied sir *Robert Dillon*; for in my judgment neither his complexion accuseth him of any disposition thereunto, nor his behaviour and manner of life giveth any token of sadnesse or desire of solitarinesse, which commonly all melancholy men are much given unto: whereas he is not onely desirous of good companie, but alwayes chearefull and pleasant among his friends.

Yea marry (said M. *Smith*) thereof he may thanke you and these other gentlemen his friends, that by comming often to visit him do keepe from him those fits which otherwise it is likely enough he would fall into; whether that his complexion draw him to it or no, which oft times deceiveth the most cunning Physitions, or whether it proceed of any accidentall cause. But (I pray you) for proofe of my words, who but one more then halfe mad or in a frensie, would of his owne accord, not being compelled thereunto, have given over such an office as he hath resigned? which besides, that it was of good reputation and profit, gave him the meanes to pleasure many of his friends, and kept him still in the bosome of the State, whereby he might in time have risen to better place, and more abilitie to do himselfe and his friends both pleasure & good? All which in a melancholy mood he hath let slip, or rather put from him: for which I, among other that love him, could find in my heart to disple[7] him very well.

In troth (quoth sir *Robert Dillon* turning to me) master *Smith* seemeth to have spoken more like a Physition, or rather like a Counseller, then like an Apothecary: and it will behove you to satisfie him wel, lest we all begin to thinke of you as he doth, and agree with him that it were expedient to give you a dose of Ellebore,[8] which the Physitions say, hath a peculiar property to purge the melancholy humour. And therefore you shall do very well (I think) to declare unto him, what reasons induced you to resigne that office, wherein I my selfe can testifie with how good contentment of all the table you did serve so many yeares. For withall some of us, that have not yet under-

8

stood upon what foundation this resolution of yours is set and grounded, shall in like sort rest the better satisfied, if from your selfe they shall be made capable of some reasonable cause that might induce you therunto. And henceforth beleeve, it hath bin well done, not because you did it, but because you have done it with reason and judgment: which although we be all sufficiently perswaded you take to be your guides in al your actions, yet these words of master *Smiths*, and the like discourses, which we heare very often among some that love you and wish you wel, doth make us sometimes halfe doubtfull to allow of this retiring your selfe from the State. Because we suppose that a man of your condition and qualities should rather seeke to be employed, and to advance himselfe in credit and reputation, then to hide his talent, and withdraw himselfe from action, in which the chiefe commendation of vertue doth consist. And to say truly what I thinke, a man of your sort, bred and trained (as it seemeth you have bin) in learning, and that hath thereto added the experience and knowledge, which travell and observation of many things in forraine countries must breed in him that hath seene many places, and the maners, orders, and policies of sundry nations, ought rather to seeke to employ his ability and sufficiency in the service of his Prince and country, then apply them to his peculiar benefit or contentment. For you that were in so good a way to raise your selfe to credite and better employment, whereunto that office was but the first step and triall of what is in you, to forsake suddenly so direct a path, leading you to preferment, and to betake your selfe to a solitary course of life, or a private at the least, seemeth a thing not agreeable to that opinion which every man that knoweth you, had conceived of your proofe: and that of you it may be said, *Gravior est culpa clara principia deserentis, quam non incipientis; Non enim magna aggredi, sed perseverare difficile.*[9] What is the end of parents in the education of their children, wherin they bestow so much care, and spend their wealth to purchase them learning and knowledge; but a desire to make them able to be employed, and a hope to see them raised to credit and dignitie in the common-wealth? Or who is he that doth not strive by all the meanes he can to advance himselfe, and to presse forward still even to the highest places of authoritie, and favour under his Prince, though oftentimes with no small hazard and danger, if he may once lay hold upon that locke,

9

which, men say, Occasion hath growing on her forehead, being bald behind; shewing thereby how foolish a thing it is to let her slip after she hath once presented her selfe to be apprehended? No doubt but this folly will be layd to your charge by many, and not without good apparance of reason, since you having had the occasion offered unto you, as well to enrich your selfe, as to rise in credite and reputation, have neverthelesse let her go, after you had fast hand in her foretop, and abandoned so great a hope, nay, so assured a reward proposed to you for your labour and paines, to be sustained some while in that place.

Sir (quoth I) to have answered M. *Smiths* imputation, I suppose would have bin very easie, since the greatest matter therein was the neglecting of my profit, and the abandoning a meane to pleasure my friends. For the first is rather a commendation (though not so conceived by him) then any just blame: and the other is no more but a partiall complaint of him and others of his disposition, that looke to their owne private interest, and consider onely what they may misse, by not having a friend in such a place, who might stand them in stead, and regard no whit the contentment or discontentment of their friend, which they are not able to measure; as wanting the generall rule by which it ought to be measured according to reason; and so consequently frame the measure according to their owne minds: using their owne judgements, even as the auncient *Greekes* were wont to say of the Lesbian rule, which being made of lead, the work-men would bend and fit to their worke, and not frame their worke by a right rule. But having added to his objection your owne censure of me, whose judgement and prudence is so wel knowne, and so much by me to be respected, I can no lesse do, then make some further Apologie for my selfe touching that point, and open so much of my counsell and purpose in that behalf as I shall thinke needfull to give you and others, that will prefer reason before their opinions, sufficient satisfaction. And first where you say, that my service in the place was acceptable unto you all, I cannot but therein acknowledge my good hap, rather then impute it to any sufficiencie in my selfe. Neither would I, in regard of that great courtesie and favour which I received therein, have willingly done any thing whereby I might have seemed unthankfull, or to have made so small estimation of so worthy a favour. But my not having bin brought up or used to much writing and long standing,

(which of ordinary that office doth require) besides the extraordinary occasions which the service bringeth forth, to travell, to
sit up late, and disorder the body, had bred such an increase of
rheume in me, and of infirmities caused therby, as I could not
without manifest and certaine perill of shortning my dayes have
continued the exercise of that place. Whereupon having in dutifull
sort made knowne the cause of my desire to resigne the office to
the Lord Deputy, who was in like sort privy to some other just
occasion I had to further that my resolution; it pleased him with
his accustomed prudence and favour towards me, to consider and
to allow of my request, and to grant me his honorable consent
to the accomplishment of the same. Neither can this be rightly
termed in me a retiring my selfe from the State, or a withdrawing
from action to hide my talent. For leaving aside the uncertaintie
and vaine issue for the most part of those hopes that commonly
draw men on into ambitious heaving & shoving for dignities and
places of credit and commoditie; from which to be freed, little
do men know or beleeve what gaine it is; as of things that, when
they obtaine them not, vexe and torment their minds, and when
they obtaine them, do soone glut and weary them. What comparison can a man of reason & judgement make betweene them,
and that contentednes which a well tempered and a moderate
mind doth feele in a private life, employed to the bettering and
amending of the principall part, which distinguisheth him from
brute beasts? Surely for my part I confess: frankly unto you,
and protest I speake truly, I have found more quietnes and
satisfaction in this small time that I have lived to my selfe, and
enjoyed the conversation of my bookes, when the care of my little
building and husbandry hath given me that ordinary intermission
which it must have, then I did before in all the time that I spent
in service about the State: the toile whereof was farre too high
a price for the profit I might make of my place, and the expectation which was left me of rising to any better. Which neverthelesse, suppose it had bin much greater then ever I conceived,
or then you have seemed to make the same: so free am I from
ambition or covetise (howsoever M. *Smith* would have me to
frame my mind thereto) as I am not only content not to flatter
my selfe with the shew of good, which the best hopes might have
presented unto me; but resolved also to put from me and tread
under foot whatsoever desire or inclination, that either nature,

11

ill custome, or daily example might urge me unto, or stirre up within me. It is a perillous thing for men of weake braines to stand in high places, their heads will so soone be giddie, and all climbing is subject to falling. Let men of great spirits, of high birth, and of excellent vertues, possesse in Gods name those dignities and preferments, which the favour of the Prince and their sufficiencie may purchase unto them: for it is they, that (as the Poet sayth) *Posuêre in montibus urbem*: and of whom you might justly say, *Gravior est culpa &c.* For as for me, I am one of those of whom the same Poet sayd, *Habitabant vallibus imis.*[10] And so I had rather to do still, then to forsake my studies which I have now begunne to renew againe: having applied my endevour to lay hold upon the foretop, which Lady Occasion hath offered me to that effect: for to any other intent, she never yet did so much as once shew her selfe to me a farre off, much lesse present her selfe to me so neare as I might reach to catch her, or fasten my hand in her golden locke. I wish my friends therefore rather to allow, and give their consents to this my resolution, grounded (as I thinke) upon a reasonable consideration, and an exact weighing of mine owne abilitie and disposition, then to concurre with M. *Smith* in opinion, or with any others that would lay to my charge folly, or lacke of judgement for the same. And that generally all men would beleeve the Italian proverbe, which sayth, that the foole knoweth better what is good and meet for himselfe, then doth the wise man what is fit for another man. Not that I would thereby reject good counsell and friendly advice, which I know well enough how beneficiall a thing it is to all men in matters of doubt and difficultie; but my meaning is onely to reserve to a mans owne understanding the judgement of such particular and private determinations, as concerne the contentment or discontentment of his mind; the circumstances of which perhaps are not meete to be communicated to others. The example whereof *Paulus Æmilius* hath given us,[11] with that grave and wise answer he made unto his friends that wold needs reprehend him for repudiating his wife, alledging her many good qualities, as her beautie, her modestie, her nobilitie, and other such like: when putting forth his leg, he shewed them his buskin, and sayd; You see this buskin is wel and handsomly made, of good leather, and to your seeming fit enough for my foote and leg, yet none of you knoweth (I am sure) where it doth wring me. Even so my selfe may haply say to any whom my former answer may not fully satisfie, that although to their seeming my state and condition was better by holding that office, not onely in respect of the benefit and commoditie my selfe and my friends might reape thereby; but also in regard of the expectation of preferment & advancement that I might have had by the exercise of the same: yet is it to them unknowne what other particulars might move me to conceive thereof otherwise, and to like rather of the privat life I now leade, then of all those benefits and commodities which the other could promise unto me.

Although the reasons by you before alledged, might well enough be answered, quoth sir *Robert Dillon*, yet this last objection you have made to conclude your speech withall, is such, as I should hold him unwise that would go about to remove you from your determination. For it were a point of overmuch curiositie, to search so farre into your mind and drift in that behalfe. But since it seemeth that your desire is now bent to the renewing of your studies, and to apply your selfe to the bettering (as you say) of that part which is proper unto man, which is the mind, or reasonable power of the soule, from whence indeed all operations worthy commendation do proceed, I pray you let us heare from you what kind of studie that is, by which you intend to purchase to your selfe this so great a good. For it is not every science that can affoord the same, since we see oftentimes men of great learning in sundry professions, to be nevertheles rude and ignorant in things that concerne their cariage and behaviour: insomuch as it hath bin fitly used for a proverbe among us, that the greatest clerkes are not alwayes the wisest men. And as I for one, am desirous to know your determination and opinion touching that point: so do I think that the rest of these gentlemen here, wil be willing and glad to spend this time which we have all disposed to visit you and keepe you companie, in hearing you discourse upon so good a Theme, by which there cannot but arise some good and profit to every of us. Because we nothing doubt, but that, as you have maturely debated with your selfe the reasons that have induced you to take upon you this resolution; so you can declare the same, and make us partakers with you of so much of your contentment, as the love and good will we beare you, will thereby fasten upon us.

Sir (said I) you have right well alledged and applied our

common proverbe, in my opinion: for it is not indeed every kind of knowledge and studie that bettereth the mind of man, as dayly experience teacheth us: since we see many men use the same as an instrument to worke their mischiefe and wickednes withall the more artificially and the more dangerously. For though nature hath engrafted in every man a fervent desire of knowledge, which discovereth it selfe in children, even in their infancie; yet have we all from the corruption of her, a disposition likewise to abuse the same, and to turne it rather to evill than to goodnesse, if speciall grace, or an excellent education (which cannot be without grace) do not fashion and frame the mind to the right use thereof. The general scope of parents, when they set their children to learning, tendeth only to the enabling of them, thereby to attaine some meanes to live by the profession either of Law, of Physicke, or of Divinitie: for of the meaner intentions I wil not speake. And too common an error it is in scholers themselves, when they are entred into the Arts, which are called liberal, to spend their time in curious searching of subtilties, frivolous, and to no use: or els in purchasing rather an apparance of learning in the science they apply their studies unto, thereby to win the shorter way to profit, then the profound and exact knowledge of sciences themselves; whereof every one neverthelesse being thoroughly attained, would yeeld no smal helpe and furtherance to that bettering of the mind, which I have spoken of.

But who is he that in the profession of the Law, aimeth at any other marke, then at sufficiencie to pleade well at the barre, to draw him the more clients, or to rise to such dignities as thereby others climbe unto: or in Physick, then to have a reputation of skil, to procure him much practise to inrich himselfe: or in Divinitie, then to be accounted a good Preacher, whereby he may get a fruitful benefice, or be invested with some Bishopricke and title of honor? Or which of them do we see, that when he hath hit the marke he shot at, and is come to the height that his profession can raise him unto. doth shew himselfe sincere, or incorrupt of mind, or so master over his owne passions, as either through covetousnes, or ambition, or love, or hatred, he will not forget the dutie which he oweth to that place, whereunto he is called, and to him that hath given him the gift as well of the meane as of the thing it selfe?

To answer you therefore directly what kind of studie I affect

14

or thinke may most better my mind, I will say that it is none of these before mentioned: for albeit I acknowledge the true study of Divinitie to include all that knowledge, which may any way be required for the perfection of mans life: yet because there is a more speciall calling thereunto, then to any other, and ought to be applied in a more reverent maner, and to a further end, then that every man might presume to take it in hand, I dare not venture to make my selfe a professor of it. As for the profession of the Law, I will not in these yeares, and with this mind, alienated from troubles and businesse, give my selfe to the same, it being the principall meane and high way to leade me againe into the labyrinth which I desire most to eschew and avoyde. To Physicke I was by my fathers choice appointed; for the perform-ance of whose wil, as became me in dutie and obedience, all the time I spent by his direction in studie, I employed in the know-ledge of the principles thereof: and sithens, as well for the use thereof to mine owne behoofe, as for the delightfulnesse, which the discovery of the secret operations and effects of nature worketh (I suppose) in every man as it doth in me, I have (when time and leisure would permit) bent my most study and reading to the authors of that science; but intention to professe it, or to practise it, in very deed as yet had I never none. But how soever the providence of my father, or mine owne industry had fashioned me to be meete to make a Physition, yet the higher providence had otherwise determined, making me to take another course of life, which before was never so much as once thought of by either of us, and made me of a scholer to become a servant. By which occasion being drawne into this countrey, and left my studies, I have so many yeares led my life here in such sort as you have seene. But having now withdrawne my selfe from the toilesome place I held, and gathered my selfe into a little compasse, as a snaile into his shell, my purpose is (if God shall please to give me his gracious assistance) to spend my time in reading such bookes, as I shall find fittest to increase my knowledge in the duties of a Christian man, and direct me in the right path of vertue, without tying my selfe to any particular kind. And as I have (God be thanked) some store of all sorts; so shall I dispense my time accordingly, sometime in perusing such as may instruct me more and more in the true maner of serving God; sometime in reading of histories, which are as mirrours or looking-glasses for every man to see the good and evill actions of all ages, the better to square his life to the rule of vertue, by the examples of others; and sometimes, and that for the most part (as thus advised) in the study of Morall Philosophie, which frameth men fittest for civill conversation, teaching them orderly what morall vertues are, and particularly what is the proper action of every one, and likewise what vice is, and how unseemly a thing, and how harmefull to a good mind the spot and contagion thereof is. To this have I ever had a speciall inclination, and a greedy desire to instruct my selfe fully therein; which hitherto, partly through the course I held whiles I was a scholer (as before I said) I could not wel do, and ever sithens my continuall busines and attendance about mine office, have diverted me therefro. And to professe plainly the truth, not any one thing hath so much prevailed to make me resolve the giving over that place, as the longing I had, and have to returne to the course of reading Morall Philosophy, which I was even then newly entred into, when I was called to be employed in that office; and the delight whereof was so great unto me, for that little which I had begun to reade, and the expectation such, which I had conceived of the use thereof (as by which a man learneth not onely to know how to carry himselfe vertuously in his privat actions, but also to guide and order his family, and moreover, to become meete for the service of his Prince and countrey, when occasion of employment may be offered unto him) that I was halfe doubtfull when I was summoned to come and take the place, whether I should accept thereof or no.

Then said M. *Dormer*, Yea but it seemeth to me that these your words imply a contradiction, when saying that you have so earnestly desired to withdraw your selfe from the exercise of your office, wherin you had so good meanes, not only to make shew of your owne sufficiency and vertue, and to do your Prince and countrey service, and withall to pleasure many of your friends, you seeme nevertheles to direct your studies to such an end, as aimeth not onely at the knowledge of vertue, but also at the practise thereof, whereby a man is made fit and enabled for such employments as the Prince or State shall lay upon him. For indeed it is an approved saying among Philosophers, *Virtutis laus, actio*: and you know what *Tullie* saith, and *Plato* before him, *Non nobis nati sumus, partem patria, partem parentes,*

16

partem amici sibi vendicant.[12] So as **Mr.** *Smiths* accusation (for ought I see) may be held as yet very reasonable against you, unles you can alledge us some better reason in your defence then hitherto you have done.

In faith (quoth I) if you be all against me, I shall have much adoe to defend my selfe, since the old proverbe is, that, *Ne Hercules quidem contra duos*:[13] and how can I then resist so many? But I hope that some of this companie will take my part, though he have forestalled me of the two chiefe men, whose patronage might best have served me, having gotten you two lawyers to pleade for him. Yet because I suppose you have not bin entertained by him for that purpose with any fee, and that you are here, not as lawyers or advocates to maintaine his cause, but rather as indifferent Judges, to determine who hath the best right on his side; I hope that upon better information, you will be drawne to judge uprightly, and not be caried away with apparances, which oftentimes hide and cast a cloud over the truth. And to answer therefore to your objection, which carieth with it some probabilitie, I would easily confesse my selfe in fault, if this resigning of my office had bin an absolute retiring my selfe from action, or that I had (as they say) forsworne any employment for the service of the State or my Prince. But if you please to consider how this my resolution hath bin grounded upon a desire to be freed onely from a place of such continuall toile and attendance, as suffered me to have no time to spare, wherein I might almost breathe, or take any reasonable recreation; and not to live idle, or sequestred so from action, as I should onely spend my time in reading or contemplation, I doubt not but you wil find my words to agree wel inough without any contradiction, and my course of life well enough fitting a man that meaneth not to live to himselfe alone. For if such had bin my purpose, I would have sought out a meeter dwelling then this so neare the citie, and I could well enough have devised to have bin farre from such controllers[14] as M. *Smith*, and to have avoided this judgement that I am now subject unto, not without hazard of my reputation, having two such persons to assist my accuser, and beare up his cause. You see that I have not so estranged my selfe from all employments, but that I can be content to take paine in the increasing of her Majesties revenue, by the care I have of her impost: I refuse not any other ordinary

employments, as of travelling in such commissions as the Lord
Deputie and Councel ofttimes direct unto me for the examining
of sundrie causes: neither do I so give my selfe to be private, but
that you and other my friends, who vouchsafe of their courtesie
sometimes to visite me, find me apt enough to keep them companie, either here at home, or else abroad: so as though I desire
to know how to do these things as perfectly well as I might, and
to that end frame my selfe as much to study as conveniently I
can, yet do I not therin contradict the reasonable and just disposition I have to employ my selfe for the service of her Majestie,
when occasion serveth: neither doth my endevour in that behalf
any way oppose it selfe to my desire, of retiring from a painefull
employment to a more quiet life, which now (I thanke God) I
enjoy: wherein I may frankly and truly protest unto you, I find
more sweetnes and contentment in one dayes expence, then I
could taste in seven yeares before, whiles I was Clerke of the
Councell. And were it but in regard of that same contentment,
I know not what man of reasonable sense and understanding,
would not esteeme the purchase thereof at a farre higher rate
then any office in Ireland whatsoever. M. *Smith* therfore may
well enough put up his pipes, and hold his peace henceforth, and
I hope not onely yee two, but all the rest of this companie will
hold him sufficiently put to silence, and begin to allow of this
my resolution, especially seeing it aimeth at so high a marke as
humane felicitie.

At which word the Primate seemed as it were to start, &
said, what sir? though we can be content to admit your reasons
against M. *Smith*, and to allow of your resolution, as having
chosen (as our Saviour said to *Martha* of her sister) the better
part; yet must you not thinke that we will let every thing go
with you which you say: but by your leave, plucke you a little
backe by the sleeve, when we see you presse forward presump-
tuously, as now in my opinion you do, when you seeme to shoote
at such a marke as humane felicitie, which is without, not your
reach onely, but all mens, whiles they are here in this low and
muddie world: for I wis that is no where to be found but above
the stars: mans felicity is placed only in heaven, where God of
his mercie hath appointed it for him to be found, and not here
on earth. I say of his mercie, because albeit he had ordained the
same for man from before all ages; yet our first father by his

disobedience depriving himselfe and all his posteritie of all possibilitie thereof, the same was eftsoones by the infinite goodnes and mercie of God purchased to him againe at a deare price, even the precious bloud of his dearest Son, which he was content to shed for the ransome of mankind, entrapped by the divell, and taken captive, whereby he might returne into his heavenly countrie againe, to enjoy that happie inheritance prepared there for him. Whosoever therfore shall seeke to get his felicitie here in this world, will find himselfe deceived: and although it be said to some purpose fitly, that he that shooteth at a starre, aimeth higher then he that shooteth at a furbush: [15] yet well ye wot, that to shoot up to the starres, is but meere follie and vanitie; and no lesse do I hold your aiming at so high a marke to be, which is so farre out of your reach.

I crie you mercie, my Lord, quoth I, if I have stepped into your marches[16] before I were aware. But I may the better be excused, because I had no intention or purpose so to do; but simply, and after the common maner of speech have used the general word in stead of the particular. For though I said I aimed at the high marke of humane felicitie, yet for so little as I have read in Morall Philosophy, I have learned that *Plato* hath made mention of two distinct felicities of man (and others besides him) the one a contemplative felicitie (which some men haply draw neare unto, but cannot perfectly attaine in this life;) the other an active or practicke felicitie, consisting in vertuous actions, and reducing of a mans passions under the rule of reason. Which practicke felicitie may not onely be atchieved here on earth by mans endevour, assisted with Gods grace and favour: but is also a great helpe and meane for such as obtaine the same, to bring them after this life unto the other in heaven. Of this latter, the rules whereof are to be taken from you Church-men and Divines; I meant not when I said, I aymed so high, at the lestwise my purpose was not properly to say, that I shot at that marke by my studie, for then I should have contradicted my former words, when I protested I durst not presume to the studie of Divinitie, which (I well understood) required a particular calling. But onely my meaning was to get your approbation, in that I had resolved by the study of Morall Philosophie to compasse, so farre forth as my endevours could prevaile, that humane practicke felicitie, which of all men in all ages hath bene so highly esteemed; and for the directing of men wherunto, so many great learned Philosophers have taken so great travell and paines to find out the ready way unto it, and by their writings to make the same knowne to others: whereby not onely particular persons might in this life attaine to live happily, but also purchase the same happines to their families, yea to whole Cities and Common-wealths. This felicitie (I think) every wel disposed man is to labor for in this life; & the better he is borne, the more ought he to bend his study to learne by what meanes the same is to be attained: and by working accordingly, to prepare himselfe to be fit and capable of that other when soever he shall be called out of this world, knowing how assured promises therof are given to them that in this life live vertuously; and how certain he may be, that the further that good which his vertuous actions shall extend to the benefite of others in this life, the greater shall be his reward in the life to come, where that felicitie is prepared for them, that by the treading downe of their passions and sensual appetites, shal endevour to reduce their soule to that purenesse and cleannes which is required in them to whom that everlasting blisse and felicitie is promised. For my part, the thing which I most earnestly desire, is to learne the shortest way to compasse the same: and happie should I thinke my selfe if I could find any man whose knowledge and learning might helpe me to direct my study to that end; because I know right well how hard it is for a man by his owne labour to search out the ready way to understand those precepts, which have bin set downe in the learned writings of Philosophers that have treated of that matter, especially in the Greeke and Latine tongues, in which it hath bin substantially handled. For although I cannot truly pretend ignorance in the Latine, in which the workes of *Plato* and *Aristotle* are to be read: yet I confesse that I do not find that facilitie in the conceiving of their writings, as I could wish, or as the greedinesse of my desire to apprehend might overtake. For *Plato* hath couched his sense thereof so dispersedly in his dialogues, as I thinke he must be a man of great learning and exact judgement that shall picke them out, and sever them from the other parts of Philosophie, which he indeed most divinely discourseth upon. And *Aristotle* is not to me so cleare nor so easily understood without deepe study, as my meane capacitie would require; specially without the interpretation of some better scholer then my selfe.

20

And herein do I greatly envie the happinesse of the Italians, who have in their mother-tongue late writers, that have with a singular easie method, taught all that which *Plato* or *Aristotle* have confusedly or obscurely left written. Of which, some I have begun to reade with no small delight, as *Alexander Piccolomini*, *Gio. Baptista Giraldi*, and *Guazzo*, all three having written upon the Ethick part of Morall Philosophie both exactly and perspicuously. And would God that some of our countrimen wold shew themselves so wel affected to the good of their countrie (whereof one principall and most important part consisteth in the instructing of men to vertue) as to set downe in English the precepts of those parts of Morall Philosophy, whereby our youth might without spending of so much time, as the learning of those other languages require, speedily enter into the right course of vertuous life. In the meane while I must struggle with those bookes which I understand, and content my selfe to plod upon them, in hope that God (who knoweth the sincerenesse of my desire) will be pleased to open my understanding, so as I may reape that profit of my reading, which I travell for. Yet is there a gentleman in this company, whom I have had often a purpose to intreate, that as his leisure might serve him, he would vouchsafe to spend some time with me to instruct me in some hard points which I cannot of my selfe understand: knowing him to be not onely perfect in the Greek tongue, but also very well read in Philosophie, both morall and naturall. Nevertheles such is my bashfulnes, as I never yet durst open my mouth to disclose this my desire unto him, though I have not wanted some hartning thereunto from himselfe. For of his love and kindnes to me, he encouraged me long sithens to follow the reading of the Greeke tongue, and offered me his helpe to make me understand it. But now that so good an oportunitie is offered unto me, to satisfie in some sort my desire; I thinke I should commit a great fault, not to my selfe alone, but to all this company, if I should not enter my request thus farre, as to move him to spend this time which we have now destined to familiar discourse and conversation, in declaring unto us the great benefites which men obtaine by the knowledge of Morall Philosophie, and in making us to know what the same is, what be the parts thereof, whereby vertues are to be distinguished from vices: and finally that he will be pleased to run over in such order as he shall thinke good,

21

such and so many principles and rules thereof, as shall serve not only for my better instruction, but also for the contentment and satisfaction of you al. For I nothing doubt, but that every one of you will be glad to heare so profitable a discourse, and thinke the time very wel spent, wherin so excellent a knowledge shal be revealed unto you, from which every one may be assured to gather some fruit as wel as my self. Therfore (said I) turning my selfe to M. *Spenser*, It is you sir, to whom it pertaineth to shew your selfe courteous now unto us all, and to make us all beholding unto you for the pleasure and profit which we shall gather from your speeches, if you shall vouchsafe to open unto us the goodly cabinet, in which this excellent treasure of vertues lieth locked up from the vulgar sort. And thereof in the behalfe of all, as for my selfe, I do most earnestly intreate you not to say us nay. Unto which words of mine every man applauding most with like words of request, and the rest with gestures and countenances expressing as much, M. *Spenser* answered in this maner.

Though it may seeme hard for me to refuse the request made by you all, whom, every one alone, I should for many respects be willing to gratifie: yet as the case standeth, I doubt not but with the consent of the most part of you, I shall be excused at this time of this taske which would be laid upon me. For sure I am, that it is not unknowne unto you, that I have already undertaken a work tending to the same effect, which is in *heroical verse*, under the title of a *Faerie Queene*, to represent all the moral vertues, assigning to every vertue, a Knight to be the patron and defender of the same: in whose actions and feates of armes and chivalry, the operations of that vertue, whereof he is the protector, are to be expressed, and the vices & unruly appetites that oppose themselves against the same, to be beaten downe & overcome. Which work, as I have already well entred into, if God shall please to spare me life that I may finish it according to my mind, your wish (M. *Bryskett*) will be in some sort accomplished, though perhaps not so effectually as you could desire. And the same may very well serve for my excuse, if at this time I crave to be forborne in this your request, since any discourse, that I might make thus on the sudden in such a subject, would be but simple, and little to your satisfactions. For it would require good advisement and premeditation for any man to undertake the declaration of these points that you have proposed, containing in effect the Ethicke part of Morall Philosophie. Whereof since I have taken in hand to discourse at large in my poeme before spoken, I hope the expectation of that work may serve to free me at this time from speaking in that matter, notwithstanding your motion and all your intreaties. But I will tell you, how I thinke by himselfe he may very well excuse my speech, and yet satisfie all you in this matter. I have seene (as he knoweth) a translation made by himselfe out of the Italian tongue, of a dialogue comprehending all the Ethick part of Moral Philosophy, written by one of those three he formerly mentioned, and that is by *Giraldi*, under the title of a dialogue of civil life. If it please him to bring us forth that translation to be here read among us, or otherwise to deliver to us, as his memory may serve him, the contents of the same; he shal (I warrant you) satisfie you all at the ful, and himselfe wil have no cause but to thinke the time well spent in reviewing his labors, especially in the company of so many his friends, who may thereby reape much profit, and the translation happily fare the better by some mending it may receive in the perusing, as all writings else may do by the often examination of the same. Neither let it trouble him, that I so turne over to him againe the taske he wold have put me to: for it falleth out fit for him to verifie the principall part of all this Apologie, even now made for himselfe; because thereby it will appeare that he hath not withdrawne himself from service of the State, to live idle or wholy private to himselfe, but hath spent some time in doing that which may greatly benefit others, and hath served not a little to the bettering of his owne mind, and increasing of his knowledge, though he for modesty pretend much ignorance, and pleade want in wealth, much like some rich beggars, who either of custom, or for covetousnes, go to begge of others those things whereof they have no want at home.

With this answer of M. *Spensers*, it seemed that all the company were wel satisfied: for after some few speeches, whereby they had shewed an extreme longing after his worke of the *Faerie Queene*, whereof some parcels had bin by some of them seene, they all began to presse me to produce my translation mentioned by M. *Spenser*, that it might be perused among them; or else that I should (as neare as I could) deliver unto them the contents of the same, supposing that my memory would not much faile me in a thing so studied, and advisedly set downe in writing, as a translation must be. And albeit I alledged for mine excuse, that I had done it but for mine exercise in both languages, not with purpose to have it seene, nor so advisedly, as had bin needful to come under their censures: yet would they have no nay, but without protracting time in excuses, I must needs fulfill their desires; and so with a courteous force they made me rise from where I sate to go fetch my papers. Which being brought before them, I said: Loe, here you may see by the manner of these loose sheetes, how farre I meant this labour of mine should come to light: and the confused lying of them, and the blots and interlinings which you see, may give you well enough to understand, how hard a thing it is to have it read before you, as you pretended. Besides that, it is of such a bulke and volume, as you may easily understand, it cannot in a short time be runne over. And therefore since you have so easily acquited M. *Spenser* of that charge which you all with me seemed so desirous to impose upon him: you may do wel in like courteous manner to discharge me of the like burthen that you would lay upon me.

Then said sir *Robert Dillon*, though it appeare indeed unto us, that the lose and disorderly placing of the papers with the interlinings, do make it unfit to be read as we desired, and that the often interrupting of the sense to find out and match the places, would take away the best part of the delight which the subject might yeeld us: yet because we know that you, having translated the whole, may easily with your memory supply the defects of the papers; I for my part do thinke, and so I suppose do the rest here present, that it is no sufficient reason to free you from so profitable a labour, as this, whereby you may acquaint us with those worthy conceits in our owne language, which you have in the Italian found to be so delightfull, and fit to be communicated by your travell to others. Therfore if you shal not think it good to reade it unto us as it is set downe in the translation precisely; at the least yet this we will urge you unto, that you will be content to deliver unto us the general points of the same, marshalling them in their order, though in the circumstances of the dialogue and persons you follow not exactly the forme of the author; and our dispensation in that case shall serve to deliver you from the blame, that otherwise as an interpreter you might be subject unto. For being done to us, and at our request, we shall be your warrants, notwithstanding any law or custome to the contrary. Be you onely willing to gratifie us, and for the rest feare you no danger; since we sit not here as in the courts, to examine whether there be as well due forme, as sufficient matter in bills & pleadings that are brought before us: but are here to passe the time with you in honest and vertuous conversation. And the drift of our speeches having growne to this issue, that we should spend this short space which we may be together, in the discoursing upon the Ethick part of Morall Philosophie, and you having the subject so ready at hand, in Gods name we pray you, delay us not by losing time in frivolous excuses, but begin to open to us this treasure, which you would so faine hide from our eyes.

Here they began all to second his speeches, and so importunatly to intreate me to accomplish their desire, that being no further able to say them nay: I answered.

Since such is your will, I can no longer resist you: onely thus much I must protest unto you, that you are guiltie, not onely of whatsoever fault or error I shal commit against the lawes of an interpreter, but also of breach of the law of hospitalitie, in overruling me in mine owne house. And as for this I may justly complaine of violence, yet perhaps find no redresse, so if any shal find fault with me for not observing the precise rules of a translator, let him impute the same not to me, but unto you, having some compassion upon me, that besides being constrained to produce that which I purposed to have kept to my selfe, I am also forced to do it, not according to mine owne choice, but in such sort as it hath pleased you to compell me. Well then, to gaine as much time as may be, I wil omit the introduction of the author to his dialogue, as a thing depending upon former matter and occasion, by which the persons introduced by him are fitted for his purpose, & supposing this present companie to be as apt to conceive the reasons by him set downe, & to make as pertinent objections as they did, I will begin even there where he, following the course of most others that have written upon that subject, maketh entry into his discourse. But with this proviso, that, because this day will not serve us to runne over the whole, you wil be content, that, as he hath devided his whole work into three dialogues, so we may meete here three severall dayes, to give every several dialogue of his one day to explane the same: for so much (I think) may well be performed every day. To which they all agreeing, I tooke my loose papers in hand, and began in this manner following. I must now presuppose that ye, whom I esteeme to be as those gentlemen introduced by this author, have likewise moved the same question, which they did, to wit, what maner of life a gentleman is to undertake and propose to himselfe, to attaine to that end in this world, which among wisemen hath bene, and is accounted the best; beginning from the day of his birth, and so guiding him therein untill he be meet to purchase the same end. And likewise where any occasion of doubt or question, for the better understanding may happen in the discourse, that some one of you desiring to be resolved therein wil demaund such questions as shal be needfull. Wherein you shall find this author plentifully to satisfie your expectations, not tying himselfe absolutely to follow neither *Plato* nor *Aristotle*, but gathering from both, and from other excellent writers besides, so much as may yeeld you the greater and fuller satisfaction. Give eare therefore unto his words.

The end in all things that men do in this world, is the first that is considered, though afterwards it be the last to be put in execution. And as, when it is brought to perfection, it beareth the name of effect, so is it the cause that moveth all other to bring it to effect. And therefore to treate of that end, which is now the motion inducing us to discourse hereupon, we must come to the first principles which may be the causes to bring a man to this end. In which respect it were needfull for me first to speake of the generation of man, since as all seeds bring forth their fruit like to themselves; so falleth it out for the most part in men: for such as are the father and the mother, such are most commonly the children. I should likewise declare, how he that wil be a commendable father, ought to have a speciall care, not of himselfe onely (for him we wil suppose to be a man endewed with all the ornaments required for a wel composed body and mind) but of the mother also. For albeit she receive the seed of generation from the man; yet howsoever it be, the children when they be once conceived, take their nourishment from the mother, and in her wombe, untill the time of their birth: whereby we see the children very often to retaine the vices of the mother. Also that in regard hereof, every man that intendeth to take a wife, ought to be very carefull in the choice of her; so that she may not be base of parentage, vitious, wanton, deformed, lame, or

26

otherwise imperfect or defective: but well borne, vertuous, chaste, of tall and comely personage, and well spoken; to the end that of father and mother, by kind gentle, vertuous, modest, and comely of shape and proportion, like children may betweene them be brought forth. For from wise men hath proceeded that warning to men, that such wives they should chuse as they wished to have their children. And *Archidamus* King of *Sparta*, was condemned by his citizens to pay a fine, for having taken to wife a woman of very low stature; because (said they) she is like to bring us forth no kings, but dandiprats.[17] Thereby declaring how they accounted no small part of the majestie of a king, to consist in the comely presence and stature of his body; and not without cause. For it is written, that the goodly shew and apparance of a man, is the first thing worthy soveraigntie. But because in the request made to me, I am required to begin onely at his birth, I thinke it shall suffice, if I declare unto you in what maner he ought to be nourished, and brought up, and instructed, till he come to such ripe yeares and judgement as he may rule himselfe, and be his owne guide to direct all his actions to that same end, which in all humane things is the last and best. Nevertheles before I begin therewith, I would have you to understand, that the first gift which the father bestoweth on the son after he is borne, is his name, by which he is all his life time to be called. Which name, is to be wished, may be decent and fit, so as it may seeme the life of the child is marked with a signe or pronostication of good hap, and of being framed to the course of vertue: for some are of opinion, that the name oftentimes presageth the qualities and conditions of the child. And therefore they are not to be commended that name their children by the names of brute beasts, as in some countries is used; where the names of *Leo*, of *Orso*, of *Astore*, of *Pardo*, of *Cane*, and such like are in use: as if their desire were that their children should resemble those wild and bruite beasts in their conditions. Let men therfore in Gods name be intitled with names meet for men, and such as may signifie or carry with them dignitie, or rather holinesse and religion, and leave to bruite beasts their owne possession.

Then, said sir *Robert Dillon*, before you proceed any further, I pray you let us understand whether that point be cleare or no, of the nourishing all manner of children. For among *Lycurgus* his lawes, there was one, whereby it was ordained, that such children as were borne unperfect in any part of their bodies, crooked, mis-shapen, of ill aspect, should not onely, not be fostered up, but also be throwne downe from the top of a high rocke, as creatures condemned by God and nature in their conception; and so marked by them, to the end that men might know, that such (if they were through ignorance bred & nourished) were likely to bring harme and ruine to the houses and common-wealths wherin they should live. Let us therfore heare your authors opinion concerning that law.

There is no doubt (said I) but that such was the opinion of *Lycurgus*, and such his law, though cruell and unjust. Nevertheles though the felicitie of man be a perfection of all the good gifts of body and mind, and he that is so borne, cannot indeed be properly termed happie in the highest degree of worldly happines: yet much more prudently have those wise men determined, who say, that the imperfections of mens bodies which are borne with them, are not to be imputed to them as hurtful or shamefull, because it is not in their power to avoid them. And who is he that can be so hard hearted as to slay an infant so cruelly, onely because nature hath shaped him unperfect in any of his lims? The mind of any good man abhorreth to thinke such a thing, much more to put it in execution.

Indeed (replied sir *Robert Dillon*) pittie ought alwaies to be before the eyes of al men, as a thing natural to them, and without which they are unworthy the name of humanitie: yet must not this pittie extend so farre for any particular compassion, as thereby to confound the universall order of things. The pittie which *Hecuba* had of *Paris* (as Poets have taught us) was the cause that *Troy* was burnt, and *Priamus* with all his worthy family destroyed: which things (say they) had never happened, if contrary to the direction of the Gods (who by her dreame forewarned her of those evils) she had not saved him. If then it were true, as *Lycurgus* affirmed, that the markes or tokens, so brought into the world by children from their mothers wombe, should foretell such to be likely to bring ruine or calamitie to their cities or countries; were it not better that he that is so borne, should rather die in his cradle, then be nourished to become the overthrow and desolation of a whole people? We know that by the opinion of the wisest, it is expedient rather one should die to save a multitude, then by sparing his life a number should perish.

That opinion (sayd I) is not unworthy wise men, but it is deepely to be considered, and their meaning to be looked into, for so shall we find no such sense therein, as you inferre: for those men spake not of children newly borne, who are not able, either by speech or deed, to give any signe or token, whereby it may be gathered, that they will prove either good or evill; but of such, as being commonly heads and ring-leaders of factious and seditious people, do make themselves authors of the destruction of noble families and whole cities: such as were both the *Gracchi* in *Rome*, and sundry others in *Greece*. And so it is to be applied, to wit, that such a man shall rather die, then for the saving of his life, a whole citie or people should go to wracke. Or otherwise, when in time of warre, by the joyning of two armies in battell, a great multitude were likly to be slaine, it were farre better that one, or two, or moe, in certaine number on each side should fight and hazard their lives in stead of the rest, then their whole powers to meet, and venter[18] the slaughter of the most part of them. As in the beginning of the State of *Rome*, the *Horatii* and the *Curiatii* did to keepe from hazard of battell both people, which were ready armed and prepared to fight together. In like manner may that saying be applied, in case a whole citie be in danger of desolation, & that the death of one man may redeeme the same. As by *Curtius* the same citie of *Rome* was preserved: who with so great courage threw himselfe armed on horsebacke into that pestilent pit which infected the whole citie, to the end that by his death he might save the people from that mortalitie and infection. And the same effect (but farre more excellently) did our Saviour likewise work, who to redeeme mankind from the bands of hell, tooke upon him all our sinnes, through which we were become thrals to Satan; and for our salvation yeelded himselfe willingly to a most bitter death. But as in such cases it is to be allowed, that one should die for the people: so is it much more to be discommended then I can declare, that an infant newly borne should be killed, though by defect of nature, want of seed, or any straine or mischance of the mother, or through abundance of ill humors, or any other strange accident, it be borne imperfect, or marked as is said.

Well, said sir *Robert Dillon*, it is true indeed that the law of *Lycurgus* was too cruell and unjust. But *Plato* in his books

29

de Repub. devised a more mild and reasonable way: for he allowed not that such children should be killed, as holding it inhumane, yet he ordained that they should be brought up in some place appointed out of the citie, and that they should be debarred all possibilitie of bearing any rule or magistracie in the Common-wealth. For it seemed, he thought that through the intemperance and disordinate living of the parents, children came to be ingendred no lesse deformed and corrupt in mind then in body: and therein the excesse of drinking wine to be a principall cause. In which respect he forbad as wel to the man as to the woman the use of wine at such times as they were disposed to attend the generation of children.

Plato (said I) must not be left unanswered, neither wil I spare to say (by his leave) that his law, though it be milder then the other, was neverthemore allowable for the causes above specified. For it is not alwayes true, that the imperfections of the body are likewise in the mind: or that a faire body hath evermore a faire mind coupled unto it. Have we not seene men of mis-shapen bodies that have had divine minds, and others of goodly personages that have bin very furies of hell? as *Plato* himselfe constrained by the force of truth and dayly experience could not but confesse. The good or bad shape of the body therefore, must be no rule for us to bring up, or not to bring up our children, though it be to be esteemed a great grace to be borne with seemely and wel proportioned members: and that it is a speciall point of happinesse to have a faire mind harbored in a comely body, because both together beare with them a naturall grace, pleasing and gratefull to the eyes of men, constraining in a sort the love of all that behold them: which thing *Virgil* wel understanding, when he spake of *Eurialus*, said,

> *Gratior & pulchro veniens in corpore virtus,*
> *Adiuuat, &c.*[19]

For although vertue of it selfe be lovely and to be highly esteemed, yet when she is accompanied with the beauty of the bodie, she is more amiable (whatsoever *Seneca* the Stoicke, more severe then need, please to say) and with more affection embraced of all them that see her. Which thing appeared in *Scipio Africanus*, when he met with *Asdrubal* his enemy in the presence of king *Siphax*: for as soone as the subtill African had beheld the comely presence and gratefull countenance of *Scipio*, he forthwith conceived that, which afterward fell out, to wit, that *Scipio* would draw *Siphax* to joyne with the Romanes, against the Carthaginians. But for all this we are not in any wise to esteeme a person in body mis-shapen or deformed, lesse worthy to be nourished, or to be admitted to magistracie, if he be vertuous, then the other that is of gratefull presence. For though *Aristotle* thinke the deformitie of the body to be an impediment to the perfect felicitie of man, in respect of exteriour things; yet he determineth, that it is no hindrance to the course of vertue. To conclude therfore this point, though children be borne weake, crooked, mis-shapen, or deformed of body, they are not therefore to be exposed, but as wel to be brought up and instructed as the other, that they may grow and increase in vertue, and become worthy of those dignities which are dispensed in their commonweales. And, me thinketh, *Socrates* that wise man spake very well to his scholers, and to this purpose, when he advised them, that they should often behold themselves in lookingglasses: to the end (said he) that if you see your faces and bodies comely and beautifull, ye may endevor to set forth and grace the gifts of nature the better, by adjoyning vertues thereunto: and if ye perceive your selves to be deformed and il-favoured, you may seeke to supply the defects of nature, with the ornaments of vertue, thereby making your selves no lesse grateful and amiable then they that have beautiful bodies. For it is rather good to see a man of body imperfect and disproportioned endued with vertues, then a goodly body to be nought else but a gay vessell filled with vice and wickednes. Children are to be bred, such as nature giveth them unto us, and we are to have patience to abide their proof, and to see what their actions will be: and if theirs that be of deformed body, do prove good and vertuous, they are so much the more to be commended, as they seemed lesse apt thereunto by their birth. And on the contrary side, they that being beautifull of body, are lewd and vitious, deserve to be driven from the conversation of civil men; yea chased out of the world, as unthankful acknowledgers of so great a gift bestowed upon them, and as unworthy to live among men. These how faire soever (be they children or men) that cary one thing in their tongue, and another in their heart, be they that deserve to be hunted out of all civill societie, that are ingrate for benefites received; who hurt, or seeke to hurt them that have done them good, and hate them, onely because they cannot but know themselves to be bound unto them. These be they that in very truth are crooked, mis-shapen and monstrous, and might well be condemned to be buried quicke: not simple innocent babes, who, having no election, can yeeld no tokens either of good or evill; against whom to pronounce sentence of death before they have offended, is great injustice and exceeding crueltie. And this (loe) is the sentence of this author touching the doubt proposed, wherein (if you rest satisfied) I will proceede.

All the companie assented to the same: and then Master *Dormer* said; Now then (I pray you) let us heare you declare what this end is, whereof you were discoursing when this doubt was proposed, and withall we must expect that you shall shew us and set us in the way wherein we are to travel for the attaining thereof, and give us precepts whereby that perfection may be purchased, unto which all men desirous to become happie in this life, direct their actions and their endevours.

Of this expectation (quoth I) you need not feare to be frustrated, for here shall you have enough (I assure my selfe) to fulfill your desire: and therewith, perusing my papers, I thus followed. The end of man in this life, is happinesse or felicitie: and an end it is called (as before was said) because all vertuous actions are directed thereunto, and because for it chiefly man laboureth and travelleth in this world. But for that this felicitie is found to be of two kinds, wherof one is called civill, and the other contemplative: you shall understand that the civill felicitie is nothing else then a perfect operation of the mind, proceeding of excellent vertue in a perfect life; and is atchieved by the temper of reason, ruling the disordinate affects stirred up in us by the unreasonable parts of the mind, (as when the time shall serve will be declared) and guiding us by the meane of vertue to happy life. The other which is called contemplation, or contemplative felicitie, is likewise an operation of the mind, but of that part thereof which is called intellective, so that those parts which are void of reason, have no intermedling with the same: for he which giveth himselfe to follow this felicitie, suppresseth all his passions, and abandoning all earthly cares, bendeth his studies and his thoughts wholy unto heavenly things; and kindled and inflamed with divine love, laboureth to enjoy that unspeakable beauty, which hath bin the cause so to inflame him, and to raise his thoughts to so high a pitch. But forasmuch as our purpose is now to intreate onely of the humane precepts and instructions, and of that highest good, which in this vale of misery, may be obtained: ye shall understand that the end whereunto man ought to direct all his actions, is properly that civill felicitie before mentioned; which is, an inward reward for morall vertues, and wherein fortune can chalenge no part or interest at all. And this end is so peculiar to reason, that not onely unreasonable creatures can be no partakers thereof, but yong children also are excluded from the same. For albeit they be naturally capable of reason, yet have they no use of her, through the imperfection of their yong age, because this end being to be attained by perfect operations in a perfect life, neither of which, the child, nor the yong man is able to performe, it followeth that neither of them can be accounted happie. And by the same reason it commeth to passe, that though man be the subject of felicitie, yet neither the child nor the yong man may be said properly to be the subject therof, but in power and possibilitie only: yet the yong man approcheth nearer thereunto then the child. And thus much may suffice for a beginning, to satisfie the first part of your demaund.

Then said Captaine *Carleil*, seeing you have proposed to us this end, which is the marke (as it were) wherat all civill actions do level, as at their highest and chiefest good, we will now be attentive to heare the rest, and how you will prescribe a man to order his life, so as from childhood, and so forward from age to age, he may direct his thoughts and studies to the compassing of this good, or *summum bonum*, as Philosophers do terme it.

That shal you also understand, quoth I, but then must the discourse thereof be drawne from a deeper consideration. Those men that have established lawes for people to be ruled by, ought to have framed some among the rest for the foundation of mans life, by which a true and certaine forme of life might be conceived, and such, as beginning to leade him from his childhood, might have served him for a guide, untill he had attained to those riper yeares, wherein he might rather have bin able to instruct others, then need to be himselfe instructed. For the foundation of honest and vertuous living, beginneth even in childhood: neither shal he ever be good yong man, that in his childhood is naught; nor a wicked yong man lightly prove good when he is old. For, such as are the principles and beginnings of things, such are the proceedings. Whereupon the wisest men of the world, have ever thought, that the way to have cities and commonwealths furnished with vertuous and civil men, consisted in the bringing up of children commendably. But among all the lawes of our time, there is no one that treateth of any such matter. There are orders and lawes both universall and particular, how to determine causes of controversie, to end strifes and debates, and how to punish malefactors: but there is no part in the whole body of the law, that setteth downe any order in a thing of so great importance. Yet *Plato* held it of such moment, as knowing that the well bringing up of children, was the spring or wel-head of honest life: he thought it not sufficient, that the fathers onely should take care of nurturing their children, but appointed besides publike magistrates in the common-wealth, who should attend that matter, as a thing most necessary. For though man be framed by nature mild and gentle, yet if he be not from the beginning diligently instructed and taught, he becometh of humane and benigne that he was, more fierce and cruell then the most wild and savage beast of the field. Wheras if he be conveniently brought up, and directed to a commendable course of life: of benigne and humane that he is, he becometh through vertue in a sort divine. And to the end the cause may be the better knowne, why so great diligence is needful and requisite, you must understand, that although our soule be but one in substance, and properly our true forme, yet hath it not one onely part, power, or facultie, or vertue (as we may call it) but divers, appointed for divers and sundry offices. For we being participant of the nature of all things living, and those being devided into three kinds; it is necessary that man shold have some part of every of those three. There is then one base and inferiour kind of life of lesse estimation then the rest, and that is the life of trees and plants, and of all such things as have roote in the earth, which spring, grow, bloome, and bring forth fruite: which fruit *Aristotle* sayth, cometh from them in stead of excrement, together with their seed. And these trees and plants, and such like growing things, have onely life, devoid of feeling (though *Pythagoras* thought otherwise) or of any knowledge: but by the benefite of nature onely, they spring, they grow, and bring forth

34

fruite and seed for the use of man, and for the maintaining of
their kind. There is another kind of life, lesse imperfect then
that, which is the same that perfect living creatures have (for of
that life, which is in maner a meane between the life of plants
and this of sensible creatures, we need not now to speake; or
if it were, we should resemble it to that which Physitions call
Embrio, and is the creature unperfect in the wombe, whiles it
is betweene the forme of seed, and of the kind whence it cometh)
which life of perfect living creatures, hath in it by nature power
to feele, and to move from place to place. For we see they stir
and feele, and have power to desire those things that are meete
for the maintaining of their life and of their nature. And by
natural inclination, and for the increase and continuance of their
kinds, they covet the joyning of their bodies, to yeeld unto nature
that, which of nature they have received, that is, to ingender the
like unto themselves. But this power of the soule, cannot use that
force and vertue which naturally it hath, if it have not withall
that former part which is proper (as is said) to plants, & is called
vegetative (you must give me leave to use new words of Art,
such as are proper to expresse new conceits though they be yet
strange, and not denizened in our language) because it giveth
life and increase to growing things, and without it the power of
feeling doth utterly faile. Next after this, cometh that excellent
and divine part of the soule, which bringeth with it the light
of reason, containing in it the powers, faculties, or vertues of
the other two. For it hath that life which proceedeth from plants;
it hath sense or feeling, & motion from place to place, proper to
the second kind; and it hath besides that other part, wherby it
knoweth, understandeth, discourseth, consulteth, chuseth, and
giveth it selfe to operation, and to contemplate things naturall
and divine: and this part is proper only to man. And as by the
two other faculties before mentioned, we are like to plants and
to bruite beasts: so by this last, we do participate of the divine
nature of God himselfe. Wherefore *Aristotle* said, that man was
created upright, for no other cause, then for that his substance
was divine, whose nature and office is to know and understand.
And truly this gift is given unto us by the maker and governour
of all things, because we might know our selves to be of a nature
most perfect among earthly things, and not farre inferiour to
the divine. And that we have received so singular a gift from

Almightie God for no other cause, but onely to the end we might perceive how all other things that grow and live on earth, are corruptible, and do resolve into their first principles or beginnings, and cease any more to be, as soone as the soule of life departeth from them: but that our minds are immortal and incorruptible, whereby we may rest assured of an eternall life. Since then these three faculties of the soule are in us, it is cleare, that as the plants, among things that beare life, are the most imperfect; so that part of the soule is most unperfect which is proper to their kind: but it is so necessary to all other kinds, as without it there is no life, and with it the rest of the faculties that are joyned therewith, though they be worthier, decay and fall. And this necessitie of nature, that without it she giveth no life, maketh the same to be most base and ignoble. For among natural things, those, which are so necessary, as without them nothing can be done, are alwaies held and reputed the most unworthy. Which thing we may see in that we call *Materia prima*: which though it be in nature before the *forme*, yet because of the necessitie thereof, it is esteemed of no nobilitie in comparison of the *forme*. And even so likewise among the senses, that of feeling is held the basest, because no perfect living creature can be without it, nor yet the rest of the senses, unlesse that be present. And therefore *Aristotle* said, that the other senses were given to man, that thereby he might live the better; but the sense of feeling was given him, because without it he could neither be, nor live. Now for so much as life may be without sense, because the *sensitive* soule is not of such necessitie as is the *vegetative*, therefore is that of more nobilitie then this somewhat, yet inferiour to the *intellective*, which can no more be without the *sensitive*, then the *sensitive* without the *vegetative*. And because the *intellective* soule is not of necessitie serving to any other facultie or power, therfore is she as Lady, Mistris, and Queene over all other the powers, faculties, or vertues of the soul; so as there is none proper unto man, but that whereby he may be either good or bad, happie or unhappie: and the same is it, whereby we understand and make choice rather of one course of life then of another. This great gift hath God bestowed upon us, to shew his great grace and goodnes, and for this purpose, that, as he hath invited us through vertue of our understanding to the knowledge of truth, and by this knowledge to become like unto himselfe; so we should bend all our study and endevours thereunto, as the end and scope of our life in this world. Of which, the occasion of this our present speech did first arise.

Here I pawsing a while, as to take breath, and withall to order some of the papers, the Lord Primate spake, saying: Having treated thus farre of the powers, faculties, vertues, or parts of the soule, I thinke it not impertinent to move a question, whether they be in man separate, and in severall places; or whether they be united all together, and seated in one place?

This question (quoth I) is very pertinent to this place, and by the author here resolved as a doubt, not lightly or easie to be answered. First, for that there have not wanted some, who would needs have that these three powers of the soule, were three distinct soules, and not joyned in one soule, appointed for severall offices. But because that opinion hath bin esteemed but vaine, it needeth not to be insisted upon; but briefly that I declare, what *Aristotle* and *Plato*, with their followers, have held. The first, with his scholers, affirme the reasonable soule to be in substance indivisible: and albeit they assigne unto her divers vertues, yet will they not have them to be indeed several and divers, but that the diversitie should proceed & consist only in the maner of understanding them: supposing them to be in the soule after such a sort, as in the line of a circle, the inner part which is hollow or embowed, and the outward which is bended. Which two parts, though we understand them diversly, yet are they but one line, and not severall. Neither do they assigne unto her divers places: but say that she is all and whole in all our body, and in every part of the same, and apt there to exercise all her functions, if the parts were apt to receive them. But because every part is not disposed to receive them, therefore she maketh shew of them onely in such as are made fit instruments to execute her powers and faculties. So giveth she vertue to the eye to see, to the eare to heare, and to the rest of the members that are the instruments of our senses. But *Plato* and his sect, have given to every power or facultie of the soule, a peculiar seate in mans body: for though they held the soul to be but one, endued with several vertues or powers; yet they affirmed that every one of those had a severall seate appointed in mans body. To the *vegetative* (from which, as from a fountaine, they said, the *concupiscible* appetite doth flow) they appointed the Liver for her

37

place. To the *sensitive*, whence cometh (say they) the fervent passion of anger, they gave the Heart. But the reasonable soule (as being the most divine thing under heaven, they assigned to hold her seate, like a Queene in a royal chaire, even in the head: unto which opinion, all the Greek authors of Physicke have leaned, and specially *Galen* the excellent interpreter of *Hippocrates*, who hath not onely attributed three severall seates to the three severall faculties of the soule, in respect of their operations; but hath also shewed with what order those members are framed, that must be the receptacles of those faculties. For he sheweth how the first member, that taketh forme after the conception, is the liver, from whence spring all the veines, that like small brookes, carry bloud over all the body. And in this member doth he place the living or nourishing soule, which we have termed *vegetative*, affirming it to be most approching to nature. Next unto this, he placeth the heart, wherein all the vitall spirits are forged, and receive their strength: for the generation whereof, the liver sendeth bloud thither, where it is refined, and made more pure and subtill; and from thence by the arteries (which all spring from the heart) the same spirits are spread thoroughout the whole body. And these two principall members, are the seates of the two principall appetites, the *irascible* and the *concupiscible*; of that the heart, of this the liver. And because all this while the creature hath yet no need (as being unperfect) of sense or motion, it is busied about nothing but receiving of nourishment. Somewhat further off from the heart, beginneth the braine to grow, and from it do all the senses flow; and then (loe) beginneth the child to take forme and shape of a perfect creature, the face, the hands, and the feet being then fashioned, with the other parts of the body, apt for feeling and voluntary moving: and from thence be derived the sinewes, the bands or ligaments, and muscles are framed, by which the motions of the members are disposed. This part is the seate of the reasonable soule, by vertue and power of which, we understand, we will, we discourse, we know, we chuse, we contemplate and do all those operations which appertaine unto reason. And as nature hath placed the braine a good distance off from the other two principall members; so hath she framed a cartilage, or thin rynd, or skin to sever the heart from the liver and other inward bowels, as with a fence or hedge betweene them and the other baser parts that are lesse pure. For the heart is purer, and so is that bloud which conveyeth the spirits from it throughout the body, then the liver; or the bloud which is ingendred in the same. And in this respect was *Aristotle* justly reprehended by *Galen*, in that he gave to the heart alone, that which appertained to all three the principall members aforesaid. For though he assigned divers vertues or powers to the soule, yet he placed them all in the heart alone; from which he said (contrary to that which common sense and experience teacheth) that all the veines, arteries and sinewes of the body were derived. But because we should go too farre astray from our purpose, if I should discourse particularly all that which may be said in this matter, I will returne (if you so thinke good) to our former purpose, which I left to satisfie your demaund.

Thus much (said the Lord Primate) hath not a little opened the understanding of this matter, and therefore you may proceed, unlesse any other of the company have any other doubt to propose. But they all being silent, and seeming attentive to heare further, I said; Now that you have understood what the powers and faculties of the soule are, it followeth to be declared, how the ages of mans life have similitude with the same. As the soule of life therfore, called *vegetative*, is the foundation of the rest, and consequently of the basest: so is the age of childhood the foundation of the other ages, and therfore the least noble, for the necessity which it carieth with it. And because upon it, the other ages are built, there ought the greater diligence to be used about the same, to make it passe on towards the other more noble then it self: so as we may reasonably conceive a hope, that from a wel-guided childhood the child may enter into a commendable youth, and thence passe to a more riper age, by the direction of vertue. But first ye must understand, that *Aristotle* wil in no wise yeeld, that this inferiour soule should be capable of reason; and therfore placeth in the sensible soule, both the *concupiscible* and the *irascible* appetites. And contrariwise, *Plato* (as before is said) distinguisheth these two affects, into both these faculties of the soule, giving to the first the *concupiscible*, and the *irascible* to the other. And because *Plato* his opinion hath generally bin better allowed then *Aristotles*, I will speake thereof according as *Plato* hath determined. This baser soule then, being that, whereby we be nourished, we grow, we sustaine life, and receive our body and being; about whose maintaining and increase, she useth continually, whether we wake or sleep, without any endevour of our owne, her vertue and operation (if food and nourishment faile not) is in her ful force, chiefly in childhood: and as soone as the child is borne, stirreth up the desire of food, to the end that by little and little it might gather strength of body, to become apt for the use of the soule, whose organ or instrument it is, for the accomplishing of the more noble operations meet for man. And because the milk of the mother, or of the nurse, is the first fit food for the infant; it were to be wished that it should receive the same rather from the mother, then from any strange woman: for, in reason, the same should be more kindly and natural for the babe then any other. In consideration whereof, the instructors of civill life, have determined and taught, that it is the fathers office to teach and instruct the child, but the mothers to nourish it. For wise men say, that Nature hath given to women their brests, not so much for defence of the hart, as because they should nourish their children: and that she hath given them two paps, to the end that they might nourish two, if by chance they shold be delivered of two at once. And truly it cannot be, but that would much increase both the love of the mother to the child, and likewise that of the child to the mother. Nevertheles, if it fal out (as oftentimes it doth) that the mother cannot give sucke to her child, or for other considerations she give it forth to be nursed to another woman; yet is there special regard to be had, in getting such a nurse as may be of good complexion, and of a loving nature, and honest conditions, that with milke it may also suck a disposition to a vertuous and commendable life.

By your licence (said M. *Dormer*) let me aske you a question, whether you thinke that the mind taketh any qualitie from the nutriment of the body: for if the mind be divine, me seemeth it is against reason, that it should not be of greater power, then to receive corruption from the nutriment of the body.

You say very well, quoth I, and here shall you be resolved of that doubt. That the mind is a divine thing, cannot be denied. And if the vertue of the mind (which is reason) could be freed from the company of those other two faculties of the soule, void of reason, in respect of themselves, it would doubtlesse remaine still in perfection of one nature, and not receive any vice from that nutriment, which yeeldeth matter to the basest facultie of the soule to maintaine and increase the body, but evermore practise her proper operations and vertue: but because it hapneth too often, partly by the ill qualitie of the nutriment, and partly for want of care in the education, that the part wherein the *vegetative* power lieth, getteth overmuch strength, and allured by the delights of the sensible part, giveth it selfe wholy to follow the pleasures of the senses, the mind being oppressed, cannot performe the offices and functions pertaining thereunto. And for this cause *Plato* affirmed, that unhealthfull bodies make the minds weake. And the body can never be sound or healthfull, when it is given to follow that baser part of the soule, and the lusts and sensualities of the same, whereby it forceth the mind prevailing against reason. Not but that the mind is nevertheles divine, but because the body being the necessary instrument of the mind, when it is wrested and drawne to an ill habit, the mind cannot use it as it would, and the light of reason is darkned & hindred, not through any defect of the mind, but onely in respect of the instrument that is become rebellious. Even as if a candle should be put into a close vessell, that the light thereof could not appeare: for the not yeelding of light, should not proceed from the defect of the candle, but of the vessell that inclosed the same. To the end therefore that the child receive not any vicious habit by the qualitie of his first food and nourishment; wise men have advised, that the nurse to be chosen for a child, should not be base or of vile condition, that the child might be the apter to be brought up to vertue: that she be not of strange nation, lest she should give it strange or unseemely manners, unfit or disagreeable to the customes and conditions of the house or citie wherein it is borne, and wherein it is to live: and lastly, that she be of good and commendable behaviour, to the end that with the milk it may suck good conditions, and an honest disposition to vertuous life. And because the nurse may be kept in house, or suffered to carry the child to her owne dwelling place; of the two, it is to be wished that the parents should rather keepe her in their owne house, to the end that even from his infancy it might learne to know the father and mother, and the rest of the family, and take by little and little the fashions and manners of the house. For the minds of children, whiles they be yong, are like to the yong tender slips of trees, which a man may bend and straighten as he list; and are fashioned to such customes and conditions as may best beseeme them. For looke what behaviour they first learne, the same they retaine and keepe a long while after. Wherefore *Phocilides* said right well:

> *Whiles yet in tender yeares the child doth grow,*
> *Teach him betimes conditions generous.*[20]

Great is the care then that fathers ought to use in framing the manners and disposition of their children, when they be yong and tender in their owne houses, and are yet in their nurses laps. Having regard not to use them either over-curstly,[21] or overfondly: for as the first over-aweth them, maketh them dull and base, and vile minded, by taking away the generositie of their minds; the other bringeth them to be wantons and waiward, so as they will never be still, but ever crying and wrawling[22] for they wote not what. For being yet but new in the world, and not acquainted with those things, the images whereof are presented to them by the senses of hearing and seeing; they easily give themselves to waywardnes and crying, when they see any strange sight or images, or heare a fearfull sound or noise, the rather by reason of the melancholy humor, which they bring with them from the mothers womb, (reason having yet little or no force in them, and their judgments being too weak to distinguish good from evill, or what is hurtfull, from what may do them good:) not that naturally they be so, for that tender age is rather sanguine and aeriall; but thorough the remnant of that bloud, from which they received their nutriment in their mothers belly: unto which their crying, the usuall remedy is the moving them from place to place, the rocking of them in their cradles, & the dandling of them; for such motions do divert them from those fearfull impressions, and make them the lesse wayward and combersome, quieting the inward passions of the mind. Besides that, such stirring of them, wakeneth and kindleth in them that naturall heate which helpeth the digestion of humors in them, and maketh them apt to be well nourished and strengthened against those outward feares, which cause their waywardnes and crying. Hereunto may be added the singing of their nurses, whereby they commonly still them, using it, as taught by nature onely: which some men thinke cometh to passe, by reason that the soule is (as they say) composed of harmony, and therefore is delighted with that which is proper and naturall to it selfe. Others (haply of better judgement) say, that children are stilled by the singing of their nurses, because one contrary expelleth and driveth away another, when it is the stronger: so as the nurses singing being lowder then the childs crying, therefore it prevaileth. But the most effectuall reason is, that the *vegetative* power or facultie being of most force in that age, and it taking pleasure in things delightfull, and abhorring those that are displeasant and noisome; when with crying it findeth it selfe annoyed, it doth more willingly admit the nurses singing, and becometh calme and still by hearing the numbers and sweetnes of the voice delighting them. Thus then are children drawne from waywardnes to be stil, from crying to mirth, and become thereby the more lively and fuller of spirit, and stirred up to a better kind of life; growing by little and little apt to understand, and to speake as nature may permit them. In which time specially, great diligence is to be used, that they neither heare any dishonest or unseemely speeches, unfit for a generous mind to conceive, nor see any sights that be shamefull or undecent to behold. For these two senses, of all the rest, are of most importance in this life; for that the images of things are represented to the mind by the eies, and by the eares do the conceits and words enter into the same. And of these two senses, do the eares so much the more helpe us towards the learning of a civill life, as the sentences of wise men passe thereby into our understanding. And whereas the things which we learne by the eyes, are but dumbe words: so do the eares heare the lively voices, by which we learne good disciplines, & the true maner of well living. And therefore *Xerxes* said, that the mind had his dwelling in the eares, which were delighted with the hearing of good words, and grieved at the hearing of unseemely. And the auncient wise men considering the great profit which the eares yeelded towards the attaining of knowledge, accounted them as consecrated to Prudence and to Wisedome. In which respect also, when they met their children, they kissed them on the eare, as if they meant to make much of that part chiefly, by which they hoped their children were to learne wisedome. And for this cause ought they that have the care of bringing up children to be very circumspect, never to pronounce any word before them, but such as are modest, and may tend to the instruction of a good life. For though it seeme not, that yong children marke such things; yet what they heare and see, doth secretly enter into their tender minds, and there take insensible rootes: which,

43

when men think least of any such matter, bringeth foorth fruite agreeable to the seed was sowne. And of ill seed, the fruite cannot but also be evill. Let fathers then take great heed to the modesty of speech and honest behaviour of all his family, and specially of the nurses, in whose bosoms their children are ever held, and in whose faces their eyes are always fixed; because they note and observe most what they do or say, having lesse regard to others. And thus, understanding, increasing in the child with yeares, as soone as he is come to be capable of any precept, before all other things it is expedient that care be had to make him conceive a knowledge of that simple, pure and omnipotent nature, the most high and everliving God, and that the same be so imprinted in his heart, as he may learne God to be the Creator of all things, the giver of life, and maintainer therof, the disposer of all gifts & graces, and the only dispenser of al goodnes: so as he may be made to understand, that he receives al goodnes from his divine Majesty. Therfore they that give unto him any thing, how smal soever a trifle it be, or a toy, shall do well to offer it unto him, as a thing sent unto him, or made for him by God, by little and little to acquaint his mind, and to fashion it to the knowledge of God, and of his divine power and goodnes. For by this meanes shall there be a sure and firme foundation layd, whereupon a strong and never-failing frame of good manners and godly in-structions may be built: and without this foundation, all other care will be spent but in vaine. For he that is void of religion, and of that feare of God, which is in effect but a due reverence unto his Majesty, can never in all the whole course of his life, do any thing worthy prayse or commendation. Whereas on the other side, he that hath this holy feare fixed in his mind, will alwayes abstaine from doing any thing unfitting or dishonest, or that may offend God, and bring him to his wrath and indigna-tion. And if perhaps through the frailtie of our nature apt to offend, by reason of the spot of sinne, wherein we are conceived, throgh the disobedience of our first father *Adam*, he happen to fall somtime into any sin, he is forthwith strucken with that same religious feare and reverence, and being ashamed of himself, seeketh to make reconciliation therfore; to the end he may not dwell in the wrath and displeasure of Almighty God, from whom he acknowledgeth as well his life and being, as whatsoever good besides he hath in this mortall life. To the attaining of this

44

religion, will the example of the father greatly further the child, if to him he shew himselfe such, as he wisheth he should become. For though the children of *Socrates* (as it is written) proved not capable of good discipline, though the father were a patterne or fountaine of honest and vertuous life, yet are we to assure our selves, that the example of the fathers life is the true and perfect mirror for the child to fashion himselfe by, that he may attaine a commendable course of life. For if the dumbe and senslesse images of excellent men, which the auncient Romanes held in their houses, were sufficient to stirre up in young men, when they beheld them, a desire to follow their steps, and to resemble those noble personages of their auncestors, whose resemblances they beheld; endevouring themselves not to degenerate from the vertues and the nobilitie of their parents: how much more, may we thinke, that it wil move the child to see in his fathers lively face, and in his actions vertue imprinted, and daily represented. I know right well, that sometimes the contrary is seene, through the inconstancy of humane things: but if we consider what happeneth for the most part, we shall find that good examples commonly are causes of good, and bad examples causes of evill. Since the child therfore is chiefly to learne of the father his forme of life, it is the fathers part to be to him in his tender yeares a lively patterne of vertue, as we have said, wherby he may (as it were) ingraft into his childs mind that good and commendable kind of life, which may bring him by vertuous actions to honour and estimation. But because it cometh oftener to passe then were requisite, that the father being busied about other matters concerning the order of his house and family, or else in the managing of the affaires of the common-wealth, he cannot attend the bringing up of his child with that care that he ought, therfore must he provide for his education, so as the same be not neglected. For as the true images of vertue are easily imprinted in the minds of children whiles they be tender: so do they quickly weare out and vanish, if they be not refreshed and revived by the discretion and industry of some meet person appointed for that purpose, and their contraries as soone ingraved in their places. The father therefore ought in any wise to make choise of some such man, to whom he may commit the charge and instruction of his child, when he is past the age of three yeares, as may be meet to give him good example of life, and season

45

him with such doctrine, as he may not degenerate or decline from that vertuous course of life which he hath endevored to put into the babes mind, even whiles he was yet in his nurses armes, and under the charge of women. For if in those first dayes of infancy, when yet he had almost no understanding, so great care was to be taken (as we have said) to lay a good foundation, how much more diligence is there now to be used, when he beginneth to have some knowledge and judgement, that the building may rise answerable to the same. Wise men have wisely said, that nature is the best mistris we can have: and the custome of vertuous behaviour and wholsome doctrine being taken in tender yeares, is converted not onely into an habite, but even into nature. Wherefore let the father at those yeares give his child in charge to some vertuous and godly man to be trained and instructed, who must be neither too mild nor too severe; but such, as may in some things agree with the manner of the nurses bringing up, to the end he may gently turne to other manners and behaviour then he had learned when he was most among women. For to take a child from the brest, and from his nurses bosome, and to put him suddenly under the hard government of a curst master, would be too violent a change, and force that tender nature overmuch. But if he that shal then have the ruling of him, shall discreetly win him with mildnes from being fond after the nurse, and by little and little draw him to a more firme kind of behaviour, in such sort as he scarse perceive that he hath forsaken his nurses lap: the child wil quickly delight to be with him as much as with his nurse, yea or with his father or mother: and pratling or childishly craving, now one thing, then another of him, there wil soone spring in his mind a desire of knowledge: which desire, though indeed it be naturall & borne with us, yet hath it need to be holpen and stirred up to come forth and put it selfe in action; for else will it lie hidden and covered with the unworthiest part of the soule, like to the fire which is covered with ashes: which though it have naturally vertue to give light and heate, yet unlesse that impediment be taken away, it wil do neither of both, nor be apt to worke his naturall effect. And therefore (as before is said) he which shall take the charge of the child after the nurse, must be very discreet to win him to his discipline without bitternes or stripes, which do rather dull and harden the childs mind, then worke any good effect. And the servile feare which the oversharpe and unadvised usage or beating of the child bringeth him unto, (not fit for a generous mind) maketh him to hate the thing he should learne, before he can come to know it, much lesse to love it. It is also a thing very profitable for his better instructing, that there be others of like yeares in his company to learne with him; for so will there arise a certaine emulation among them, through which, every of them will strive to step before his fellow: besides that the conversation of such as are like in age and qualitie, wel bred and brought up, is a very fit occasion to make them all wel mannered and of good behaviour, those yong yeares being (as before is sayd) apt for the simplicitie thereof, to take whatsoever forme is given unto them. And for this cause was *Merides* King of the Aegyptians greatly commended among the auncient wise men, for that as soone as his sonne *Sisostres* was borne, he caused all the children that were borne in the citie that same day, to be gathered together, and brought up with his said son, where they were instructed in all those disciplines and noble arts, that in those dayes were in estimation, and meet to direct to a commendable life. And that the manner of good education is to proceed by degrees, it appeared by the order which the Kings of Persia held in the bringing up of those who were to succeed them in their Empire. But because our discourse tendeth not to the instructing of Princes children, but onely of such gentlemen of meaner qualitie as may be fit instruments for the service of their commonwealth or country: it will be best to passe that over in silence.

Whiles in this place I was pawsing a while, as to take some breath, Captaine *Carleil* sayd in this sort: I hope your author giveth not over so this matter. For howsoever his purpose was to discourse of the civill life of private men, yet the declaring of the order which was held in the instructing and training up of the children of those Princes, cannot but be as well profitable as delightfull. Therefore let us (I pray you) heare what is sayd by him touching the same.

That shal I willingly do, said I, for that the like request was made to him by one of that company; and thus he proceedeth, saying, that though it might suffice to refer them to what *Xenophon* in his *Ciropædia* hath left written of that subject, having learnedly and diligently under the person of *Cirus*,

47

framed an *idaea* or perfect patterne of an excellent Prince: yet he meaning to follow *Plato* and *Aristotle* in his treatise, will therefore report what he hath gathered out of *Plato* to that purpose, and adde therunto briefly as much out of *Aristotle* as may serve for the better understanding of the rest. You shall understand then that the custome among these kings, was to give the child who was to succeed in the kingdome, soone after he was borne, into the hands of those Eunuchs that were esteemed of best life in the court: whose care was chiefly to fashion his body with all diligence, that it might be straight and most comely of shape and proportion; because the first thing that is offred to the sight in a King, is the grace and comelinesse of his person, which maketh him to be reverenced of his people, and beloved of his Peeres. His infancy being past, he was given in charge to others, that exercised him in handling his weapons, horse-manship, and feates of armes; and likewise in hunting, as a meet exercise to frame him fit for military discipline. And this the father did, because he was perswaded that the knowledge of warre was one of the surest foundations for the upholding of a State or kingdome. When he was come to the age of 14. yeares, then was he delivered over to foure other excellent personages, who were called the royall schoole-masters, the one most wise and prudent, the other most just, another most temperate, and the last most valiant. The first instructed him to know and honour God, and taught him the knowledge of things divine and eternall, and withall, such as appertaine to the life of a good Prince: by which he became learned, as wel in things contemplative, as in things concerning the actions necessary and convenient for a King. For they exercised him dayly in the understanding of sciences, and in the knowledge of good and vertuous behaviour, as two most necessary things to humane life, and which should leade him the ready way to his felicitie and happines in this world; making him to know, that nothing was more miserable in man then ignorance, and how by the generall consent of the most wise men, he that is ignorant is esteemed an ill man. To which purpose it is said by *Cicero*, that there is no greater evill can befall a man then to be ignorant. And *Plato* (from whom the other drew his sentence) sayth, that all ignorant persons were in that respect also miserable. For Temperance being the rule and measure of Vertue, upon which dependeth mans felicitie; the opinion of this divine Philosopher was, that he that was ignorant could not know temperance, and consequently must be to seeke in the way of vertue: the defect whereof estrangeth a man from God, even as the having of this singular vertue of temperance (wherof we shall speake hereafter more at large) doth draw him neare unto his Majesty, to his great comfort and satisfaction. Ignorance therfore being a mortall infirmitie unto mans mind, and such a one as suffereth him not to enjoy his felicitie, to which (as to the marke proposed) he levelleth all his actions: it is written that they of *Mitilene* intending severely to punish certaine of their confederates, who being armed with them in the field, had forsaken them, made a decree against them, that from thenceforth they should not set their children to schoole to learne arts or sciences. This first schoole-master teaching him thus, Religion and the feare of God; and training him in the manners and behaviour appertaining to a King, did so long hold him under his governance, till it appeared he had taken well and perfectly that discipline. Then the second master taking him in charge, taught him that which in consequence next followeth to religion, that is, that there is nothing more fitting for a King then truth and veritie; that speciall care was to be taken so to embrace the same, as he should never have one thing in his mouth, and another in his heart, as wicked and deceitful men have, who are borne for the destruction of vertue, and of honest and wel-disposed persons: and that those, who were to be taxed therewith, were not only deceivers, but worthy the name of traitors. In regard wherof (as *Philostratus* writes) among the Indians, if any man bearing magistracy, were detected of a lie, he was presently deprived of his magistracy, and disabled for ever after to beare any. And this they did, because they conceived (and that rightly) that he which respected not truth in matters of moment, destroyed as much, as in him lay, the societie and civill conversation of men, since no man can trust or beware of a lyer. Therfore (as *Plutarch* reporteth) *Epenetus* affirmed, that all injuries and wickednes proceeded from a lyer. This schoole-master gave him to understand, that as the nature of God is pure and simple, never deceiving us, whether we sleepe or wake: so, seeing there was no dignitie under God so great as the Kings, he ought first, and above all things, to conforme himselfe and his actions unto that high and eternall truth, the feare & knowledge

49

of whom, had bin formerly taught him. And as it seemed to them, that by truth he attained a resemblance of God himselfe: so did they think that by lying, a man was worthy to loose the title of a man. Which thing haply he meant, who devised *Pan* to be the son of *Mercury*, the inventer of speech, as Poets have fained; signifying by the shape of *Pan*, under which is comprehended as well the false speaker as the true; that the upper part of his body bearing humane shape, betokeneth truth (then the which nothing is more proper to a man of vertue) but by the lower parts being crooked, and of shape like a goate, false and untrue speaking was signified: inferring that man by speaking untruth, becometh monstrous, and of a reasonable creature falleth to be a bruite beast: whence also proceeded that among the Persians, a lie was reputed a most hainous offence. And we see that even now among us, it is reputed so great a shame to be accounted a lyer, that any other injury is cancelled by giving the lie; and he that receiveth it, standeth so charged in his honor and reputation, that he cannot disburden himselfe of that imputation, but by striking of him that hath so given it, or by chalenging him the combat.

Captaine *Norreis* hearing thus much spoken of truth, and of the lie, interrupting me, said; God grant your author follow this theame a while, that we soldiers may also have some instruction from him. For this matter of the lie giving and taking, is growne of late among us to be confused and dangerous, so as a man can hardly tell, how to carry himselfe in so many occasions, and sundry cases, as dayly happen in companies, wherein perhaps the authoritie and reasons of such a man may yeeld us no small light.

Your wish therin (quoth I) shal not be frustrate, for the matter is by him handled at large: but let us heare what be the points that you would specially be resolved in; for it is not unlikely but that they will jump with the question proposed by one of those persons supposed in his dialogue.

Marry sir (said he) I would gladly know, since he hath spoken of truth and untruth, and declared how the injury received by taking the lie, cannot be cancelled, but by striking or chalenging the partie who gave it; whether this kind of chalenging and fighting man to man, under the name of *Duellum*, which is used now a dayes among souldiers and men of honour, and by long custome authorized, to discharge a man of an injury received, or for want of proofes in sundry causes, be ancient or no? whether it concerne honor or no? and whether it appertaine to civill life, and that felicitie which we are discoursing upon or no?

You have (said I) moved your question very right, and to the purpose; which to answer at full, would require a long speech: so deepe rootes like an ill weed, have the opinions of men taken concerning the same in this our age; which to cut downe or roote up, many sithes and howes[21] would scarce suffice. But as briefly as may be, you shall be satisfied in part; and he will make it appeare unto you, that the reasons which are set downe in defence of this foolish custome and wicked act, are false and absurd. And first of all you shall heare him say, that this maner of combatting, which through the corruption of the world hath taken strength, and is permitted of some Princes, is nothing aunciant at all. For in histories it is not to be found, that for revenge of injury, for want of proofes, for points of honour, or for any such like causes, this wicked and unlawfull kinde of fight, was ever graunted or allowed in auncient time. For when any difference or controversie fell out among men of honor, which might concerne their credit and reputation for matter of valor, they never tried the quarrell by combat betweene themselves, but strove to shew which of them was most worthy honor, by making their valour well knowne in fight against their common enemies, as in *Cæsars* Commentaries we have a notable example. And the singular fights or combats, that are mentioned in the Greeke or Latine histories, or fained by the Poets, happened evermore betweene enemies of contrary nations, or otherwise in time of publike warre, though perhaps the quarrell might be privat betweene some of the chiefe men of both camps, as betweene *Turnus* and *Æneas*, *Paris* and *Menelaus*. *Turnus* labouring that *Æneas* might not have *Lavinia* to his wife: and *Menelaus* seeking to recover his wife whom *Paris* had taken from him. Or else they fought for the publike quarrell, one to one, or more in number on each side, for preventing of greater bloodshed, as did the *Horatii* and the *Curiatii* before Rome. Or by the ordinance of some publike games, as those called *Pithii* and *Olimpici* among the Greeks, and those called *Circenses* among the Romanes, whether they were celebrated in honour of their Gods, or at the funerals of their dead, or for other causes. In which games or spectacles were produced certaine men, named by the Romanes *Gladiatores*, and by the Greeks *Monomachi*, to fight together; the first invention wherof, appeareth to have come from the people of *Mantinea*. But other private combats for causes above mentioned, was never so much as heard of among them, much lesse received or allowed in their common-weales, which were well ordered and maintained by honest and vertuous lawes. The name of *Duellum* was given by the Latins, not to singular fight betweene man and man, but to the generall warre betweene two nations or States, as may be seene by *Plautus*, *Horace*, *Livie*, and other authors. And as for them that say, the name of *Duellum* was unproperly applied to an universall warre, they are not to be heard or beleeved, because they that so used it, were the fathers of the Latine tongue, who knew better the proprietie of the words of their owne language, then these fellowes now do. But rather they are to be blamed for wresting that auncient name to so wicked a fight, which they rightly gave to the generall warre allowed by the lawes, and by all civill and politike constitutions.

The Primate, who had bin attentive to this speech, said, as concerning the Latins, it is true that hath bin alledged: but it seemeth, the Greeks knew very well this combat, as may be gathered by the word *Monomachia*, which signifieth the fight of one man against another. And I remember *Plato* in his dialogue intituled *Laches*, maketh mention of this same singular fight, which sheweth, that in his dayes the combat of body to body was knowne and used.

Two things (said I) the author hath said, the one, that this sort of battell or fight which is now in use, and called *Duellum*, was not knowne to the ancient Greeks nor Romanes in their wel-ordered Common-weales, and that therefore they gave no such name unto the same: the other, that the Romanes gave that name of *Duellum* to the publike warre betweene two people or nations, being enemies. But that the Greeks gave not the name of *Monomachia* to those singular fights which were used among them, that hath he not said. But though the name of *Monomachia* were used among them, yet was it not meant of this kind of combat which we speake of, but of that onely which was sometimes used in their publike games and spectacles, or else might fall out sometimes accidentally in their warres. And

that same place of *Plato* which you have alledged, doth sufficiently declare it. For if my memory faile me not, he saith there,
that when the generall battell ceaseth, and that it is requisite
either to fight with them that resist, or to repulse those that
would assault, in such a case the *Monomachia*, or fight of man
to man was meet to end all strife. Which word of *Monomachia*,
nevertheles I remember not to be used by *Aristotle* in any place
of all his works, from whom nevertheles these men that defend
this folly, seeme to fetch their arguments, as hereafter I shall
declare. But by this you may perceive that the use of *Monomachia*, was a fight betweene two men in their publike games
and shewes, not for private quarrell or hatred, nor for want of
proofes, or for points of honour. And further I will say, that in
well ordered martiall discipline, and warres lawfully enterprised,
after the fury of the battell was ceased, it was not lawfull to kill
or hurt the publike enemy. Which thing is cleerly set foorth by
Xenophon in the person of *Chrisantas*, who although he had cast
downe his enemy, and fastned hold in the haire of his head, ready
to have stricken it off; yet hearing the trumpet sound the retreit,
forbare to strike him, but let him go: holding it not fit to offend
his enemy after the time of fight was past, signified by the retreit
sounding. This sort of fight was likewise suffered against publike
enemies by the Romanes when their state flourished. For we
reade in their histories of sundry that have in the warres fought
hand to hand with their enemies; but yet could not the Romane
souldier, though he were provoked by his enemy to singular
battell, fight with him without the licence of his General or
Captain. And this was so religiously observed among them in
that Common-weale (which was the patterne of all others) that
the father spared not to condemne and slay his owne sonne, who
had gotten a notable victory in his absence, because he had
without his fathers licence attempted to fight with the enemy.
True it is, that for contention of valor, we reade that *Alexander*
granted a combat betweene *Diosippus* and his adversary, both
being his souldiers and in his campe, though the one were a
Macedonian, and the other an Athenian; which *Diosippus*
unarmed, having onely a clubbe for weapon, overcame the
Macedonian armed with speare and sword, and other armour
on his body. But this was not for quarrell of injury received,
for revenge or want of proofes. Neither from this one example,

53

is any conclusion to be drawne, that for strife of valour the combat should be granted. For the not admitting it afterwards in wel-ordered commonweales, nor by any other generall that we can reade, above once, doth plainly shew that it was rather a toy of *Alexanders* head, then grounded upon any reason: who among so many vertues as he had, wanted not other disordered motions, which stained his noblest and most glorious actions, as that of the death of *Calisthenes* and some others. By this then you may understand that among the Greeks our maner of combat was unknown, & that it was not that which they cal *Monomachia*. But this wicked and detestable custom of the combat sprong first among the Longobards, a barbarous people; & much more barbarous is the thing it selfe growne, by the abuse therof in our daies. For though they in some cases granted the combat, yet suffered they not their champions to fight with weapons of steele or iron, but only with staves & targets, unles it were in cases of treason. But now upon every quarrell they come to fight with swords & daggers, and other like sharp weapons, and with minds cruelly bent to murder and mischiefe like most wild and savage beasts. And thus much concerning the first question may serve, since time wil not permit to treate of every one at large.

Yea but, I think, said captain *Carleil*, that if the combat be lawfull in cases of treason or injury to the Prince, the same reason should make it lawfull also for other causes.

Not so, said I, for treasons or offences against the Princes persons, offend the publike State, which reposeth upon the person of the Prince, and therefore the injuries of private men are not to be compared unto them. And as touching the second point, whether it concerne honor or no: my author saith, that he that taketh so unjust a course to revenge his private wrong, is so farre from getting honor thereby, as he rather looseth whatsoever honor or reputation he had before; the combat being a thing odious and offensive unto God. For it is said, that he reserveth revenge unto himselfe; which, they that by combat seeke to wreake themselves, take upon them to do by their owne power and strength, against all lawes divine, naturall and positive, in contempt of magistrates, contrary to the orders and constitutions of all wel-founded Common-weales: and finally contrary to all equity, and all civill and honest conversation. Howbeit I know there want not some, who with their confused arguments go about to make men beleeve, that so great an injustice should be equitie: not knowing, or faining not to know, that equitie is the tempering or mitigating the rigor of the law, which otherwise (like a tyrant) condemneth without mercy; being farre from favouring the rigor of so unreasonable and so sharpe a conflict, then the which, none can be imagined more furious or contrary to the nature of man. Yet forsooth to equitie do these maintainers of the combat seeke to draw this crueltie; arguing that of two evils, it is the lesser; and that the lesser evill is to be reputed in liew of a good, if not truly, yet respectively. Which argument is no way to be admitted, since that (God be thanked) without this lesser evill, so many good Common-weales have ever bin ruled, and at this day are not knowing, or faining not to know, that equitie ruled with good and politike governement; and the same never permitted, but where men forsake to follow reason, and like mad and desperate people are transported by rage and fury. For what commonwealth, either auncient or moderne, well framed upon honest and godly lawes, 'hath ever admitted this lesser evill? And yet, Iwis, in all places and in all ages have injurious words and deeds past betweene men. Nay, the same hath evermore bin forbidden utterly, and the inquirie and punishment of the wrong-doers bin reserved to the magistrates. Neither doth their allegation of being included within the kind of warre generall, serve to their purpose. For the combat is not contained under warre, as the particular under the universall: for those things that are contained under any universall, are of the same nature that the universal is: as we see man hath the nature of the living creature, under which he is contained, even as is the bruite beast; but the combat is cleane contrary of nature to the universall warre, as shall be declared. First great Lords and Princes who make warre, have no magistrates over them to decide by justice, and to end their controversies, as private men have. Besides that, when warre is moved against any Prince, the State and Common-weale is offended, publike orders are perverted, honesty put in danger, the way layd open to all injury to the offence of Almightie God, and finally, whatsoever is good or honest in citie or country, brought into confusion. And man being borne for the behoofe of his country, his Prince, his kinred and friends, and for the defence of religion, publike honesty and of vertue; it is the dutie of every man of vertue and honor, to oppose himselfe against the fury of the enemy for the defence of all those things above specified. Furthermore, the universal warre is allowed by the lawes of all those who have bin founders of famous Common-weales, to take away seditions, and reduce such as were rebellious to obedience, and to maintaine temperance and order among all subjects. And God himselfe is called the God of hoasts, but not the God of combats: for they are none of his works, but of the divell himselfe. Whereupon it is also sayd in the Scripture, that the strength of warre consisteth not in the multitude of souldiers, but that it commeth from heaven. And S. *Augustine* sayth, that warre is not unjust, unlesse it be raised with purpose to usurpe or to spoyle: and S. *Ambrose* in like sence affirmeth, that the valour of those men that defend their countrey from barbarous people, is full of justice. By all which may clearly be seene how farre they are astray, that would bring this kind of combat to be comprehended under the kind of warre universall. And if in all ages, civill warres have bin odious and accounted cruell, what praise or commendation can be justly given to two gentlemen of one citie or country that fight together with purpose to kill one another? whereas then the circumstances above mentioned make the universall warre just and lawfull: this wicked kind of private fight or combat, is voyde of them all, and cannot therefore be but most unjust and unlawfull. With like wrong do they also labour to make it seeme commendable, affirming that men thereby shew their valour and fortitude. For valour or fortitude being a principall vertue, how can it have place in so unjust and so unnaturall an action, proceeding onely from anger, rage, fury, and rashnes? Finally, these men that will needs have *Aristotle* to be their warrant, might (if they list) see that he in his Ethikes, where he directeth man unto vertue, and to civill felicitie, putteth not among those whom he calleth *fortes*, or men of valour, such men as are delighted in revenge, but giveth them the title of warlike or *bellicosi*. And in the same bookes he sayth, that whosoever doth any thing contrary to the lawes, is to be accounted unjust. And (I pray you) what can be more directly contrary to the lawes then this kind of combat or private fight? And if by taking justice from the world, all vertue must needs decay, because she is the preserver and defender of vertue; how can this so excellent a vertue of fortitude be in them, that despising the lawes and the magistrates, and neglecting all religion, and

56

good of their cuntrey and weale publike, do practise this wicked combat. Moreover, they perceive not, that *Aristotle* in his Ethikes (from whence the rules of civill life are to be drawne, and not from his Rhetorikes, out of which these men fetch their doutie arguments, because elsewhere they can find none for their purpose) saith, that to fight for cause of honour, is no act of fortitude. Whereupon ensueth, that such as come to the combat upon points of honour, as men do now a dayes for the most part, make not any shew of their fortitude, but onely of their strength and abilitie of body, and of their courage: whereas true fortitude, is to use these gifts well and honestly, according to reason. And what honestie or reason can there be in this so mischievous and wicked a fight? which nevertheles these men so farre allow and commend, as they are not ashamed to say (moved surely by some divellish spirit) that a man for cause of honour may arme himselfe against his country, the respect whereof is and ever was so holy; yea even against his father, and with cursed hands violate his person, unto whom (next after God) he must acknowledge his life and being, and what else soever he hath in this world. This cannot be but a most pestiferous opinion, and a speech hardly to be beleeved could come out of the divels owne mouth of hell; who though he be the author of all evill, yet scarce thinke I that he durst father so abhominable a conceit or sentence. But it is a world to see how solemnly men will become starke mad, when they once undertake to defend a mad cause. For to make their frantike fancie to seeme reasonable, they utter such absurdities as are not only detestable to men, but even bruite beasts also abhorre. For among beasts, many there are, that by naturall instinct, not onely feare and respect their begetters, but do also nourish them diligently when they are waxen old, and not able to purchase foode for themselves, repaying thankfully the nouriture which themselves received whiles they were yong, as it is certainly knowne the Storke doth. But here to colour their assertions, they say, that so ought children to do to their parents, and citizens to their country, so long as the one ceaseth not to be a father, and the country forgetteth not her citizens: a saying no lesse foolish then the other. For when can that come to passe? what law of nature, or what civill constitution hath taught us this lesson? or out of what schoole of Philosophie have they learned it? what injuries can a father or a mans country do unto him that may make him not to acknowledge his countrey, which ought to be deerer unto him then his life, or to cast off the reverence due to his father? Good God what els is this but to invite men, and as it were to stir them up to *parricide*, a thing odious even to be mentioned. It is no marvel therfore, if such as attribute so much to points of honor, & wil needs defend the combat in that respect, fall by Gods sufferance (as men blinded of the light of naturall reason) into such absurd opinions, fit for senslesse men: which opinions, in very truth, are no lesse to be condemned then wicked heresies, and the authors of them worthy sharpe punishment to be inflicted upon them by such as have authoritie in that behalfe. And this do they the rather deserve, because they seeke to maske and disguise the good and commendable opinions of the best Philosophers, and to wrest them in favour of their damnable and wicked doctrine. But I should digresse too far if I should say all I could to confute this impietie, and these wicked writings and cruell opinions: and therefore returning to our purpose of honour, whereof we were speaking, you may understand by that which I have already sayd, that honour there is none to be gotten by the combat; yet because among other things they say the combat hath bin devised for cause of honour, I must let you know that in true and sound Philosophie, they that respect honour as the end of their actions, are not onely unworthy to be accounted vertuous men, but deserve blame and reproch. But hereof I shall have occasion to speake more amply in a fitter place. Onely this I wil now adde, that no actions are commendable but those that are honest, and where honestie is not, there can be no honour. And honestie in truth there is none (as before hath bin said) in such a fight contrary to all vertue, odious to all lawes, to all good magistrates, and to God himselfe; though the folly of the favourers of this divellish device seeke most wrongfully to draw the summe of all vertues to this injustice. Furthermore, either the offences done to men, may be avouched before Princes and magistrates in judgement, as no wrongs, but lawfull acts, or not. If they may be so avouched and proved, then a thousand combats cannot take them away: neither is there any cause of combat if so wicked a custome were allowable. If not, then he that hath done the injury, is already dishonest and dishonored; and the victorie over such a man, in faith what honour can it purchase? *Plato* the divine Philosopher, and *Aristotle* his disciple after him, considering the nature of injury, and finding that it caried with it alwayes vice and reproch, affirmed that it was better to receive an injury then to do it. And *Plato* concludeth, that he that doth injury, cannot attaine to happinesse: both which sayings are most agreeable to Christian religion. *Aristotle* affirmeth, that the magnanimous or great minded man, utterly despiseth all injuries, for that an ill man cannot by any injury he can do unto him, blemish those vertues wherewith he must be adorned to be truly magnanimous. With these worthy men therefore I conclude, that injuries are to be contemned and light set by, specially of magnanimous men. For, as *Seneca* saith, a magnanimous man will never thinke that a vicious man hath done him injury, though his meaning were to do it; but referre the punishment of his ill intention to the magistrate, and the revenge to God. And whosoever doth otherwise, entring into this revengefull humour of the combat, he doth not onely not purchase any honor to himselfe thereby, but heapeth on his owne head Gods wrath and indignation, and shame of the world in the judgement of wise men, who know what is honest, and what not, what things deserve praise, and what blame; and how, when, and wherefore a man of vertue ought to venture his life. For he that thinketh by the combat to right himselfe, taketh upon him the office of God, and of the magistrate, as if himselfe were superiour to them both, and were able of himselfe (as soveraigne Lord) to do justice: which thing how dangerous it is in a wel-ordered Common-weale, all lawes, and reason it selfe doth plainly teach us.

But yet these goodly defenders of this abuse say, that a man, both by order of nature, and by the opinion of Philosophers, may well repulse an injury by his owne vertue, and not by law. And I say (as before) that if the injury be done unto a man of magnanimitie; the way to shake it off, is to despise it, because the excellencie of his vertue is greater then any injury that can be done unto him: and if it be done to him that is not come to that degree of vertue as to be magnanimous, he may perchance at the instant repulse the same, or revenge himself in hot bloud without any great reproch. But to reserve a malice or hatred any long time, and therupon to come to the combat with a revengefull mind, as bruite beasts do; will alwayes be esteemed of wise men, a vicious action, and contrary to all lawes and civill order. And they that are of such revengefull minds, are termed by

Aristotle bitter and sharpe men, as if he would say without reason. In which respect he judgeth them to be (as hereafter shal be shewed) men unworthy of civil conversation. And by him it is esteemed the part or office of a vertuous civill man, and a point of magnanimitie to pardon and forgive offences and injuries. For *Plato* and his followers were ever of opinion, that magnanimite was given to man, not because he should dispose himselfe to hatred, fury, revenge and wrath, but to honestie and vertue. Wherefore *Seneca* also said, that it was a kind of revenge to forgive. And the temple of the *Graces* (according to *Aristotles* opinion) was placed in the midst of the citie of *Athens*, because all men might thereby understand, that they were to render good for good, not ill for ill. For as by the first, cities are the better preserved and maintained: so by the other, they are destroyed and brought to ruine. Yet if the magnanimous man would wish him chastised that hath offended him, he will not vouchsafe himselfe to file[24] his hands upon so base and vicious a person as those be (by *Plato* and *Aristotles* judgement) who are injurious to others; but suffereth the magistrates according to the order of law to revenge his cause by the punishment of the offender, according to his desert, to the end the vertue of the one, and the vice of the other may be manifested, and the one chastised, and the other honored thereby. And what more glorious revenge can a man desire, or what more notable testimonie of his vertue, then to have him corrected, and rest infamous by the punishment which law shall inflict upon him who hath done him injury? Or what else do these furious minded men seeke in fine by their combat? But yet they alledge further (as wiling to maintaine their wrong opinions with some shew of reason) that combats are sought only in cases of injuries, not determinable by law. Which answer is as inconsiderate as the rest. For what kind of injuries can grow betweene man and man, whereunto the authoritie of the Prince and of the Magistrates doth not extend? who indeed are not to regard the obstinacie of the parties, but to punish them by imprisonment, and such other meanes as law doth allow and permit; to bridle the insolencie and disobedience of such as will not obey and be ameinable. For if in civill actions that course be held, wherefore should not the same rigor be the rather used in this so unlawfull and beastly a debate? Neither is there any reason in that they speake of publike and private injuries, since the cases are farre unlike. For publike injuries come from lawfull enemies, such as offend or offer wrong to States or Cities: but they that are privatly injuried in their person, cannot call them their lawfull enemies that so have done them injury: rather they themselves are to be esteemed lawfull enemies to their countrey, whiles in following their rage and furious appetite of revenge, they oppose themselves against the publike and civill governement, and deserve in that respect to be severely punished by the magistrate, as men that esteeme more their private injustice than publike justice. And thus much for the second part of your question. Now touching the last point, whether it appertaine to civill felicitie or no: you may easily gather by that which is already said, that there can be nothing more contrary to good discipline in a wel-ordered commonweale, then this wicked and unjust kind of fight, which destroyeth, so farre foorth as it beareth sway, all civill societie. For it breedeth the contempt of God and his commandements, of Religion, of lawes, constitutions and civill governement, of Princes, of magistrates, and finally of countrey, parents, friends and kinred: to all which men are bound by reason naturall and civill, and for defence of them to spend their lives in maner aforesaid: but not at their owne appetite, instigated by rage and furie to be prodigall thereof, or for revenge of private quarrels or injuries. Will you see how absurd and senslesse a thing these men maintaine, that set up and magnifie this glorious combat? then take but this one instance. They say, in good sooth, that if two gentlemen, subject to the selfe and same lawes, stirred by this furious conceit, have chalenged the one the other to the combat, and that their soveraigne Lord or Prince forbid them to proceed therein, that they are not to obey him, but to seeke to accomplish their chalenge elsewhere out of his jurisdiction. And can any reasonable man, or a good subject endure to heare such a proposition maintained without stomacke or displeasure? That which among the Painims and Gentiles was not lawful without speciall licence of the superiours to be attempted against a publike enemie, armed to the ruine of their State and Common-weale: will these jolly politicians have now to be lawfull among Christians in dispite of their naturall and lawful Lords and Princes, upon whom the foundation of well pollicied States is layd, and in the obedience towards whom, civill felicitie it selfe doth rest?

But we neede not to marvell, if such men contemne humane lawes and ordinances, when they sticke not to disobey God himselfe; unto whom they knowing manifestly this kind of fight to be odious and displeasing; yet are they not ashamed by publike writings to maintaine it, and thereby to draw souldiers and men of valour into their error of a wilfull madnesse and mischievous mind. It is a meere mockery, and a thing worthy to be laughed at, to see how busily such fellowes build upon a false foundation, as if their building were like to stand. For leaving and forsaking the patterne and true rules of vertuous behaviour, of policie and states, and of good lawes written by that excellent Philosopher *Aristotle*, they take hold (forsooth) of some fragments or parcels of his Rhetorikes to worke upon: as though from thence men were to take the precepts of civill conversation or politike governement, whence onely the rules and method of well speaking are to be taken, and not of civill felicitie. Out of his Rhetorikes they have culled out namely this place, where he saith, that God helpeth those that are wronged, not understanding, or seeming not to understand, that *Aristotle* in that place speaketh of civill judgements or criminall; and not of battels or combats, such as this that he never knew, ne yet ever heard spoken of: and if he had, would have sought to have driven it out of the frantike fancie of all men. It is not to be denied, but that in good and godly judgements managed by men desirous to maintaine justice, God is alwayes at hand to help and uphold the right, and to tread downe and overthrow the wrong. For by him have judgements bin appointed and ordained, and magistrates to rule and oversee them, not only for the common benefit of men, but also for the defence of truth and righteousnesse, and for the punishment of untruth and wickednesse. Moreover it is to be understood, that onely such places in *Aristotles* Rhetorikes are to be approoved and allowed in civil or politike life, as are by him confirmed in his Ethikes and Politikes: as that it is lawfull for a man to repulse an injury, and to defend himselfe, and such other like. For, as himselfe affirmeth, the drift of his booke of Rhetorikes, is to instruct a man how to frame his speech to perswade, and how to move the minds of Judges to anger, hatred, revenge, compassion, and such like other affects, which oftentimes wrest the truth, and make wrong to prevaile. So as if the Orator prevaile, and attaine the end he seeketh, which is to perswade, or use the meanes to attaine it artificially, he hath done his dutie. By which it appeareth, that Rhetorike is ordained for judgements and controversies, but not for instruction of civill life and manners. But let us see what they get by this place taken out of the Rhetorikes. For my part, I see not wherfore any man should looke or hope for any helpe or favour at Gods hands in this so unjust, unlawfull and wicked an action, most offensive to his divine Majestie, as contrary to his expresse commandement, and a worke most pleasing and acceptable to the divell, by whose instigation the same is wholy set forward. Nay rather may the prevailing of them that have the wrong cause to defend, as oftentimes we see it happen in the combat, serve for a most cleere argument, that it falleth out by Gods speciall permission to unseele the eyes (if it were possible) of such as are so wilfully blinded, to the end they might see how unjust the conflict is, which, these men say, was first invented (among other causes) that truth might be knowne, and right from the wrong. But how is truth or right found out, if he which hath right on his side be overcome, as oftentimes it falleth out? Forsooth they answer, that it so hapneth by reason of some other offences of him that is overcome, and that God will have him so punished for the same. By which reason it should follow that God (who is truth it selfe) suffereth in this fight (which they say was devised for trying out of the truth) that in respect of punishing him for other offences that maintaineth the truth, the other who hath the wrongfull cause in hand, should triumph in his unjust victory, and truth should be borne downe and defaced. Then which reason, what can be imagined more contrary to the goodnes, justice, and power of God? as if he could not otherwise punish sinners, then by a meane that should spot and overthrow truth, in which he is so well pleased. It is therfore a most evident signe & certaine testimonie, that this kind of proofe or trial of truth is most uncertain, and the fight to that end unjust and wicked. And that it is no other then the work of the very divell, who being the author of all discord, hatred, debate, falshood, seditions, unjust wars, of death, & mortal enemy to truth, rejoiceth when he seeth right overwhelmed with wrong, reason oppressed by injustice, truth defaced by falshood, and by meanes thereof, men drawne to everlasting damnation. And when it doth come to passe, that he which maintaineth the right doth prevaile (if any right or reason

63

may be supposed in so wicked and unlawfull an action) even that it selfe is to be imputed to the subtiltie of the divell, to draw men on as with a baite, because he is loth to lose the great gaine of soules which he maketh by the humor of this detestable combat. By which, not onely the champions themselves, but they that having power, permit them or grant them libertie to fight; all they that counsel them therunto, & all they that give them the looking on in so damnable an action, become subject unto him, and enemies to God their Creator and Redeemer. And indeed there is no vice or sinne in the world, whereby he winneth more to his kingdome, then by this; because at once he purchaseth thousands of soules: so foolishly do men flocke to be the beholders of a bloudie spectacle, with inhumane desire to see the spilling of mans blood. But now to conclude this matter, it is a lamentable thing that any Christian Prince, or other generall commander, should permit so pernicious and so damnable a thing, and consent, that under their authoritie it should be lawfull for one man to kill another for private quarrell, and they to sit themselves *pro tribunali*, to behold so unjust and cruell a fight. For they ought rather to consider, that they are Gods ministers, and by his divine providence called to so high and so eminent a place, not to favour or give reputation to the divels works (among which there is none more wicked then this) but to execute his will, to which the combat is directly and expressly contrary, though it have bin accepted and allowed by ill use, or rather abuse, and bene entituled by the name of a custome by such as defend the same: who consider not that custome is to be observed in good and commendable things, and not in wicked and unlawfull, as this is. And if it happen that any abuse do grow and shrowd it selfe under the name of a custome, the same ought to be taken away and abolished; and thereto do all Philosophers agree. Of which kind, this combat being manifestly one, it should be rooted out, and not suffered to continue under that name. For good customes are agreeable to Nature, in which respect it is said, that custome is another nature. But that which is contrary to nature (as this is) ought not to be named a custome, but a vile abuse, be it never so much cloked with the name of custome: the rule whereof is prescribed by *Aristotle* in his second booke of Politikes, and should therefore not only not be permitted or maintained, but being crept in, be removed and banished as a most pestilent and dangerous thing. And wheras *Aristotle* in his Rhetorikes saith, that revenge is better then pardon, that is to be ruled according to the civill orders and constitutions of good common-weales. For he sayth not so universally, but onely in respect of an Orator, and (as is said already) he in his Rhetorikes teacheth but what is requisite for an Orator to consider, to perswade, and not what is meete in civill life, as he doth in his Ethikes.

And thus much this author having said effectually to the purpose of your demaund, I may, if you please, proceed to the former matter, from which this question hath occasioned him and us to digresse.

All the companie agreed thereunto, and having well allowed of the discourse, framed themselves attentively to heare the rest.

Wherefore I said, You remember well (I doubt not) that the next was to speake of the third master of the Kings son; who after the good instructions given by the former two to their disciple, taught him that his appetite was in all things to be subject to reason, and that he ought never to suffer himselfe to be drawne from that which was honest by any inticement: for that honestie was the end and scope of all vertue. He sought to perswade him, that the chiefest thing that maketh a King to be knowne for a King, was to know how to rule himselfe before he ruled others, and to master his owne appetites rather then other mens. So the first having fashioned him to Religion, and the second to truth, this third framed him to be temperate and just. Whereby it came to passe, that although he know himselfe to be above the law, yet did he not onely not seeke to over-rule the law, but became a law to himselfe: so as he was never led, either by love or hatred, in his judgements (whether he punished or rewarded, nor by anger, or desire to benefite any man) from that which was just and honest. Thus holding under reasons awe the disordinate appetites of his mind, with the direct rule of justice, (under which, *Plato* saith, all vertues are contained, because it is grounded upon truth) he alwayes directed his actions to the marke of honestie, ever doing good, but never harming any. And knowing, that who so is subject to his owne appetites, deserveth not the title of a free man, much lesse of a King: he framed himselfe to be most continent, and shewed in himself an example of honest life and behavior to all his subjects. His benignitie he declared to them by his liberalitie, and by shewing more care of the publike good then of his owne; and that he would rather give of his owne, then take from them their goods. With his mildnesse and affabilitie he made himselfe singularly beloved, and wan[25] their hearts, and with gentlenesse in word and deed, and with love towards his people, & truth in al his actions, he made them understand that indeed he approched as neare to God in these excellent qualities, as a mortall man could do. By meanes whereof, no man fearing harme from him, he was beloved and reverenced as a God among them. Now having learned of his three first masters, Religion, Prudence and Wisedome, Truth, Justice and Temperance, with those other vertues belonging unto them; the fourth then taught him all that appertained to Fortitude, and made him understand, that onely he is to be esteemed a man of fortitude and valour, who can hold a meane between furie and feare. And that when occasion of perill and danger is offred unto him, bearing with it honestie, and wherein he might make shew of his vertue and courage, did readily embrace and take hold of the same. And that albeit he were deare to himselfe, in respect of those vertues which he knew himselfe to be possessed of; yet esteeming more an honest and a glorious death then a naturall and reprochfull life, he would make no difficultie to hazard his life for the benefite of his countrey, knowing that an honorable end would be crowned with immortall fame. And forasmuch as it is seldome seene, that men can use this princely vertue as it ought to be used, and when it should be used, with such other circumstances as are requisite thereto; therefore did his master instruct him and make him understand, that he which matcheth not his naturall courage with Prudence, and those other vertues, which the former masters had taught him, could not rightly be called a valiant man. And how that this vertue, being stirred up by magnanimitie, stoutly pursued honest things without respect of difficulties: and that though things formidable and terrible be naturally shunned of men, yet the valiant man despiseth them, and feeleth them not in respect of justice and honestie, whereby such men became equall to the Gods, as Poets fained. And that if Prudence and Temperance were not joyned with this royall vertue of Fortitude, the same was turned into foolish hardinesse. And because his disciple should know how to avoid this vice, he declared to him how such men as, to avoyde infamie, onely exercised their valour, and exposed their lives to perill, or onely to purchase honour, were not to be called properly valorous men; but they onely who for honesties sake made triall of their valour, because honestie is the onely end of vertue, by which humane felicitie is to be atchieved. And that he likewise was not to be accompted valiant, who for feare of paine or punishment, tooke in hande fearefull and dangerous enterprises, nor yet they that through long experience in warfare, or because they have bin often in the brunt and danger of battels, went cheerfully or couragiously into the warres to fight, as it were by custome, for that they did it rather by art and practise then by free election, without the which can be no vertue. Neither he that by rage and furie suffered himselfe to be transported to attempt any danger; since there can be no vertue, where reason guideth not the mind. And for this cause wilde beasts (though they be terrible and fierce by nature) cannot be termed valiant, because they being stirred onely by naturall fiercenesse, wanting reason, do but follow their instinct, as do the Lions, Tygers, Beares, and such other like. Nevertheles he denied not but that anger might accompany fortitude; for that it is rather a help unto it, then any let or impediment, so long as reason did temper them, and that it served but for a spurre to pricke men forward in the defence of just and honest causes. Moreover he declared unto his scholer, that there is a kind of fortitude that hath no need of any such spurre of anger: which kind concerned the bearing of grievous and displeasing accidents, and the moderating of a mans selfe in happie and prosperous successes. And this is that blessed vertue which never suffereth a man to fall from the height of his minde, being called by some men patience: who will not onely have her to be a vertue separate from the foure principall vertues, but also that she should be above them. But this opinion of theirs is not well grounded, since in truth she is but a branch of fortitude: through which (as *Virgil* sayth) men beare stoutly all injuries, whether they proceed from wicked persons, or from the inconstancie and changeablenesse of fortune; but remaineth alwayes invincible and constant against all the crosses, thwarts and despites of fortune. This vertue is fitly described by *Cicero*, where he saith, that it is a voluntary and constant bearing of things grievous and difficult, for honesties sake. And in the Scriptures it is said, that it is better for a man to beare with invincible courage such things, then to be otherwise valiant, or to hazard himself, how, where, & when it is fit. For who so beareth stoutly adversities, deserveth greater commendation and praise then they which overcome their enemies, or by force win cities or countries, or otherwise defend their owne, because he overcometh him selfe, and mastereth his owne affects and passions. Having respect to these things, this wise schoole-master shewed his disciple, that the valiant man was like a square solid body, as is the die, whereunto *Aristotle* also agreeth, which in what sort soever it be throwne, ever standeth upright: so he being still the same man, which way soever the world frame with him, or the malice and envie of wicked men, or the freakes of fortune tosse him; which fortune, some call the Queene of worldly accidents, though, as a blind cause, she alwayes accompanieth her selfe with ignorance. Moreover he added that hope of gaine or profit ought not to move a man to put his life in apparant danger: for if it chanced (as often it doth) that the hope began to quaile, forthwith courage failed withall, and the enterprise was abandoned, because vaine conceived hope, and not free choice of vertue had guided him. A thing which never happeneth to them that in honest causes hazard their lives. For though an unexpected terror chance unto them, so as on the sudden they cannot deliberate what were best to do: yet even by habite which they have made in the vertue of fortitude, they loose not their courage; but the more difficult and fearefull the accident appeareth, the more stoutly will they resist and oppose themselves against the same. Likewise he declared to him, that it was not true fortitude, when men (not knowing what the danger was which they entred into) did undertake any perillous enterprise: for it must be judgement, and not ignorance, that shall stirre men to valorous attempts. Neither yet that they were to be esteemed properly valiant, who like wilde savage beasts, moved by rage and fury, sought revenge, and to hurt them that had provoked them to wrath: for such were transported by passion, and not guided by reason. Last of all he concluded that he was justly to be accounted a man of valour, who feared not everie thing that was perillous, yet of some things would be afraid. So as true fortitude should be a convenient mean betweene rashnesse and fearefulnesse: the effect whereof was to be ready and hardie to undertake dangerous actions, in such time, place, and maner as befitted a man of vertue; and for such causes as reason commanded him so to do: and because the doing thereof was honest and commendable, and the contrary was dishonest and shamefull. All these points did this worthy schoolmaster seeke to imprint in the yong Princes mind, that he might become stout and haughtie of courage, to the end that he (who was borne to rule and commaund) might not through any sudden or un-looked for accidents be daunted with feare, or become base and cowardly minded: nor yet by overmuch rashnesse or furie waxe fierce and cruell; but with mild, yet awfull behaviour, governe and commaund the people subject unto him. These were the seeds of vertue, which these wise and worthy masters did cast into the tender mindes of those yong Princes, from whence (as out of a fertile soile) they hoped to reape in their riper yeares fruite answerable to their labour and travell. And this is all (said I) that this author hath discoursed upon this matter, and as much (I suppose) as is needfull for the education of children, till they come to yeares of more perfection, wherein they may begin to guide themselves.

And then sir *Robert Dillon* (who as well as the rest had given a very attentive eare to the whole discourse) sayd: Truly these were right good and worthy documents, and meete to traine a Prince up vertuously; neither could any other then a glorious issue be expected of so vertuous principles and education. And though this diligence and care were fitting for so high an estate as the son of a mightie monarke, yet hath the declaration therof bin both pleasing and profitable to this companie, and may well serve for a patterne to be followed by private gentlemen, though not with like circumstances; since the same vertues serve as well for the one as for the other to guide them the way to that civill felicitie, whereof our first occasion of this dayes discourse began. But evening now hasting on, and the time summoning us to draw homeward, we will for this present take our leaves of you; having first given you harty thanks for our friendly entertainment, especially for this part thereof, whereby with your commendable travell in translating so good and so necessary a worke, you have yeelded us no small delight, but much more profite; which I am bold to say as well for all the companie as for my selfe: where-unto they all accorded.

But, said the Lord Primate, we must not forget one point of your speech, which was, that you tied us to a condition of three dayes assembly; that as the author had devided his work into three dialogues, so we should give you three dayes time to runne over every day one of his dialogues. Supposing therefore that you have finished his first, we will to morrow (if this company please to give their consent thereunto) be here to understand whether he have as sufficiently set downe rules for the fashioning a yong man to the course of vertue, as he hath done for the education of his childhood. Therefore you may looke for us, & prepare your tongue, as we will bring attentivenesse to heare his doctrine by your study made ready for our understanding. And so they departed all together towards the citie.

THE SECOND DAYES MEETING, AND DISCOURSE
OF CIVILL LIFE.

When the next morning was come, which appeared faire
and cleare, the companie (which the day before had bin with me)
came walking to my house, all, save onely M. *Smith* the Apothecary, whose businesse being of another sort, was not so desirous
to spend his time in hearing discourses of that nature, which
brought no profit to his shop. And being entred into the house,
they found me ready to go walke abroade to take the sweete and
pleasant ayre: wherefore though they had already had a good
walke from the citie thither, being somewhat more then a mile;
yet were they not unwilling to beare me companie, and would
needs go with me. So I led them up the hill to the little mount,
which standeth above my house, along a pleasant greene way,
which I had planted on both sides with yong ashes: from whence
having the prospect not onely of the citie, but also of the sea
and haven, we there sate us downe, and some commending the
ayre, some the delightfulnesse of the view, we spent the time in
sundry speeches, until one of the servants came to summon us
to walk home to dinner. Whereupon returning home, and finding
the meate on the table, we sate us downe; I telling them that
they found a Philosophers dinner, for so I would now begin to
take upon me to entitle my selfe, since they had made me (at the
lest) the trucheman [26] or interpreter of one that was worthy that
name. And that I had the rather prepared no greater store of
meate for them, because I would imitate the temperance of a
Philosopher, as we were in number a convenient companie for
a Philosophicall dinner.

Why, said the Lord Primate, what meane you by that? is
there any determinate companie appointed for such meales as are
fit for Philosophers?

Yea sir, quoth I, if my memory faile me not, I have read
that to such refections as might as wel feed the mind as the body,
there would not be any such great company of guests invited, as
by the confusion of their talke and communication, the serious
and yet delightful discourses that might be proposed, should not

be imparted to all, nor yet so few, as for want of matter the same were to be omitted. Therefore it was determined that the number should be betweene the Graces and the Muses, that is to say, not under three, nor above nine. We are therefore a fit companie for a Philosophicall dinner, and your entertainment shall be according for your cheere.

Wel, said sir *Robert Dillon*, you shal need no shifts with us, for as we wil not commend your cheere (which is the thing is commonly begged by the excusing of want of meate) so shal you not need to take any care, either for the satisfying of our appetites with dainty fare, or to entertaine us with Philosophicall discourses at dinner: for we expect such a banket[27] at your hands after dinner in that kind, as we shall the better passe over our dinner without them, which we desire in that respect may be the shorter, to the end that our bodies being fed temperatly, our mindes may be the sharper set to fall to those other dainties which you have prepared for us.

Yea but let not our dinner I pray you (said Captaine *Dawtrey*) be so temperate for sir *Robert Dillons* words, but that we may have a cup of wine: for the Scripture telleth us that wine gladdeth the heart of man. And if my memory faile me not, I have read, that the great banket of the Sages of Greece, described by *Plutarke*, was not without wine; & then I hope a Philosophical dinner may be furnished with wine: otherwise, I will tell you plainly, I had rather be at a camping dinner then at yours, howsoever you rerebanket[28] will haply be as pleasing to me as to the rest of the company.

Whereat the rest laughing pleasantly, I called for some wine for Captaine *Dawtrey*; who taking the glasse in his hand, held it up a while betwixt him and the window, as to consider the colour: and then putting it to his nose, he seemed to take comfort in the odour of the same.

Then said the Lord Primate, I thinke (Captain *Dawtrey*) that you meane to make a speculation upon that cup of wine, you go so orderly to worke, as if you were to examine him upon his qualities; whereof two principall you have already resolved your selfe of, by the testimony of your two principall senses. The colour, we all determine with you is good, the smell seemeth not to mislike you: it is consequent therefore that when you have drunke it up, you will also resolve us whether all three the

72

qualities concurring together, it may deserve the title of *vinum Cos* or no: for such was the wine wont to be entituled among the ancient Romanes, that caried the reputation to be the best.

And what (I pray you, said I) might be the cause that their best wine was so called? for I have heard that question sundry times demaunded, but I could never heare it yet answered sufficiently to my satisfaction.

It is no marvell (sayd the Lord Primate) for although the matter have bin long in controversie, and debated by many ful learned men, and among them some that loved wine so well, as their experience might make them beeleve that their verdit shold be very sound; yet for ought I find, we may say *adhuc sub judice lis est.*[29] Some say it should be taken for *vinum Cossentinum*, as coming from a territory so named, which commonly bare the best wines neare about Rome. Others interprete it by letters, saying that *Cos* is to be taken for *corpori omnino saluberrimum.* But they that presume most to have hit the marke, say that it is so to be understood, that *Cos* should signifie the wine to be best by these three qualities, which Captaine *Dawtrey* seemeth to insist upon, that is to say, *coloris, odoris,* and *saporis*; which three recommending a wine, it cannot but be called very good. And this is as much as I have read or heard, and will be content to be of the Jurie with Captaine *Dawtrey* to give my verdit whether this of yours be such or no.

In good faith (said Captaine *Dawtrey*) if I be the foreman of the Jurie, as I have bin the first to taste the wine, I will pronounce it to be indeed singular good, and well deserving the title of *Cos*: for all three those qualities which you have sayd wine is to be commended for.

If the wine be good (said I) you may be sure I am right glad, as well because I have it to content such my good friends, as because I have made my provision for my self so well; whereby I hope you will all thinke me worthy to be a taster for the Queenes advantage,[30] and my office to be well bestowed upon me, since I can taste a cuppe of wine so well; for it is indeed of mine owne choice.

Marry sir (said M. *Dormer*, who had even then finished his draught) me thinkes it fareth not with you according to the common proverbe, which saith, that none goeth worse shod then the shoomakers wife: for in good sooth this is a cup of wine

73

fit to recommend your taste, and consequently your selfe to be employed in your office. But since you asked my Lord Primate the meaning of *vinum Cos*: and withall said that you never heard that question answered to your contentment; let us (I pray you) heare what is your conceit therein, and whether you can give any more probable sence thereof then those which he hath told us.

Nay in good faith, said I, that wil I not presume to do; for I am not so affected to mine owne conceits, as to preferre them before other mens. A better interpretation I will not therefore offer unto you: but if you will needs have me tell you how I, among others, conceive of that *vinum Cos*: which is read of, I thinke that it was so called for that the custome being in those dayes, that wheresoever the Romane Consul came, when he went in his jorney towards his government, or els within his province, they of the good townes or cities presented him with such dainties as the place affoorded, and specially with the choisest wines that were there to be had, thereupon the best and most excellent wine was termed *vinum Consulare*, to wit, such as of choise was taken for the Consul himselfe. And the common abbreviation of Consul being written in all aunceint authors with these three letters *Cos*: so commeth *vinum Cos*: to be understood (as I have said) for *vinum Consulare*, which was the best. And this is my opinion, which if it be worthy to be admitted to go in companie with the rest, I will not desire it should go before them: and if you will be pleased to accept of this my interpretation of *vinum Cos*: together with the wine which you say is so good, and let the same supply the badnesse of your fare, (wherein my wife hath the greatest fault) I shal go the more cheerfully to the rest of my taske, which I am comforted by your speeches, you are so well disposed unto, as it maketh you hasten to make an end of your bad dinner. Fruite therefore being brought, and the table taken up, sir *Robert Dillon* said; It is an approved opinion of all antiquitie, that after dinner a man should sit a while, and after supper walk a mile: we must not therefore so suddenly rise from dinner to go to our rerebanket; yet may we gather up some of the crums of yesterdayes feast, how full soever our bellies be with the good meate we have eaten here. I remember then that the substance of a childs education, that was to be set in the right way to his civill felicitie, was yesterday declared by the example of the order held by the Kings of Persia, in the training of their

74

sons, which were to succeed them in their kingdome. Which order, though it were both pleasing and profitable to be understood, and that with change of circumstances it might well serve for the direction of a private gentleman how to bring up his child: yet I for my part thinke that it would have bin very good that there had bin set downe a course more particularly, in what learning or study of the liberal arts the child should have bin exercised. For I have found by experience, that the care and diligence of parents may advance very much the forwardnesse of their children, so as some being well plied, shall not onely reade perfectly, but be also well forward in his Grammer, when the other of like wit and capacitie shall for lacke of plying drag and come very farre behind.

That is (said I) most true, and I can verifie it in my self; for such was my fathers care (who not onely in the education of his children, but also in the ordering of his houshold, was second to no man of his degree that ever I know) as before I was full five yeares of age, I had gone through mine Accidence, & was sent to schoole to Tunbridge, 20 miles from London, and if either the aire of the place, or some other disposition of my body had not hindred my health by a quartaine ague that tooke me there, I might have bin a forward scholer in my grammer at 6 yeres old, and have bin ready to have accompanied my learning with those corporall exercises which by some are set downe as fit to be used by children betweene the yeares of five and ten, as well to harden their bodies and to make them apt for the wars (if their disposition be thereunto) as for health. But by that unhappie accident, not onely the health and strength of my body, but my learning also met with a shrewd checke, which I could never sithens recover sufficiently. Neverthelesse as much as my father could performe, he omitted not to have me trained both to my booke and to other exercises agreeable to his calling & abilitie, following (as I suppose) such precepts as he had found set downe by some worthy authors treating of that matter. The exact forme of which education perhaps is hard to be observed, but by such as have together with a fatherly and vigilant care, wealth and meanes answerable to finde in their owne houses schoole-masters to instruct and fashion their children according to those rules and precepts. For by them, before the child attaine the age of 14. yeares, he should not only have learned his Grammer, but also Logike, Rhetorike, Musike, Poetrie, drawing and perspective, and be skilfull at his weapons, nimble to runne, to leape and to wrestle, as exercises necessary upon all occasions where fortitude is to be employed for the defence of his countery and Prince, his friends, and of his faith and religion. And this is that which I conceive your meaning was, when you said, that you thought it had bin needfull there had bin some more particular course set downe for the dispensing of the childs time in his learning. All which *Piccolomini* hath so exactly set downe in his learned booke of Morall institution, written first in the Italian tongue, as it may seeme he rather proposed or set foorth a perfect child, as *Cicero* hath a perfect Orator, and *Castiglione* a perfect Courtier, then that it were easie to bring up or traine any in that sort or according to that patterne. And therefore since that which our author hath sayd of the education of the Kings children of Persia, seemeth enough if it be fitly applied for the instruction of any children during their childhood, we may (if you please) now proceede to his second dialogue, treating of the instruction of a yong man from his childhood forward: for I have made ready my papers, so as I hope without much interruption I may in English deliver unto you his mind, set downe in his owne language, though not with like smoothnesse of style. But since yesterday I heard you find no fault, I may the better be encouraged to go on this day with my plaine manner of penning, though it be unpolished.

Yea marry, answered sir *Robert Dillon*, very willingly: and all the company assenting thereunto, I arose, intreating them not to stirre, for that I would presently returne unto them with my bookes.

Which being done, and every man lending an attentive eare, thus I began: As yesterday the infancy or childhood of man was resembled unto that part of the soule which giveth life, and is called *vegetative*, being the foundation of the other parts: so must youth now be likened to that part which giveth sense and feeling, and is named *sensitive*. And as it is harder to rule two horses to guide a coach or charret then one: so is there farre greater difficultie in guiding a yong man then a child: for he is stirred much more with passions then the simple age of a child, and is more violently caried away with things that delight him; because he hath now the second power of the soule in force to

76

draw him, which for the most part is much more contrary to reason then the first. For wheras that first coveted only that which was profitable, and which might nourish the bodie without any great regard of that which was honest, as whereof it had no knowledge at all; this other being wholy bent to delight, respecteth little any other thing: which delight having greatest force in yong mindes, draweth them sundry wayes, and by allurements maketh them so much the more greedy to attaine the things they take pleasure in, as the spurres wherewith they be pricked are more sharpe and poignant. This appeareth by their actions most manifestly. For hunting egerly after pleasure, they are never quiet untill they compasse their desires: and albeit that their desires be vehement in every thing they fancie, yet do they most of all discover themselves in the lusts of the flesh, which in them are firie, by reason of the abundance of blood and naturall heate that is in them, increasing those their disordinate desires beyond measure, yea they grow infinite in them, and variable, as themselves are inconstant, misliking this day that, which yesterday they liked; which proceedeth onely because their said desires are not forged in that part of the mind where reason hath her firme seate, and proper dwelling. To this imperfection of lust, is also added the violent motion of anger, to which they are subject, and thereby soone drawne from the course of reason and justice. By this passion are they provoked to enter into debate and quarrels upon every light occasion, and as people desirous of honour and reputation, as soone as they thinke they receive any injury, they feare no perill nor danger of their lives, but boldly and rashly undertake to fight, led by a desire of revenge, and hope to have the victorie over their enemies. Of money or goods they make smal reckoning, through lacke of experience, because of their youth, and want of prudence, which groweth from experience: and therefore little know they, how necessary the goods of fortune are to humane life, and into what inconveniences they fall that are without them. So as they spend and consume without discretion, not regarding the time to come, but supposing the world will alwayes be at one stay. They be easily deceived, not knowing the saying of *Epicarmus*, that not to beleeve rashly was the sinewes of wisedome. And because they consider not how variable are the resolutions of this world and humane affaires, they are ever full of good hope, seldome fearing that any thing may befall them other then wel: which hope layeth open the way to such as lie in waite to intrap them and deceive them. They seeme likewise to have a touch of magnanimity, by reason of the heate of their youth, which stirreth them up to undertake great matters, but yet inconsideratly, as folke moved rather by nature then by election: and so are they inclined rather to attempt things seeming honorable, then things profitable. They love their friends much more fervently then any other age, because they delight more in company, and measure not friendship by profit or by honestie, but onely by their delight, as they find them conformable to their appetites. They flie easily into that which is in all things vicious, that is, too much; which too much, is harmeful even in justice it self: whereupon is growne (I thinke) our English proverbe, that too much of a mans mothers blessing is not good: not considering the precept of *Chilo*, who with three words taught the summe and effect of all vertue, *Ne quid nimis*.[31] Whereby we may understand, that vertue consisteth in the meane betweene two extremes, which on either side are too much or too little, wherein yong men do most incline to that extreme of too much: for they love too much, they hate too much, they hope too much, they feare too much, they trust too much, they spend too much, they beleeve too much, they presume too much: and by presuming too much, they build more then they ought to do upon the uncertaine and variable chances of fortune, without setting before their eyes those good courses by which men through vertuous and commendable acts do attaine a happie life. And this is the cause why they give so deafe an eare to friendly admonitions, and to wise & grave advice & counsel. For they, not knowing their owne ignorance, thinke they know all things, such is the quicknesse and vehemencie of spirit which raigneth in them, and giveth them a certaine shadow of nobilitie of courage, by which they presume they are able to do all things of themselves well and commendably; but they find themselves farre deceived when they come to the triall. They do oftentimes injury to others, rather unadvisedly then maliciously of purpose to harme or offend. And having generally a good opinion of all men, simply measuring others words by their owne hart: they are soone moved to compassion and pittie. They delight exceedingly (as voide of care) to laugh, to sport, and to be merrie: and with quips and biting speeches to taunt their fellowes, and such as converse with them:

and heare more willingly pleasant conceits and merrie tales, then grave sayings or aunciet admonitions of wise and learned men.

In faith (said Captaine *Norreis*) you have painted or described a yong man in so strange a figure, as to me it seemeth, I see a monster before mine eyes, with moe heads than the auncient Poets said that *Hydra* had, the same that gave *Hercules* so much to do to overcome her: and it is to be marvelled, that all yong men are not soone weary of that age, which bringeth with it such varietie of imperfections, and all contrary to reason and vertue. You make us almost to conceive an opinion, that there can be no Art nor prudence sufficient to deliver us from such a multitude of errors that environ us on every side.

If there were cause of complaint that youth should be thus described, said I, yet am not I the man you should complaine of, but rather of mine author, or of *Aristotle*, who long before described the same even as he hath done: and of *Horace* in like sort, who taking the matter out of *Aristotle*, concluded it in substance much like, though in fewer words, saying:

> *The yong man on whose face no beard yet shewes,*
> *When first he creepeth out of others charge,*
> *Delights to have both horse and hound at will,*
> *With them to hunt, and beate the woods and fields,*
> *Like waxe to vice is easie to be wrought,*
> *And sowre to them that tell him of his fault:*
> *Too late he learnes his profit for to know,*
> *And in expence, aye too too lavish still,*
> *His heart is high, and full of hote desires,*
> *And soone he loathes that earth he loved deare.*[32]

And truly the nature of a young man is very perillous, and unapt of it selfe to be ruled and directed to any good course; partly because of the ignorance accompanying that age, and partly for that following the vanities and delights which the worser part of the soule or mind doth set before him, he respecteth not that which is honest and vertuous, as a thing he never knew or tasted. And therefore being intent onely to pleasures and delights, he considereth not any thing but what is present before him. For wanting (as is said) experience, meete to foresee accidents to come, he beleeveth much more them that intice him & flatter him, by praising all he doth, then those men that reprove or check him for doing ill, or shew him the way to vertue, by telling him the truth. Neither is there any thing that more setteth a yong man astray from the course of vertue, then flattery: and specially are yong Princes to take heede thereof, about whom are continually flatterers to winne their favor, and by harming them with that subtil engin, to purchase to themselves as much gaine & profit as they can. These, who (as *Aristotle* saith) bend all their wits to evill, with continuall lying and soothing, make yong men beleeve that they are excellent in all things above course of nature; whereunto they (simple) giving a readier care then they should, become so blind and foolish, that they discerne not their owne good: but pricked forward with those false praises, apply themselves to that onely which is pleasant and delightfull, and become a prey unto their flatterers, who like Parasites affirme all that they heare their master say, and denie whatsoever he denieth. In which respect *Diogenes* did right well say; that flatterers were worse then crowes, who feed but on the carcasses of the dead, but these jolly companions devoure the mindes of men alive, making them become (as *Seneca* saith) foolish or mad. From whose conceit *Epicarmus* varied not much, who said, that crows pick out the eyes but of dead carcasses, but flatterers pick out the eyes of the mind, whiles men are yet alive. And to say truly, this cursed generation, with their leasings and soothing, induce such as harken to them and beleeve them, to be their own foes, and to barre themselves from the attaining of true glory, whiles they make them glory in the false praises of wicked flatterers. Who to the end they may be the better beleeved when they flatter, use all art possible to shew themselves affectioned (though counterfetly) to them, in whose harts they seeke to poure their poison. For they kill in them all seeds of vertue, and they take from them the knowledge of themselves, and of all truth: to which, flattery is a most pestilent and mortall enemie. And happy might indeed Princes thinke themselves, if they had about them men that would frankly and resolutely resist the attempts of flatterers, such as was *Anaxarcus Endemonicus* about *Alexander* the Great. This *Anaxarcus* misliking that *Alexander* throgh the flattery & false praises of such as magnified his acts, grew so prowd, as he wold needs be esteemed a God, & seeing on a time his Physition to bring him a potion to ease the griefe of his disease when he was sicke, said, *Is it not a wofull case, that the health of our God should consist in a draught of licour and drugs*

composed by a man?[33] Words full wel beseeming the sincere mind
of a free harted man. As on the other side it was vile adulation
which *Demades* the Athenian used, who being at an assembly
of Councell, proposed a decree, by which he would have had
Alexander to be reputed for the thirteenth of the great Gods.
But the people perceiving his flattering purpose and small reverence to divine things, condemned him in a fine of an hundred
talents. If Princes, and such as manage States, would follow this
example, and have an eye to such fellowes, there would not be
such store of Sycophants as now a dayes there are; and the
vertues and merites of honest men, worthy honour and favour,
would be better knowne and regarded then they are; and rewards
and recompences would be given to such men, and not to flatterers, who seeke to put them besides themselves. This I say of
such as suffer themselves to be seduced by these charmers, but
not of wise Princes, who give no more eare to their inchantments,
then doth the serpent to the charmer; because they know that
their praises and soothings are but strangling morsels smeared
over with hony. *Philip* of Macedon, the father of *Alexander*, had
a flatterer in his Court, called *Cisofus* (or as some say *Cleophus*)
who did not onely affirme and deny all that *Philip* sayd or denied,
but also on a time when *Philip* had a sore eye, and ware some
band or scarfe before it, he in like manner came before the King
with the like: and another time when *Philip* having hurt one of
his legs, limped upon it, and had clothes wrapped about it, the
flatterer came likewise with his leg so wrapped and halting into
the Court; seeking thus not only by his words as other Parasites
do, but also with his gestures and whole body to transforme the
King, and put him beside himselfe. But although *Philip* tooke
delight in this skim[34] of men, yet could they never draw him by
their charming to incurre those vices which his sonne ranne into:
who albeit he was of a most noble nature and mind, yet did he
so much attribute to these bad companions, and was so caried
away with their flattering praises, that he could not endure the
truth that *Calisthenes* told him, but miserably slue him, spotting
with so cruell and barbarous a fact, all that ever he did before
or after, were it never so noble and worthy of glorie. But contrariwise, *Agesilaus* did so despise and hate all flatterers, that he
wold never give any man leave to commend his vertues, but
onely such as had authoritie to reprehend his vices. Whereas

Alexander was so distraught & ravished with the delight of such flatterers, that he not onely suffered himselfe to be perswaded by them that he was the sonne of *Jupiter*, but became also so foolish as to endure sacrifices to be made unto him, and to be worshipped like a God. From which folly he could never be brought, untill such time as he was grievously wounded in an incounter with an arrow. Out of which his wound *Dioxippus* the Athenian wrastler seeing the blood to run aboundantly, said, to taxe *Alexanders* vaine glory; Why then, do the Gods immortal bleed as we mortal men do? which his words *Alexander* hearing, and feeling the pain and smart of his wound, he perceived himself to be mortall and no God; opening thereby in such sort the eyes of his mind, as when *Anaxander* the Philosopher (though unworthy that name because he was a flatterer) standing once by *Alexander* when it thundred, asked him, whether it were he that had caused that thunder-cracke, as the son of *Jupiter*? No, said he, mildly rejecting his flattery, I will cause no such terror unto men. And another time when a medicine which he had taken troubled him grievously in the working, and *Nicesias* had said unto him, What shall we mortall men do, if ye Gods endure such paine and agonie? he looking angrily upon him, answered, What Gods? I feare me rather that the Gods do hate us. This noble King likewise, after sicknesse and hurts had made him know himselfe, did a worthy and noble act towards *Aristobulus* the Historiographer. For this *Aristobulus* having written a booke of the deeds of *Alexander*, and being with him in boate upon the river *Hidaspe* in *India*, he besought leave that he might reade his booke unto him: which when he had obtained, and that *Alexander* perceived, by the untrue reports made in his praise beyond all measure, that he was a flatterer, and no Historiographer: despising his shamelesse flattery, he tooke the booke out of his hands, in a rage throwing it into the river, and fiercely turning to him, said, Thou wretch, thou hast thy selfe deserved to be throwne after thy booke, since thou hast not bin ashamed to set downe to the memory of posteritie the reports of my acts in such a false and flattering manner. By this, which we have sayd, may easily be gathered, that they, who once give eare to flattery, cannot discerne the harme and deceit of flatterers towards them, untill some bitter storme or crosse of froward fortune befall them, to open their eyes, and to give them to understand how

82

they have bin deceived by such lying companions, and harmed more then by their mortall enemies. Which thing this wicked generation well considering, lest Princes should perceive their flatterie, they never cease, as soone as they have gotten trust and credit by their lies, to use all meanes and devices possible, to put into their disgrace and hatred all such as they think may be like to discover their subtilities, and to make knowne the harme which they procure. To which purpose of inventing false and colourable causes, they labor to remove them from being about the Prince, that they may the better turne topsie-turvie all at their pleasure. By this meanes they so blind the eyes of those poore Princes whom they possesse, that whiles they are in prosperitie they not onely love them and hold them deare, but also bestow upon them offices, lands, and great Lordships. As by *Philip* before named it appeared, who made *Thrasideus* the flatterer, Lord of his countrey, though otherwise he were a man of little worth and wisedome. And that *Philip* who was the last King of Macedon overcome by the Romanes, had a flatterer in his Court, whose name was *Proclides*: who albeit he were a stranger (to wit, a Tarentine) and a very vaine fellow, yet crept he so farre into the said Kings favour, that he was able to breede great broyles and troubles in the kingdome. These and such like inconveniences would not happen, if the ignorance of yong men (not discerning themselves) did not open the way to flattery, and leade her as it were by the hand into the presence of Princes, inducing them to delight in her. Hereof I have spoken the more, because, the number of flatterers being infinite, and very many those that by them are blinded and seduced to esteeme them and raise them into reputation, all yong gentlemen, and Princes specially might be forewarned of the harme they may do unto them, if before they offer their poison of lies and soothing praises, they be not armed to repulse their practises, and advertised of their snares. Which thing the Thessalians considering, when they had taken a citie called Melia, they razed it, only because it bare the name of flattery in the Greeke language, so much did they hate and abhorre even the name of so abhominable a vice. And where some Princes haply think themselves wise inough to take heed of such caterpillers, and therefore care not to rid their Courts of them: let them assure themselves that therein they do like men that will feede on hurtfull meates, and presume they shal not offend their stomacks. For these gallants can so cunningly watch and espie their times to worke their feate, that in the end they cast out their poison, and infect their minds with some fawning device or other before they be aware: so as there is no other meanes to avoid this mischiefe, but onely to keepe it farre off, and not to suffer it to approch. True it is neverthelesse, that if Princes (having flatterers about them) would looke well into themselves, and learne the precept of *Nosce teipsum* (which onely precept is of such importance, as without it no man can be happie) they might reape profit by their flattery: not by delighting in it, but by using it as a rule or a square to examine their mindes and their actions by. For when they shall find themselves praised and magnified by any flatterer, they wil endevor themselves to garnish their minds with those vertues, for which they were by him commended and extolled, and were not before in them; to the end they might afterwards be truly and deservingly praised for the same by men of vertue and honestie, whose propertie is to exalt and celebrate the actions of worthy and famous men, and not to lie and flatter, to purchase favour to themselves, and to draw ruine upon the heads of those that they shal have put besides their wit, as flatterers do. *Diogenes* was so great an enemy to flattery, that he chose rather to live in his tub, then in the courts of mightie Princes, who offered him favour and entertainment, disdaining to have abundance of things gotten by so vile a vice. Contrariwise *Aristippus*, though he were one of the disciples of *Socrates*, did so degenerate from the doctrine and behavior of his master, that he became a parasite to *Dionysius* tyrant of Sicile, esteeming more the profit he got that way, then the reputation he might have won by the profession of Philosophie: and grew in the end to be of so base a mind, that although the Tyrant did spit in his face, yet would he not be angry; but being rebuked for enduring so vile a disgrace, he laughing at them that rebuked him, sayd: If fisher-men to take a small fish can be content to go to sea, and to be washed all over with the waves; shall not I endure that the King with a little spittle wet me, to the end I may catch a Whale? This same *Aristippus* seeing *Diogenes* on a day to wash a few herbes which he had gathered for his supper, he said to him: Go to sirra, if you would frame your selfe to follow the humor of Princes, you should not need to feed upon herbes. Neither thou (said *Diogenes*) if thou knewest thy selfe to be (I will not say) a Philosopher, but a man, thou wouldst not be (as thou art) the dog of *Dionysius*. For dogs for their meate fawne upon their masters; and so did this Philosopher shew how base and vile a thing it is to be a flatterer. Which, by this digression, my author hath in like sort laboured to make apparant by reasons and examples. But now returning to his former matter, because he hath rather shewed the harme that comes by flattery, and how it increaseth vice in yong mens minds, then instructed them which way to roote it out, you shall heare how he goeth about to pull up the ill weeds that choke the naturall good seeds in their minds, that by the increase of the good, they may have sufficient store to furnish them in the way of their felicitie. It is already declared what bad qualities and conditions the two worser powers of the soule stirre up in yong mens minds, for that they be mightie and vehement, and apt to oppose themselves against reason, and to resist her. And how reason in yong folkes is scarce felt or perceived, such is the force of the two foresaid faculties, which draw them to lustfull appetites and disordinate passions. The cause whereof, *Heraclitus* ascribeth to the humiditie, wherwith these two ages abound: for it seemed to him that drinesse was the cause of wisedome, and therefore sayd, that the wisest mind was nothing else but a drie light. To which opinion *Galen* leaning, thought the starres to be most wise because they be most drie. But leaving them with their opinions, and imputing the cause onely to the worser powers or faculties of the soule, let us follow our two first chosen guides, *Aristotle* & *Plato*. They say then, that the soule which giveth sense or feeling, and containeth in it the other that giveth life, is not yet so rebellious against reason, but that she maybe subdued, and brought to be obedient. So as you must not think, but that youth, though it be incombred with those passions and desires before mentioned, may neverthelesse be directed to that good course which leadeth man to his most perfect end in this life, and for which all vertues are put in action. For above or over these two powers or faculties, is placed a third, like a Ladie or Queene to commaund if she be not hindred in the execution of her charge. And if these two unruly and wild powers, which are the spring and fountaine head of all disordinate affections, be once wel tamed and broken, they do no lesse obey her commaundements, then the wel taught horses obey the coach-man.

For we are all drawne as it were by two unbridled colts in this life, by these two baser powers of the soule. Wherof the one sheweth it self in most vigour and strength in childhood, and the other in youth. Concerning the first of which, *Aristotle* and his master do disagree. But when they both are joyned together, and strong, they become the more unruly, unlesse the former (as was said yesterday) be well tamed and made meeke by good instruction and diligent care of education. For if childhood be fashioned according to the good precepts of the learned; that first power commeth humble & obedient to be coupled with the other, and thereby is there the lesse labor requisite for him that shall have the guiding of them both in youth. But in youth described even now, as you have heard, in whom both these faculties are rude and undisciplined, the passions are altogether incited and ruled by the naturall powers. For though nature (if she be not hindred) bring forth her effects perfectly in respect of their substances; yet are they often unperfect in regard of the accidents. And for this cause is Art and industry needful to induce vertuous habits, to supply that wherin nature accidentally may be defective. Whereby it cometh to passe, that although the vertues and faculties of the soule have all that which nature can give unto them; yet have they need of mans wit and discipline to bring forth laudable and perfect operations. And this is done by that part of Philosophie which is called Morall, because from it we do draw the forme of good manners, which being actually brought into the mind of a yong man, as well as by the doctrine and wise instruction of others: and so by long custome, converted into an habite, do breake and make supple those parts which by nature are rebellious to reason. And of so great importance is the well training up of childhood, even from the first, that it may be assuredly beleeved, that the youth succeeding such a childhood as was yesterday prescribed, must needs be civill and well disposed: and on the contrary side, that the life of such youths will be wicked and disordered, as having bin ill brought up in their childhood, do enter into so hopelesse a course, as may be likely to be the foundation of all vice and wickednesse during the whole life to come. And hopelesse may they be thought indeed, who by ill doing beginne even from their tender yeares to induce an ill habit into their minds: for from age to age after it increaseth and taketh roote in such sort, as it is almost impossible to be rooted out or taken away. Neither can there be any greater evil wished to any man, then that he be ill-habituated, which thing by *Ælianus* report, the Cretans were wont to wish to their enemies whom they hated most extremely, and not without cause. For he that is fallen into an ill habite, is no lesse blind to vertuous actions, then he that wanteth his sight to things visible. And as the one is ever plunged in perpetual darknes: so doth the other live in everlasting night of vice, after he hath once hardned himselfe to evil. And this is the worst kind of youth that may be, which *Aristotle* advised should be driven out of the citie, when neither for honesties respect, nor for admonitions, nor shame, nor for love of vertue or feare of lawes, they could possibly be reclaimed to vertuous life.

I pray you (said Captain *Norreis*) let me interrupt you a little, so shall you the better take breath in the meane while. I noted not long sithens a saying of your author, which me seemed somewhat strange, and that is, that the substance of the soule should be made perfect by the accidents.

You say right, quoth I, but let not that seeme strange unto you: for it ought rather to seeme strange unto you if it were otherwise; because the substance of every thing is so called, by reason that it is subject unto accidents; neither can there be any accident (to which it is proper to be in some subject) but it must fall into some substance: and hardly would the substance perhaps be discerned by sense, but that the accidents do make it to be knowne. Yet hath nature given to the substance all that she could give to enable the same, to wit, that it might by nature be of it selfe alone, having no need of any other thing in respect of being; and that it should be so necessary to all things else that is not a substance, as without it they should be nothing. Therefore the nature of the soule is such, as the parts thereof have their vertues and faculties perfect: but in that concerneth the directing of them to civill life, man cannot by nature onely compasse it, nor attaine to that end of which we treate.

Then said Captaine *Norreis,* If it be so, as by nature we cannot have that wherewith we should compasse our felicitie, it must belike be in us contrary to nature. And, all things contrary to nature, being violent, and of no continuance; I cannot perceive how this felicitie of ours may stand.

Sir (said I) it followeth not, that whatsoever is not by nature,

87

must needs be contrary to nature. But most true it is that the meanes to guide us to this felicitie; or our felicity it selfe, is in us not by nature: for if it were so, all men should naturally be happy, and by nature have the means to purchase the same, because all men should of necessitie worke after one sort. For things naturall, unlesse they be forced or hindered, do alwayes bring foorth the same effects, wheresoever they be; and the powers which nature bestoweth, are indifferently dispensed to all alike. Which thing is to be understood by the *vegetative* part of the soule, which in plants and in creatures sensible attendeth onely by nature, without counsell or election, to nourish, to increase, to procreate, and to preserve: ne ceaseth at any time from those offices, but alwaies produceth like effects in al things that have life. And the sensible soule evermore giveth the power and vertue of feeling to creatures sensible, and never altereth her operation, nor ceaseth to yeeld the same whiles life endureth, except by some strange accident she be forced. Seeing therefore the diversitie of mans will, the varietie of his operations, and how differently they use the faculties of the soule, we must needes conclude, that in respect of civill life, they work not according to nature. But we must not therfore say, that their working to purchase their felicitie, and the end we speake of, is contrary to nature. For such things are properly said to be contrary to nature, as are violently forced to that which is not naturall, and whereunto they have no aptnesse or disposition at all. As for example, if a stone (which is naturally heavy, and therfore coveteth to move to the center of the earth) be cast upward into the aire by force, it is to be said, that the motion of that stone so forced upward is contrary to nature; because it hath no instinct or moving from nature to go upward: and though it were throwne up ten thousand times, so often wold it fal downe again, if it were not retained otherwise from falling. And if fire, which is light, & covets to ascend, should be forced downeward, that force would be contrary to nature, and the force ceasing, it would by nature ascend again, because it hath not any vertue, or principle, or motion to descend, but onely to ascend, by which it striveth to come to the place which is proper to it by nature, as it is fire, and by which it is fire naturally. For the elements have alwayes their essence most perfect, when they are nearest to the place assigned them by nature. But man being a creature capable of reason, and thereby apt to receive those vertues, the seeds whereof nature hath sowne in his mind, it cannot be said, that the meanes (by which he is to be led to so noble an end as his felicitie) should be in him contrary to nature. For never any thing worketh contrary to nature, in which is the beginning of that operation that it is to do.

Why, said Captaine *Norreis* againe, since you say that the seeds of vertues are in our minds naturally, it seemeth strange to me that they should not bring forth generally in all men their fruite; as the seed which is cast into the earth, springeth, buddeth, flowreth, and lastly in due season yeeldeth fruite according to kind.

Marry (said I) and so they do. For if mans care and industry be not applied to manure the earth diligently, and to weed out the il weeds that spring among the good seed which is sowne, they would so choke the same as it would be quite lost. And even so, if the seeds of vertue be not holpen with continuall culture, and care taken to pul up the vices which spring therewith, and whereof the seeds are naturally as well in our mind, as those of vertue, they wil over-grow and choke them, as the weeds of the garden over-grow and choke the good herbes planted or sowne therein. For so grow up the disordinate appetites, unreasonable anger, ambitions, greedie desires of wealth, of honour, wanton lusts of the flesh, and such other affections spoken of before, which have their naturall rootes in those two baser parts of the soule devoyde of reason. And as we see the earth, without manuring to bring forth wyld herbs and weeds more plentifully then other good seed, which by industry and labor is cast into the same: so do those passions, affects, and appetites of those baser parts of the soule, spring and grow up thicker and faster then the vertues; whereby (for the more part) the fruit of those good seeds of vertue is lost, if the mind be not diligently cleaned from them by the care of others. And these ill qualities are in yong men the worse, when they suffer themselves to be transported without regard of reason or honestie, and their right judgement to be corrupted, and their crooked to prevaile. Which crooked judgement is in effect the cause of all vices and ill affections, & turnes the braine, making them like drunken men, much like as coccle[35] doth to them that feed thereupon. But this hapneth not unto that youth which succeedeth a well fashioned childhood, such as yesterday was spoken of; though it be not sufficient to have a childe either well brought up or well instructed. For a new care must be taken, and new diligence be used to cherish the growth of the good seeds bestowed & manured in the mind of the child: which made *Aristotle* say, that education onely was not enough to make a man vertuous. For though the child be so well bred as hath bin prescribed, yet unlesse some care be had to bridle it (so unpleasing a thing it is for youth to live within the compasse of modestie and temperance) it is easily turned to that part, to which pleasure and delight doth draw it. Nevertheles that first culture bestowed upon childhood, doth so much availe, as the yong man that is disposed to hearken, to good admonitions, shall have the lesse to do to live vertuously, and to tame that sensitive part which he hath onely to strive withall, and to make obedient to the rule of reason.

Captaine *Carleil* then said, I pray you (before you go any further) let me aske this one question, why until now your author having spoken of this moral science, hath all this while made no mention of the speculative sciences, wherein me thinketh a yong man hath special need to be instructed? for they also (I suppose) are necessary to happinesse of life.

That doubt the author answereth thus, said I: Vertues are generally devided into Speculative and Practike; or we may say, into Intellective and Active. The speculative habites are five in number, viz: Understanding, called by the Latines *Intellectus*, Science, Wisedome, Art, and Prudence. And because hitherto he hath spoken onely how men in civill life may attaine to be good, or decline from being evill; and that the speculative sciences declare, but how wise, how learned, or how prudent they be, and not how good or vertuous they be: and that these two first ages are not of capacitie sufficient to embrace them, therefore he reserveth the treating thereof untill a fitter time, which the course of our speech will leade us unto.

Yea but *Aristotle* saith (quoth the Lord Primate) that yong men may be Arithmeticians and Mathematicians, and finally therin wise, but yet he affirmeth that they can not be prudent.

That place of *Aristotle* (said I) is to be understood, not of this first degree of youth, whereof the author hath spoken hitherto, but of the perfection and ripenesse that in time it may attaine, as after shall be declared when time doth serve.

That time (said Captaine *Carleil*) we will attend. But because we see both vertues and sciences are to be learned, and that I have heard question and doubt made of the manner of learning them, I pray let us heare whether your author say ought thereof, and specially whether our learning be but a rememorating of things which we knew formerly, or else a learning a new.

This is indeed (said I) no light question which mine author handleth also even in this place: and there are on either side great and learned authors, as *Plato* and *Aristotle* first, whereof the one was accounted the God of Philosophers, and the other the master of all learned men: and ech hath his followers, who with forcible arguments seeke to defend and maintaine the part of their master and captaine. But before we enter into that matter, you must understand that *Plato* and *Aristotle* have held a severall way each of them in their teaching. For *Plato* from things eternall, descended to mortall things, and thence returned (as it were by the same way) from the earth to heaven againe; rather affirming then prooving what he taught. But *Aristotle* from earthly things (as most manifest to our senses) raised himselfe, climing to heavenly things, using the meane of that knowledge which the senses give, from which his opinion was, that al humane knowledge doth come. And where sensible reasons failed him, there failed his proofes also. Which thing, as it hapned to him in divine matters, so did it likewise in the knowledge of the soule intellective (as some of his interpreters say): which being created by God to his owne likenesse, he hath written so obscurely thereof, that his resolute opinion in that matter cannot be picked out of his writings; but that reasons may be gathered out of them, in favour of the one part and of the other: as though the treatie[36] of a matter so important and necessary to our knowledge, were (as schoole-men say) a matter contingent, about which arguments probable may be gathered on both sides: yet had he before him his divine master, who (as far as mans wit could stretch without grace) had taught him cleerly that which was true, that mans soule is by nature immortall, and partaker of divinitie; howsoever some of the *Peripatetikes* seeme out of *Aristotle* to affirme that *Plato* was contrary to himself, as making the soule somewhiles immortall, and otherwhiles not: which in truth is not in *Plato* to be found, if he be rightly understood. But to the purpose. The opinion of *Aristotle* was, that our soule did not only not record any thing, but that it shold be so wholy voyd of knowledge or science, as it might be resembled to a pure white paper: and therefore affirmed he, that our knowledge was altogether newly gotten; and that our soule had to that end need of sense; and that sense failing her, all science or knowledge should faile withall. Because the senses are as ministers to the mind, to receive the images or formes particular of things: which being apprehended by the common sense, called *sensus communis*, bring foorth afterwards the universals. Which common sense, is a power or facultie of the sensitive soule, that distinguisheth betweene those things that the outward senses offer unto it; and is therefore called common, because it receiveth commonly the formes or images with the exteriour senses present unto it, and hath power to distinguish the one from the other. But as those senses know not the nature of things; so is the same unknowne also unto the common sense, to whom they offer things sensible. Wherefore this common sense being (as we have said) a facultie of the *sensitive* soule, offereth them to the facultie *imaginative*, which hath the same proportion to the vertue *intellective*, as things sensible have to the sense aforesaid. For it moveth the understanding after it hath received the formes or images of things from the outward senses, & layeth them up materiall in the memory where they be kept. This done, *Aristotle* and his followers say, that then the part of the soule capable of reason, beginneth to use her powers; and they are (as they affirme) two: the one *intellectus possibilis*, and the other *intellectus agens*: these latin words I must use at this time, because they be easie enough to be understood, and in English would seeme more harsh; whereof the first is as the matter to the second, and the second as forme to the first. Into that possible facultie of the understanding, do the kinds or *species* of things passe, which the fantasie hath apprehended, yet free of any materiall condition: and this part is to the understanding, as the hand is to the bodie. For as the hand is apt to take hold of all instruments; so is this power or facultie apt to apprehend the formes of all things, from whence grow the universals: which though they have their being in the materiall particulars which the Latins call *individua*; yet are they not material, because they are not (according to *Aristotle*) yet in act. In which respect it is sayd, that sense is busied about things particular, and that onely things universall are knowne, because they be comprehended by the understanding, without matter.

It is neverthelesse to be understood, that the kindes of things are in this possible part thus separated from matter, but blind and obscure: even as colours are stil in substances, though the light be taken away; which light appearing and making the ayre transparent which before was darkened, it giveth to things that illumination, by which they are comprehended and knowne to the eye, whose object properly colours are. And the Sunne being the fountaine of light, wise men have said, that the same Sunne giveth colours to things; for that by meanes of his light they are seene with those visible colours which naturally they have neverthelesse in themselves, though without light they could not be discerned, and remaine there as if they were not at all. This part of the soule then, wherein reason is, worketh the same effect towards things intelligible that the Sun doth towards things visible; for it illumineth those kinds or formes which lie hidden in that part possible, dark and confused, devoyde of place, time, and matter, because they are not particular. And hence it cometh that some have said this possible understanding (as we may terme it) to be such a thing, as out of it all things should be made, as if it were in stead of matter; and the other agent understanding to be the worker of all things, and as it were the forme, because this part which before was but in power to things intelligible, becometh through the operation of the agent understanding to be now in act. And for this cause also is it said, that the understanding, and things understood, become more properly and truly one selfe same thing, then of matter and forme it may be said. For it is credible, that both the formes of things and the understanding being immateriall, they do the more perfectly unite themselves, and that the understanding doth so make it selfe equall with the thing understood, that they both become one. To which purpose *Aristotle* said very well, that the reasonable soule, whiles it understandeth things intelligible, becometh one selfe same thing with them. And this is that very act of truth, to wit, the certain science or knowledge of any thing: which knowledge or science is in effect nought else then the thing so knowne. And this knowledge is not principally in man, but in the soule, wherin it remaineth as the forme therof. This is briefly the summe of the order or maner of of knowledge, which those that follow *Aristotle* do set downe: who therefore affirme that his sentence was, that who so would understand any thing, had need of those formes and images which the senses offer to the fantasie. From which sentence some (not well advised in my opinion) have gone about to argue, that the soule of man should be mortal, because *Aristotle* assigned no proper operation unto her, as if such had bin his opinion. But they consider not that *Aristotle* in his bookes *de Anima,* spake of the soule as she was naturall, and the forme to the body, performing her operations together with the body, and as she was the mover of the body, and the body moved by her, but not as she was distinct or separate from the bodie. And right true it is, that whiles she is tied to the bodie, she cannot understand but by the meanes of the senses: but that being free and loosed from the body, she hath not her proper operations, that is most false. For then hath she no need at all of the senses, when being pure and simple, she may exercise her owne power and vertue proper to her, (which is the contemplation of God Almightie, the highest and onely true good) nor yet of any other instrument but her selfe. And in this respect, perchance the better sort of *Peripatetikes* following their masters opinion, have said, that the soule separated from the body, is not the same she was whiles she was linked there-unto, as well because then she was a part of the whole, and was troubled with anger, desire, hatred, love, & such like passions common to her with the body; as because being imprisoned in the body, she had neede of the senses; but now that she was freed from that imprisonment, nor any way bound to the body, she might use her selfe and her vertue much more nobly and worthily then before. And therefore *Aristotle* said, that the soule separated from the body, could no more be called a soule, but equivocally. But here is to be noted, that it is one thing to speake of the intellective soule which is divine and uncorruptible, and another thing to speake of the soule simply. For doubtlesse, the *vegetative* and *sensitive* soules, which cannot use their vertues and operations but by meane of the body, die with the body. But the intellective soule, which is our onely true forme, not drawne from the materiall power, but created and sent into us by the divine majestie, dieth not with the body, but remaineth immortal and everlasting. And thus much touching the maner of our learning, according to *Aristotles* opinion may suffice. But *Plato* doubtlesse was of opinion that our soule, before it descended into us, had the knowledge of all things: and that by comming into this mortall prison (which his followers have termed the sepulchre of the soule) she was plunged as it were into profound darknesse from a most cleere light, whereby she forgat all that erst she knew. And that afterwards by occasion of those things, which by meanes of the senses come before her, the memory of that she knew before being stirred up and wakened, she came to resume her former knowledge, and in this sort by way of rememorating, and not of learning a new, she attained the knowledge of sciences; so as we learned nothing, whereof before we had not the knowledge. In conformitie of which their masters sentence, the *Platonikes* say, that since the body bringeth with it the seeds that appertaine unto it by nature, it is to be beleeved, that the soule likewise, being much more perfect, should bring with it those seeds that appertaine to the mind. And to this reason they adde, that men even from their first yeares desiring things that are good, true, honest, and profitable: and since no man can desire a thing which he knoweth not after some sort, it may be concluded, that we have the knowledge of those things before. But because it would be too long a matter to rehearse all the arguments which *Plato* his followers bring to prove this, by our desiring of things, by seeking them, by finding them, and by the discerning of them; it may suffice to referre you to what *Plato* hath left of this matter written under the person of *Socrates*, in his dialogs intitled *Menon* and *Phaedon*, and divers other places. And likewise to that which his expositors have written, among whom *Plotinus*, though he be somewhat obscure, deserveth the chiefe place, as best expressing *Plato* his sence and meaning. But let our knowledge come how it will, either by learning anew, or by recording what the soule knew before; she having need (howsoever it be) of the ministery of the senses, and seeing it is almost necessary to passe through the same meanes from not knowing to knowledge: we shall ever find the like difficulties, whether we rememorate or learne anew. For without much study, great diligence, and long travel, are sciences no way to be attained. Which thing *Socrates* (who haply was the author of *Plato* his opinion) shewed us plainely. For when the curtizan *Theodota*[37] scoffing at him said, she was of greater skill then he: for she had drawne divers of *Socrates* scholers from him to her love, where *Socrates* could draw none of her lovers to follow him: he answered, that he thereat marvelled nothing at all: for (said he) thou leadest them by a plaine smooth way to lust and wantonnesse; and I leade them to vertue by a rough and an uneasie path.

Here Captaine *Norreis* said, Though this controversie betweene two so great Philosophers be not (for ought I see) yet decided, and that if we should take upon us to discerne whose opinion were the better, it might be imputed to presumption: yet would I for my part be very glad to know what was the reason that induced *Plato* to say that our soule had the knowledge of all things before it came into the body; and I pray you, if your author speake any thing thereof, that you will therein satisfie my desire.

Yes marry doth he sir, said I, and your desire herein sheweth very well the excellencie of your wit, and your attention to that which hath bin said: and both may serve for a sufficient argument, what hope is to be conceived of a gentleman so inclined and desirous to learne. Thus therefore he saith to your question. That whereas we according to truth beleeve, that our soules are by the divine power of God, incontinently created and infused into our bodies, when we beginne to receive life and sense in our mothers womb. *Plato* contrarily held, that they were long before the bodies created, and produced in a number certaine by God, and that they were as particles descended from the Gods above into our bodies: and therfore he thought it nothing absurd, that they should have the knowledge of al things that may be knowne. For that they being in heaven busied in the contemplation of the divine nature, free from any impediment of the body: and that divine nature containing in it (as he said) the essentiall *Ideas* of all things, which *Ideas* (according to his opinion) were separate and eternall natures remaining in the divine minde of God, to the patterne of which, all things created were made, they might (said he) in an instant have the knowledge of all that could be knowne.

If this opinion were true, said Captaine *Norreis*, happie had it bin for us, that our soules had continued stil, after they were sent into our bodies, to be of that sort that they had bin in heaven, for then should we not have needed so much labour and paine in seeking that knowledge which before they had so perfectly. And being so perfect to what end did he say, they were sent into our bodies to become unperfect?

His opinion (said I) was, that the soules were created in a

certaine number, to the end they might informe so many bodies: and therfore if they should not have come into those bodies, they should have failed of the end for which they were created. In which bodies, the *Platonikes* say further, that they were to exercise themselves, and were given to the bodies, not onely because they should give them power to move, to see, to feele, and to do those other operations which are naturall; but to the end that they should in that which appertaineth to the mind, not suffer us to be drowsie, and lie (as it were) asleepe, but rather to waken and stirre us up to the knowledge of those things that are fit for us to understand: and this was the most accomplished operation (sayd they) that the soule could give unto the bodie whiles it was linked thereunto.

I cannot see (said the Lord Primate) how this hangeth together. For I have read that these kind of Philosophers held an opinion, that our soules all the while they were tied to our bodies, did but sleepe: and that all, which they do or suffer in this life, was but as a dreame.

It is true (said I) that the *Platonikes* said so indeed; and that was, because they knew that whatsoever we do in this life is but a dreame, in comparison of that our soules shal do in the other world, when they shal be loosed from those bands which tie them to our bodies here: through which bands they are hindred from the knowledge of those things perfectly which here they learne. In regard whereof *Carneades*, *Arcesilas*, and others the authors of the new Accademie said constantly, that in this world there was no certaine knowledge of any thing. And *Nausifanes* affirmed, that of all those things which here seeme to us to be, we know nothing so certainly as that they were not. Unto which opinion *Protagoras* also agreed, saying, that men might dispute of anything *pro & contra*; as if he should say, that nothing could be assuredly knowen to us whiles we are here, as our soules shall know them whensoever they shall be freed from our bodies, and lie no more inwrapped in these mortall shadowes, because then they shall be wholy busied in the contemplation of truth: neither shal they be deceived by the senses, as in this life they are oftentimes, who offer unto them the images of things uncertainly, not through default of the senses, but by reason of the meanes whereby they apprehend the formes of things. For the sense by his owne nature (if he be not deceived or hindred in

97

receiving of things sensible) comprehendeth them perfectly, nay becometh one selfe same thing with them. And this is the cause why it is said, that our soules sleepe whiles they remaine in this life, and that our knowledge here is but as a dreame. According to which conceit, the inamoured Poet, speaking of his Ladie *Laura*, said very properly upon her death in this sort:

> *Thou hast (faire Damsell) slept but a short sleepe,*
> *Now wak'd thou art among the heav'nly spirits,*
> *Where blessed soules interne within their maker.*[38]

Shewing that our life here is but a slumber; and seeming to infer that she was now interned or become inward in the contemplation of her maker, being wakened from her sleepe among those blessed spirits, as she had bin, before she was inclosed in this earthly prison. And likewise he seemed to leane to *Plato* his opinion in another place, when speaking of her also, he said she was returned to her fellow star. For *Plato* thought the number of soules created, was according to the number of the starres in heaven: and that every soule had a proper starre to which it returned after this life. But as for our knowledge, in truth it is but a shadow in respect of the knowledge our soules shall have by the contemplation of the divine essence. Whereupon *Socrates*, one of the wisest and most learned men that ever were, yet evermore affirmed resolutely, that the only thing he knew, was, that he knew nothing. And to say truly, this his knowing of nothing, might well be termed a learned ignorance.

Well (said the Lord Primate) captain *Carleil* and captaine *Norreis* have by their demaunds ministred a very fit occasion unto you, to discourse out of your author the considerations of the maner of our knowledge, and consequently of the soule of man, and to declare withall the opinions of two so excellent Philosophers and of their followers. But though both agree in this, that whether the soule learne of new, or by rememorating, she hath alwayes need of the senses as her ministers to attain knowledge: yet is it to be beleeved, and that assuredly, that the soule of man being created by God Almightie to his owne image and likenesse, she hath also some proper operation or action resembling his; to the accomplishment whereof, she hath no need of the sense. And that being dissolved from the body, or after, when he shall be re-united to the same in the resurrection, she having then the same image and likenesse of God still in her, she shall everlast-

98

ingly be wholy and onely intent to the contemplation of his divine majestie, who is the onely true and perfect good and happinesse. The perfection of which divine majestie, is the knowledge of himselfe; and knowing himself to know all things by him created and produced. But it is time now for you to returne to the matter you had in hand, when you were drawne by their demaunds to make this digression.

And even so will I, since you be so pleased, quoth I, and so proceeded in this maner. In the beginning of youth, the yong man is fitly to be resembled to a traveller that is arrived in his journey to a place where the way is devided into two parts, and standeth in doubt which of them he shall take: for in either of them he seeth a guide standing ready to leade him; whereof, the one inviteth him to pleasure, and the other to vertue. The first proposing to him his delights[39] and ease, and the other labour and travell. And forasmuch as that age is inclined naturally to pleasures, and enemy to paine-taking and labour, it is greatly to be doubted that the yong man leaving the way that leades to vertue, wil betake himselfe to the other guide to follow the way that leadeth to delight. Wherefore if at any time it be needfull for the father to have a watchfull eye upon his sonne, it is then most important when his child is to make his passage from his childhood into his youth: and at that time to set before his eyes continually instructions, wherby he may conceive how honestie and good behaviour, with civill conversation, are the foundation of good and happie life: and this chiefly is he to do by his owne example. For though it be very good, that his son in those yeares, and at all other times, should see the whole family so ordered, as he may learne nothing therein but vertue and honesty; yet must he not thinke but that his sonne will better beleeve and follow what he shal see himselfe do or say, then all the family besides. And if *Aristotle* advise masters to endevour themselves to give good example to their servants and slaves; how much more ought the father to be carefull to do the like to his own children, who are dearer to him then his servants, being his owne lively images. For as it is the mothers care and office to breed and nourish her childe; so is it the fathers dutie to see him well instructed and taught in vertues and good behaviour: and the speeches and demeanour of the father in his houshold or family, are to his children as lawes in a citie to the citizens, and do assuredly enter into the mindes of children with farre greater force then men would think. Which made *Xenocrates* to say, that the stopping of young mens eares was more needful then the arming of their bodies against the strokes of their enemies; because the danger was greater which they incurred by hearing an unseemely speech, specially from their parents mouth, then that which they might feare by fighting with their enemies. The father therefore must be very circumspect that his sonne heare him not speake any word undecent or dishonest: for nature with a certain hidden vertue perswadeth youth, succeeding a weltaught childhood, to beare great reverence and respect to the grave and ripe yeares of their parents, and of all aged persons; who even in the first view represent unto them vertue, prudence, and all good and grave behaviour. And such is he to shew himselfe to his sonne, as even in his countenance, gestures and words he may as in a table behold therein the lawes of honest life. And that his actions may be in all points to his son a patterne and example of civill conversation and vertuous living.

It is a very necessary and important instruction and advertisement (said M. *Dormer*) that you have last mentioned for fathers to observe. But I would faine that you shold tel me, whether you have not seen (as I oftentimes have done) wicked children begotten of very good and honest parents.

Yes (quoth I) oftener then I would. Neither can it be denied, but that as there are some young men by nature and through their happie constellation wholy bent to vertuous and honest conditions; so are there others naturally disposed to vice and lewd behaviour: yet since it seemeth not credible, that of good parents ill children should come; and that diligent care in bringing them up should not plucke up (if not wholy, yet in part) those evil weeds which choke the good seeds, so as the fruit might in due season be expected: seeking to finde the reason hereof, I have called to mind the precept of *Hippocrates* given to the Physitions, to wit, that it is not sufficient for recovery of the sicke patient, that the Physition be well disposed to cure him, and employ his diligence to that effect: but that other things must likewise concurre for the recovery of his health, as the care and sollicitude of such as watch and tend him, with other exteriour things. For even so me thinketh, that to the good proofe of a young man, besides the example of the father, and of the rest of the family,

be it never so vertuous, there must also concurre the goodnesse
of his conversation abroade, to make his domesticall familiaritie
worke due effect: since many times I have seene it fall out, that
the haunting of ill company from home, hath done a young man
much more hurt, than all the good instructions or vertuous
examples domesticall could do him good. So soft and tender are
the minds of yong men, and apt (as was formerly said) to be
wrought like waxe to vice. And this cometh to passe, by reason
that the sensitive part calling youth to delight, and diverting it
from the travell and paine which learning and vertue require, is
hardly subdued and brought under the rule of reason, by which
it esteemeth itselfe forced, when it is barred from that it desireth.
And if by any exteriour occasion it be pricked forward, it farreth
as we see it oftentimes do with young hard-headed colts, who take
the bit in the mouth, and run away with the rider, carrying him,
will he, nill he, whether they list. It ought therefore to be none
of the least cares of the father to provide, that the forraine conversation of his son may be such as shall rather help then hinder
his care and home example. To which effect, it would be very
good, if it might be possible, that the young man were never from
his fathers side. But forasmuch as many occasions draw men to
attend other waightier affaires, as well publike as privat, wherby
they are driven to have their minds busied about exterior things,
and to neglect their children who are their owne bowels. Therefore is it their parts in such cases to appoint for their children,
when they are past their childish yeares, some learned and honest
man of vertuous behaviour to governe them and take care of
them, whose precepts they may so obey, as they shall feare to
do any thing that may breede reproch or blame unto them. For
such things are mortall poison to yong mens minds, and not only
put them astray from the path that should leade them to vertue,
but imprint in them also a vitious habit that maketh them unruly
and disobedient to all wholesome admonitions and vertuous actions.
This man so chosen to have the charge of youth, must be carefull
among other things to foresee, that his disciples may have such
companions, as the Persian Princes had, provided for them, to
wit, equall of age and like of conditions, with whom they may be
conversant & familiar. For such similitude of age and conditions
doth cause them to love and like one another, if some barre or
impediment fall not betweene them. The auncient wise men

assigned to youth the Plannet of *Mercury*, for no other cause (as I suppose) but for that *Mercury* being (as Astronomers say) either good or bad, according as he is accompanied with another plannet good or evil: even so youth becommeth good or bad, as the companies to which it draweth or giveth it selfe. And therefore ought not yong men to have libertie to haunt what companie they list, but to be kept under the discipline of wise men, and trained up in the companie of others of their age well bred, untill it may be thought, or rather found by experience, that they be past danger, and become fit to guide themselves: having brought their mind obedient to reason so farre, as it cannot any more draw him to any delights, but such as are honest and vertuous. This delight in vertue and honestie, is best induced into a yong mans mind by that true companion of vertue that breedeth feare to do or say any thing unseemely or dishonest: which companion *Socrates* sought to make familiar to his scholers, when he would tell them how they should endevour themselves to purchase in their minds prudence, into their tongues truth with silence, and in their faces bashfulnesse, called by the Latins *verecundia*, deriving it from the reverence which yong men use to beare to their elders. This we call shamefastnesse, and is that honest red colour or blushing which dieth a yong mans cheekes when he supposeth he hath done or said any thing unseemely or unfit for a vertuous mind, or that may offend his parents or betters: a certaine token of a generous mind, and well disciplined, of which great hope may be conceived that it will prove godly and vertuous. For as a sure and firme friend to honestie and vertue, like a watch or guard set for their securitie, it is ever wakefull and carefull to keepe all disordinate concupiscences from the mind, whereby (though of it selfe it be rather an affect then a habit) neverthelesse she induceth such a habite into a yong mans mind, that not onely in presence of others he blusheth, if he chance to do any thing not commendable, but even of himselfe he is ashamed, if being alone he fall into any errour. For though some say, that two things chiefly keepe youth from evill, correction, and shame, and that chastisement rather then instruction draweth youth to do well; yet I for my part never think that yong man well bred or trained up, who for feare of punishment abstaineth from doing things shamefull or dishonest: punishment being appointed but for them that are evill: which made the Poet say:

102

For vertues sake good men ill deeds refraine :
Ill men refraine them but for feare of paine.[40]

For the wickednesse of men hath caused lawes to be devised and established for the conservation of honest and vertuous societie, and civil life, whereunto man is borne: which lawes have appointed penalties for the offenders, to the end that for feare thereof, as *Xenocrates* was wont to say, men might flie from ill doing, as dogs flie harme doing for feare of the whip. And because *Plato* formed his Common-weale of perfect and vertuous men, therfore set he downe no lawes in his bookes *de Repub.* because he supposed the goodnesse of the men to be sufficient for the governement thereof without a law, either to commaund good order, or to punish offenders. Nevertheles the same divine Philosopher considering how the imperfection of mans nature will not suffer any such Common-wealth to be found: he wrote also his bookes of lawes to serve for the imperfection of other Common-weales, which were composed of men of all sorts, good and bad, meane or indifferent, in which both instruction and punishment were needfull, as well to make the evill abstaine from vice, as to confirme the good, and to reduce those that were indifferent to greater perfection. Lawes therefore have appointed punishments, that vertue might be defended and maintained, civill societie and humane right preserved. But yong men bred as our author would have them, are by all meanes to be framed such, as for vertues sake, for feare of reproch, for love and reverence to honestie, and not for feare of punishment to be inflicted on them by the magistrates or their superiours for doing of evill, they may accustome themselves never to do any thing, for which they should neede to blush, no not to themselves alone. Which thing they shal the better performe, if they use to forbeare the doing of any thing by themselves, which they would be ashamed of if they were in company. It is written, that among the auncient Romanes one *Julius Drusus Publicola* having his house seated so as his neighbours might looke into it, a certaine Architect offered him for the expence of five talents to make it so close as none of his neighbors should looke thereinto, or see what he was doing. But he made him answer againe, that he would rather give him ten talents to make it so, as all the citie might see what he did in his house; because he was sure he did nothing within doores whereof he neede be ashamed abroad, though every man should see him.

103

For which answer he was highly commended. True it is that *Xenophon* esteemeth this blushing to a mans self, to be rather temperance then bashfulnes: but let it be named how it wil, it is surely the propertie of a gentle heart so to do. And therefore *Petrarke* said well:

> *Alone whereas I walkt mongs woods and hils,*
> *I shamed at my selfe : for gentle heart*
> *Thinkes that enough, no other spurre it wils.*[41]

Yet would I not neither, that our young man should be more bashfull then were fit, as one over-awed or doltish, not able to consider perils or dangers when they present themselves, not yet to loose his boldnesse of spirit. For *Antipater* the sonne of *Cassander* through the like qualitie cast himselfe away, who having invited *Demetrius* to supper with him at such a time, as their friendship was not sure but stood upon doubtful termes, and he being come accordingly: when *Demetrius* afterwards as in requital of his kindnesse invited *Antipater* likewise to supper, though he knew right well what perill he thrust himselfe into if he went, considering the wyly disposition of the said *Demetrius*: yet being ashamed that *Demetrius* should perceive him to be so mistrustful, would needs go, and there was miserably slaine. This is a vice, named in the Greeke *Disopia*, and which we may in English call unfruitfull shamefastnesse, wherewith we would not wish our yong man should be any way acquainted, but onely with that generous bashfulnesse that may serve him for a spurre to vertue, and for a bridle from vice. But because *Plato* saith, that though bashfulnesse be most properly fit for young men, yet that it is also seemly inough for men of al yeares. And that *Aristotle* contrariwise thinketh it not meete for men of riper years to blush: it may therefore be doubted to whether of these two great learned mens opinions we should incline. For cleering hereof, you must understand that the *Platonikes* say two things among others are specially given for a divine gift unto man: Bashfulnesse the one, and Magnanimitie the other: the one to hold us back from doing of any thing worthy blame & reproch: the other to put us forward into the way of praise and vertue; whereby we might alwayes be ready to do well onely for vertues sake, to the good and benefit of others and to our owne contentment and delight. Of which course, the end is honour in this world, and glory after death. But because the force of the Concupiscible appetite is so great, and setteth before us pleasure in so many sundry shapes, as it is hard to shun the snares which these two enemies of reason set to intrap us, and that the coldnesse of old age cannot wholy extinguish the fervour of our appetites; for my part I think that as in all ages it is fit that Magnanimitie invite us to commendable actions; so also that we have neede of shamefastnesse to correct us whensoever we shal go beyond the bounds or limits of reason in what yeares soever, and to check us with the bridle of temperance. For though *Aristotle* say, that shame ought to die red in a mans cheekes, but for voluntary actions only: yet *Plato* considering that none but God is perfect without fault; and that every man, even the most vertuous falleth sometimes through humane frailtie, thought (according to Christianitie) that ripenesse of yeares or wisedome should be no hinderance to make them ashamed, but rather make them the more bashfull whensoever they should find in themselves, that they had run into any errour undecent or unfitting for men of their yeares and quality. Not intending yet thereby that the errors of the ancienter men were to be of that sort that yong mens faults commonly are, who through incontinencie runne oftentimes into sin wilfully: whereas men of riper yeares erre or ought to erre only through frailty of nature. Much better were it indeed for men of yeares not to do any thing of which they might be ashamed, if the condition of man would permit it, then after they had done it to blush thereat: and much more reprochfull is his fault, if he offend voluntarily then the young mans. But since no man (though he have made a habite in wel-doing) can stand so assured of himselfe, but that sometime in his life he shal commit some error: it is much better (in what age soever it be) that blushing make him know his fault, then to passe it over impudently without shame. And accordingly Saint *Ambrose* said in his booke of Offices, that shamefastnesse was meet for all ages, for all times, and for all places. And for the same cause perhaps have wise men and religious held, that an Angell of heaven assisteth every man to call him backe from those evils, which the ill Angell with his sugred baite of delight and disordinate appetite inticeth him unto, onely for his ruine. For they thought that our forces were not able to resist so mighty provocations. As for *Plato* and *Aristotle*, it seemeth they differed in opinion, for that, the one considered humane nature as it ought to be, and the other as it commonly is indeed. Which may the better be beleeved, because *Aristotle* in his booke of Rhetorike, restrained not this habite of shamefast-nesse so precisely to young men, but that it may sometimes beseeme an aged mans cheekes also, though so farre as grace and wisedome may prevaile, it would best beseeme him never to do the thing whereof he need be ashamed, as before was sayd. And the same rule ought young men also to propose to them-selves, whereby they shall deserve so much the more commenda-tion, as the heate of their yeares beareth with them fierie appetites, and they the lesse apt to resist so sharpe and so intollerable prickes. The way to observe that rule, is to strive in all their actions to master themselves, and to profit in vertue: whereunto will helpe them chiefly, that they endevour themselves to bridle such desires as they find most to molest them, not suffering them to transport them beyond the limits of honestie. But because the day goeth away, and that to treate particularly of all that might be said concerning the direction of youth to vertue, which leadeth him to his felicitie, would require more time then is remaining, I wil briefly knit up the rest that concerneth this matter. Young men have naturall heate so much abounding in them, that they cannot rest, but be still in motion as well of body as of mind. The one with running, leaping, and other exercises, and when all they faile, the tongue ceaseth not, which by reason of their age is the more bold and ready. The other with passing from one discourse to another, and from one passion to another; now loving, now hating, now boyling with anger and choler, now still and quiet, with such like motions of the mind. And because the motions of the body, and the affections of the minde must have their measure and their rule, and the one and the other convenient exercise and moderate rest: therefore did the auncient wise men devise two speciall Arts, most apt and fit for both these purposes. Whereof, the one they call *Gymnastica*, which is a skilfull and moderate exercise of the body; and the other Musike, by which name it is well knowne in all languages. And when they had caused their youth to spend part of the day in learning those sciences and disciplines which they thought fit for that age (for of all other things they abhorred the training them up in ignorance, because seldome can an ignorant man be good, and supposing that men without knowledge and learning are but figures of men, and images of death without soule or life) then would they draw them to honest exercises of the body by degrees. For they held it a thing most necessary for the wel-founding of a Common-wealth, to be continually carefull of the framing youth both in body and mind; because they knew right well that good education maketh young men good: and that such are Common-wealths and States, as are the qualities and conditions of the men which they do breed. Touching the body therfore, they did devise to strengthen and harden it with convenient and temperate exer-cises: as the play at ball, leaping, running, dansing, riding, wrast-ling, throwing the barre, the stone or sledge, and such like. For the minde, they thought best to stay and settle it selfe with the harmonie of Musike: and from these two they resolved, that two great good effects did ensue: From the first, strength of body and boldnesse of spirit; and from the latter, modesty and temperance, inseparable companions for the most part unto forti-tude. For some of them were of opinion, that our soules were composed of harmonie; and beleeved that Musike was able so to temper our affects and passions, as they should not jarre or discord among themselves, but be so interlaced the one with the other in a sweet consent, as wel guided and ordered action should proceed from the same, even as sweet and delightfull Musike proceedeth from the wel-tempering of tunable voices, or well consorted instruments. Neither would they have the one to be exercised, and the other omitted: for that they thought, if yong men should give themselves onely to the exercises of the body, they wold become too fierce and hardy; and so be rather hurtfull to their commonweales then otherwise. And if they should follow onely Musike, which is proper to rest and quietnes, and used as a recreation of the mind, as *Aristotle* saith, they would become soft minded and effeminate. But by joyning both these faculties together in one, they sought to make a noble temper, and to induce a most excellent habite, as well in the mind as in the body. So that if valor were required for the defence of their countrey, or vanquishing of their enemies, they were made fit and apt thereunto by the exercises of the body; but with such measure and temper as should not exceed. Which measure and temper, they obtained from that harmonie which Musike im-printed in their mindes: under which they comprehended not onely the ordering of the voice and sounds of instruments, but all other orderly and seemely motions of the body; which upon their stages, or Scænes in the acting of Tragedies, was chiefly to be discovered. And that all orderly motions were comprehended under Musicke, was held so certaine by *Pythagoras, Archetas, Plato, Cicero,* & other famous Philosophers, that they were of opinion, that the orderly course and motions of the heavens could not be such as it is, or continue without harmony, though *Aristotle* do oppose him selfe to their opinion. And for this cause did *Lycurgus* devise that Musike should be conjoyned with the military discipline of the *Lacedemonians,* not onely to temper the heate and furie of their minds in fight; but also to cause them to use a certaine measure in their marching, and other occasions of war. In which respect they never went to battell without certaine pipes, according to the times whereof they understood how to use their bodies and weapons: from which respect also cometh our using of drums and trumpets to give souldiers knowledge when to march, when to stand, when to assault, and when to retire: and consequently how to joyne order and measure with their valour against the enemy: and the Lansknight and the Switzer[42] use also the fife at this day with the drum. And to say truth, great is the force of Musike skilfully used to stirre up or to appease the mind. For we reade, that *Pythagoras* finding a wanton yong man enraged with lust, ready to force the doore of an honest woman, he so calmed his mind, onely by changing the Phrigian tune and number into the Spondean, that he gave over his wicked purpose. And *Therpander,* when a great sedition was raised among the *Lacedemonians,* he with his musike so quieted their mindes bent to fury, that he reduced them to a perfect peace. It is also written of the great *Alexander,* that he was so moved by that tune and number of Musikes, which the greeks called *Orthios nomos,* which was a kind of haughtie tune to stirre men to battel, that he rose from the boord to arme himselfe, as if the trumpet had sounded the allarme. But what talke we of the auncient opinions concerning the force of Musike to move mens minds, when we find they beleeved that their Gods were forced by the vertue of Musike to appease their wrath? For, the *Lacedemonians* being infested with a great pestilence, *Thales* of *Candia* was said by musike to have mitigated their anger, and so to have delivered them from that mortality. The which thing *Homer* also signified, when he said, that the yongmen of Greece with their songs did appease *Apollo* his wrath, and caused the

108

plague to cease which had infected their campe. And the Romanes likewise being annoied with a great pestilence, received then first the singing of Satires into the Citie though but rudely tuned then, as a remedy for that infection. The force & efficacie of musike then being such as I have declared, it is no marvel that the Ægiptians, after they had once received it into their Commonwealth, as meet for the instruction of their youth, wold never after allow that it sholde be altered or changed, but such as it was when they first admitted it, such they continued it without altering the space of ten thousand yeres, according to their manner of contemplation, having a conceit or rather a firme opinion that they could not alter musike but with danger to their State. Which opinion the Lacedemonians likewise so embraced, that when *Timotheus* an excellent Musition in Sparta, had presumed to adde but one string to the Cyther, they banished him out of the citie and territories, as a violater of lawes, and a corrupter of honest discipline. Albeit with *Phrine* they dealt more mildly, who having added to the Cyther two cords, one sharpe, and another grave or flat, they onely caused him to take them away againe, supposing that seven strings were enough to temper the sound thereof, as a number comprehending all musike; and that the increasing therof was but superfluous and harmefull. These ancient examples & considerations, are not sleightly to be passed over: for though many other occasions of corruption in our age may be assigned; yet one of the principall, in the judgement of wise men, may wel be imputed to the qualitie of that corrupted musike which is most used now a dayes; carrying with it nothing but a sensual delight to the eare, without working any good to the mind at all. Nay, would God it did not greatly hurt and corrupt the mind. For as musike well used is a great help to moderate the disorderly affections of the minde: so being abused it expelleth all manly thoughts from the heart, and so effeminateth men, that they are little better then women: and in women breedeth such lascivious and wanton thoughts, that oftentimes they forget their honestie, without which they cannot be worthy the name of women. Not that I would hereby inferre, that musike generally were to be misliked, or unfit for women also: but my meaning is of this wanton and lascivious kind of musike, which is now a dayes most pleasing, and resembleth the Lydian of old time, which *Plato* so abhorred, as he would not in any sort admit it into his Common-weale, lest it should infect the minds of men and women both. And from him may we learne what kinde of musike he would have men to embrace, to stirre their mindes up to vertue, and to purge the same from vice and errour. Like as also from *Aristotle* in his 8. book of Politikes, taken perchance out of the writings of his master. But if that auncient kinde of musike, framed and composed wholy to gravitie, were now knowne and used, which kinde was then set forth with the learned and grave verses of excellent Poets, we should now also see magnificall and high desires stirred up in the minds of the hearers. Which verses contained the praises of excellent and heroicall personages, and were used to be sung at the tables of great men and Princes, to the sound of the Lyra; whereby they inflamed the mindes of the hearers to vertue and generous actions. For the force of Musike with Poesie, is such, as is of power to set the followers and lovers thereof into the direct way that leadeth them to their felicitie. *Socrates* demaunding of the Oracle of *Apollo*, what he should do to make himselfe happie: he was willed to learne Musike; whereupon he gave himselfe forthwith to the studie of Poesie, conceiving with himselfe, that verses and Poeticall numbers are the perfectest Musike, and that they enter like lively sparkes into mens minds, to kindle in them desires of dignitie, greatnesse, honor, true praise and commendation, and to correct whatsoever is in them of base and vile affection. In auncient time therfore men caused their children to be instructed in Poesie before all other disciplines, for that they esteemed good Poets to be the fathers of wisedome, and the undoubted true guides to civill life, and not without cause. For they raise mens thoughts from humble and base things, such as the vulgar and common sort delight in, and make them bend their endevours wholy to high, yea heavenly things. As who so list to attend diligently the excellencie of the Psalmes and Hymnes composed by the Kingly Prophet *David*, and others called the singers of the Hebrew Church, shall easily discerne. But since our musike is growen now to the fulnes of wanton and lascivious passions, and the words so confusedly mingled with the notes, that a man can discerne nothing but the sound and tunes of the voices, but sence or sentence he can understand none at all; even as it were sundry birds chanting and chirping upon the boughes of trees : yong men are much better in the judgement of the wise, to abstaine from it altogether, then to spend their time about it. For as good disciplines are the true and proper nourishment of vertue: so are the evill the very poison of the same.

Then said Captaine *Carleil*, as concerning the difference between the auncient musike and ours in this age, I do easily agree with you, and wise it were otherwise, that we might see now a dayes those wonderfull effects of this excellent Art, which are written of it in auncient authors. But where you so highly extoll the studie of Poesie, you make me not a little to marvel, considering how *Plato*, being so learned a man, did not onely make small estimation thereof, but banished it expressly from his common-weale.

Let not that seeme strange unto you, said I: for *Plato* condemned not Poesie, but onely those Poets that abused so excellent a facultie, scribling either wanton toyes, or else by foolish imitation taking upon them to expresse high conceits which themselves understood not. And specially did he reprehend those Poets, who in their fictions did ascribe to the Gods such actions as would have bin unseemely for the most wanton and vicious men of the world: as the adultery of *Mars* and *Venus*, those of *Jupiter* with *Semele*, with *Europa*, with *Danaë*, with *Calisto*, and many moe. Though some have under such fictions sought to teach morall and marvellous sences, which *Plato* likewise in his second *Alcibiades* declareth. But he blamed not those Poets, who frame their verses and compositions to the honor of God, and to good examples of modestie and vertue. For in his books of Lawes he introduceth Poets to sing Himnes to their Gods, and teacheth the maner of their Chori in their sacrifices, and to make prayers for the Common-weale. Howbeit, to say truth, though he so do, he would not have it lawfull for every man to publish any composition that he had made, without the allowance and view of some magistrate elected in the citie for that purpose. Which magistracy he would have to be of no fewer in number then fiftie men of gravitie and wisedome: of such importance did he hold the compositions of Poets to be. Which regard if it were had now a dayes, we should not see so many idle and profane toyes spred abroade by some that think the preposterous turning of phrases, and making of rime with little reason, to be an excellent kinde of writing, and fit to breed them fame and reputation. Supposing (as men blinded in their owne conceits) that they exceed all other

111

writers, and that from them only others that write in that kind shold take their rules and example. So drowning their corrupted judgements in their ignorance, that where they be worthy blame, they esteeme themselves comparable to the most famous and excellent Poets that ever wrote, and that they ought to be partakers of their glory and greatest honors. But to men of judgement, and able to discerne the difference betweene well writing and presumptuous scribling, they minister matter of scorne and laughter, when they consider their disjoynted phrases, their misshapen figures, their shallow conceits lamely expressed, and disgraced, in stead of being adorned, with unproper and unfit metaphors, well declaring how unworthy they be of the title of Poets. Such are they, who being themselves ful of intemperance and wantonnes, write nothing but dishonest and lascivious rimes and songs, apt to root out all honest and manly thoughts out of their mindes that are so foolish as to lose their time in reading of them. These indeed ought to be driven out, and banished from al Commonweales, as corrupters of manners, and infecters of young mens mindes: who may well be compared to rocks that lie hidden under water, amid the sea of this our life, on which, such yong men as chance to strike, are like to suffer shipwracke, and sinking in the gulfe of lust and wantonnesse, to be drowned and dead to all vertue. But true Poesie well used, is nothing else but the most ancient kind of Philosophie, compounded and interlaced with the sweetnesse of numbers and measured verses. A thing (as saith *Musæus*) most sweet and pleasing to the mind, teaching us vertue by a singular maner of instruction, and covering morall sences under fabulous fictions: to the end they might the sooner be received under that pleasing forme, and yet not be vulgarly understood, but by such onely as were worthy to tast the sweetnesse of their inventions. For so did the Philosophers of old write their mysteries under similitudes, to the end they might not be straight comprehended by every dul wit, and lose their reputation, by being common in the hands and mouth of every simple fellow. This maner first began among the wiser Ægiptians, and was afterwards followed by *Pythagoras* and *Plato*. And *Aristotle*, though he wrote not by similitudes and allegories, yet wrapt he up his conceits in so darke a maner of speech and writing, as hardly were they to be understood by those that heard himselfe teach and expound his writings. But to make an end

112

with Poets, he that marketh those fictions which *Homer* hath written of their Gods, like as those of *Virgil*, and other of the heathen Poets, though at the first they seeme strange and absurd; yet he shall find under them naturall and divine knowledge hidden to those that are not wise and learned: which neither time nor occasion would, that I should here insist upon. Let it suffice that yong men are to make great account of that part of Musike which beareth with it grave sentences, fit to compose the mind to good order by vertue of the numbers and sound; which part proceedeth from the Poets, whom *Plato* himself called the fathers and guides of those that afterwards were called Philosophers. But this that by varietie of tunes, and warbling divisions, confounds the words and sentences, and yeeldeth onely a delight to the exterior sense, and no fruit to the mind, I wish them to neglect and not to esteeme.

Indeed (said captain *Carleil*) I agree with you, that our musike is far different from the ancient musike, and that well may it serve to please the eare: but I yeeld that it effeminateth the minde, and rather diverteth it from the way of blisse and felicitie, then helpeth him thereunto. But are there not other disciplines, besides these two which you have specified last, wherein yong men are to be instructed to further them to the attaining of that end, about which all this our discourse is framed?

Yes marry (said I) and so far as youth is capable, it might well be wished that he had knowledge of them all. But of these our author hath first spoken, supposing that from Grammer, and such other the liberall Arts, as those first yeares could reach to understand, he should be straight brought to the excercise of the body and to Musike. Nevertheles it is requisite withal, that, as his yeares increase, he should apply himselfe without losse of time to learne principally Geometry and Arithmetike, two liberal arts, and of great use and necessitie for all humane actions in this life; because they teach us measure and numbers, by which, all things mans life hath need of are ordered and ruled. For by them we measure land, we build, we devise Arts, and set them forth, all things are directed by number and measure, as occasions serve: and without the help of these two faculties all would be confused and disordered. And therefore did the Ægyptians set their children carefully to learne them: for that by them they decided the discords and differences growing among the dwellers along the banks of the river of Nyle, which with her inundations, and breaking of their meares[43] and limits did give them often cause to fall at variance and strife among themselves. For navigation likewise how needfull they are, all men do know, that know the necessitie of the use thereof for humane life, since all that nature produceth to all people and nations in the world particularly, is thereby made common to all, with the helpe of commutation and of coyne. From these two also cometh the exact knowledge, not onely of the earth and of the sea, but of the heavens likewise and of their motions, of the starres and course of time, of the rising and setting of the plannets: and to conclude all in few words, of the whole frame and order of nature, and of her skill, by which she knitteth and uniteth together in peace and amitie things in themselves most contrary. All done so cunningly by number and measure, as a whole yeares discourse would not serve to display the same at large. The Art of warre in like maner, so needful for States and Commonweales, to keepe in due obedience stubborne and rebellious subjects, and to repell the violence of forreine enemies, if it were not directed by measure and number: what would it be but a confusion, and a most dangerous and harmfull thing, which would soone fall from the reputation it hath and ever had. For these considerations therefore and others, is youth, that bendeth his course to vertue, to exercise it selfe in Geometry and Arithmetike, which in ancient times men would acquaint their children withall, even from their childhood: as Arts that have more certainty then any other. But they are not to be attained without Logike, because from it are gotten the instruments and the maner to devide, to compound, to invent and find out reasons and arguments; and finally to discerne and judge of truth and falshood. But here I must tel you, that he meaneth not of that Logike which is used now a dayes most in schooles, standing for the most part upon brawlings and contentions, and propounding of frivolous questions, serving to nought else but subtilties, and inextricable knots, fitter to nourish arguments then to teach or explane the truth. Which abuse *Antisthenes* misliking, said, it was meeter to instruct him that contended, then by contention to overcome him. For Logike being indeed, the way and meane to instruct and teach, and (as before is said) the proper instrument of sciences, such as learne it onely to contend, forsake the right end and scope of that Art, and are as fruitlesse to their followers or scholers, as myre is to the way faring man, which besides the defiling of his garments, doth oftentimes make him also to fall. Therfore *Plato* in his time cried out upon the same, judging it not without cause to be a meer folly that hindred the knowledge of truth, and the learning of those things which the soundest and wisest Philosophers taught as well touching vertuous and civill actions, as naturall and divine sciences: from which, this vaine science putteth men astray, so long as it teacheth onely to argue and to contend. Whereby it commeth to passe, that whiles they are more intentive to the words and circumstances then to the matter, the more they strive to seeme learned and subtill, the lesse they shew themselves to understand. Next to Logike is Rhetorike to be placed, or the Art of Oratory, which *Leontinus* did preferre before all other, because it maketh it selfe Ladie over mens minds, not by force or violence, but by their owne consents and free-will. And as *Zeno* expressed the difference betweene these two Arts, by resembling the former to his hand closed, and the latter to his hand stretched out. So doth Rhetorike use arguments with lesse force and efficacie then Logike; yet fetcheth them from Logike, as from a fountaine or well head, not to seek out the truth exactly, but only to perswade or disswade with them that, which he thinketh most profitable for the speaker, or the person for whom he speaketh. And of this Art, have all publike and private actions appertaining to civill life need to perswade what is good and profitable, and to disswade what is hurtfull or unprofitable, to appease tumults and dissentions, to treate of leagues and peaces, to stirre up the mindes of men to the defence of their friends, their parents, their Prince and country, and their Religion: to search out and investigate the truth of all things, to assist the innocent and oppressed in courts of judgment, to accuse the faultie and offenders: and finally to give unto vertue her due praise and commendation; and unto vice due blame and reproch. By these meanes and studies which we have briefly touched, rather then perfectly declared, ought a young man to be framed to civill conversation, and instructed with all carefulnesse, that he may learne to bridle his concupiscible desires, his angry and disordinate motions, occasioned by the senses, and stirred up by those two parts of the minde, which are rebellious and contrary to reason: whereby he may give himselfe wholy to honest and vertuous endevours. And because store of wealth oft times causeth young men (when they possesse it) to turne aside from vertue, because riches is the nurse of wantonnesse in those yeares, great regard is to be had, that as the father, so farre as his state requireth, is not to suffer his son to want any thing that is necessary for his calling; so must he take heede that he be not so fed with money, as feeding therby his lusts and sensuall appetites, he may abandon the good thoughts of vertue, and receive in steed of them the seeds of unruly and disorderly affections, which of themselves are by nature in youth much more mightie then were fit, and need not to be holpen by plenty of riches. For to give a yong man money at will, to dispose as he list (unlesse the father find, as in some yong men it happeneth, that he hath prevented his yeares with staidnesse and discretion) is even as much as to put a sword into the hands of a furious or mad man.

By this the Sun was so farre declined towards our horizon, as all the companie thought it time to depart, that they might before sun-set reach to the citie.

Wherfore sir *Robert Dillon* rising up, said: Howsoever the latenes of the day call us away, yet the desire to heare on further the discourse of so good a matter, hath drawne us on in such sort, as we have scarce perceived how the time is past. And for your second feast, you have right daintily and plenteously entertained us. We must now expect the third, which to morow (God willing) we wil not faile to come and accept: in hope that though we be combersome & troublesome unto you, yet as wel in regard of discharging your promise, as of accomplishing the desire of so many your friends, you will not thinke it much to affoord us your patience and your breath in delivering to us the substance of your authors third dialogue of Civil life; by which we may learne as much as he hath written of the Ethike part of Moral Philosophie, teaching the ready way for every man in his private course of life to attaine his felicitie, and that end, of which all this discourse of yours hath had his beginning. And so taking their leave all together they departed.

THE THIRD DAYES MEETING, AND DISCOURSE OF CIVILL LIFE.

I was not yet fully apparelled on the next morrow, when looking out of my window towards the citie, I might perceive the companie all in a troupe coming together, not as men walking softly to sport, or desirous to refresh themselves with the morning deaw, and the sweete pleasant ayre that then invited all persons to leave their sluggish nestes; but as men earnestly bent to their jorney, and that had their heads busied about some matter of greater moment then their recreation. I therefore hasted to make me ready, that they might not find me in case to be taxed by them of drowsinesse, and was out of the doores before they came to the house: where saluting them, and they having courteously returned the good morrow unto me; the Lord Primate asked me whether that company made me not afraide to see them come in such sort upon me being but a poore Farmer: for though they came not armed like soldiers to be cessed[44] upon me, yet their purpose was to coynie[45] upon me, and to eate me out of house and home. To whom I answered, that as long as I saw Counsellers in the companie, I neede not feare that any such unlawful exaction as coynie should be required at my hand: for the lawes had sufficiently provided for the abolishing therof. And though I knew that among the Irishry it was not yet cleane taken away, yet among such as were ameynable to law, and civill, it was not used or exacted. As for souldiers, besides that their peaceable maner of coming freed me from doubt of cesse, thanked be God the state of the realme was such as there was no occasion of burthening the subject with them, such had bin the wisedome, valour and foresight of our late Lord Deputie, not onely in subduing the rebellious subjects, but also in overcoming the forreine enemie: whereby the garrison being reduced to a small number, and they provided for by her Majestie of victual at reasonable rates, the poore husbandman might now eate the labors of his owne hands in peace and quietnes, without being disquieted or harried by the unruly souldier.

We have (said sir *Robert Dillon*) great cause indeed to

117

thanke God of the present state of our country, and that the course holden now by our present Lord Deputie, doth promise us a continuance, if not a bettering, of this our peace and quietnesse. My Lord *Grey* hath plowed and harrowed the rough ground to his hand: but you know that he that soweth the seede, whereby we hope for harvest according to the goodnesse of that which is cast into the earth, and the seasonablenesse of times, deserveth no lesse praise then he that manureth the land. God of his goodnesse graunt, that when he also hath finished his worke, he may be pleased to send us such another Bayly to oversee and preserve their labours, that this poore countrey may by a wel-ordered and setled forme of governement, and by due and equall administration of justice beginne to flourish as other Common-weales do. To which all saying Amen, we directed our course to walke up the hill, where we had bene the day before; and sitting downe upon the little mount awhile to rest the companie that had come from Dublin, we arose againe, and walked in the greene way, talking still of the great hope was conceived of the quiet of the countrey, since the forreine enemie had so bin vanquished, and the domesticall conspiracies discovered & met withall, and the rebels cleane rooted out, till one of the servants came to call us home to dinner. Where finding the table furnished we sate downe, and having seasoned our fare with pleasant and familiar discourses, as soone as the boord was taken up, they sollicited me to fetch my papers that I might proceede to the finishing of my last discourse of the three by me proposed. But they being ready at hand in the dining chamber, I reached them, and layd them before me, and began as followeth. Hitherto hath bin discoursed of those two ages, which may for the causes before specified, be wel said to be void of election, and without judgement, because of their want of experience. For which cause have they had others assigned to them, for guides to leade them to that end, which of themselves they were not able to attaine, that is, their felicitie in this life. And now being to speake of that age which succeeds the heate of youth; we must a litle touch the varietie of opinions concerning the same. *Tully* saith, that a citizen of Rome might be created Consul (which was the higest ordinary dignitie in that citie) when he was come to the age of 23. yeares. *Plinie* in his *Panegyrike* saith, that it was decreed *lege Pompeia*, that no man might have any magistracie before he were thirtie yeeres old. And *Ulpian, lege S. Digest.* treating of honours, writeth, that under the age of 25. yeares no man was capable of any magistracie. Among these three opinions, the last of the civill lawyer holdeth the *medium,* and is therefore the fittest to be followed: for then is a young mans mind setled, and he is become fit (being bred and instructed as hath bin before declared) to be at his owne guiding and direction: and then doth the civill law allow him libertie to make contracts and bargaines for himselfe, which before he could not do, being in pupillage[46] and under a tutor. Howbeit our common law cutteth off foure yeeres of those, and enableth a yong man at 21. yeers of age to enter into his land, and to be (as we terme it) out of his wardship. Which time being (I know not for what respect) assigned by our lawes, may well be held not so well considered of, as that which the civill law appointeth, if we marke how many of our yong men over-throw their estates by reason of their want of experience, and of the disordinate appetites which master them: all which in those other foure yeares from 21. to 25. do alter to better judgement and discretion. Whereby they are the better able to order their affaires.

Why, said Captain *Dawtry,* I have knowne, and know at this day some young men, who at 18. yeers of age are of sounder judgement and more setled behaviour, then many, not of 25. yeeres old onely, but of many moe, yea then some that are grey-headed with age.

Of such (said I) there are to be seene oftentimes as you say some, that beyond all expectation, and as it were forcing the rules of nature, shew themselves stayed in behaviour, and discreete in their actions when they are very yong, to the shame of many elder men. Of which companie, I may well of mine owne knowledge, and by the consent I thinke of all men, name one as a rare example and a wonder of nature, and that is sir *Philip Sidney;* who being but seventeene yeeres of age when he began to travell, and coming to Paris, where he was ere long sworne Gentleman of the chamber to the French King, was so admired among the graver sort of Courtiers, that when they could at any time have him in their companie and conversation, they would be very joyfull, and no lesse delighted with his ready & witty answers, then astonished to heare him speake the French language so wel, and aptly, having bin so short a while in the countrey. So was he likewise esteemed in all places else where he came in his travell,

119

as well in *Germanie* as in *Italie*. And the judgement of her Majestie employing him, when he was not yet full 22. yeeres old, in Embassage to congratulate with the Emperour that now is his comming to the Empire, may serve for a sufficient proofe, what excellencie of understanding, and what stayednesse was in him at those yeeres. Whereby may well be said of him the same that *Cicero* said of *Scipio Africanus*, to wit, that vertue was come faster upon him then yeeres. Which *Africanus* was chosen Consull being absent in the warres, by an universal consent of all the tribes of Rome, before he was of age capable to receive that dignitie by the law. But these are rare examples, upon which rules are not to be grounded: for *Aristotle* so long ago said, as we do now in our common proverbe, that one swallow makes not summer. Among young men there are some discreete, sober, quicke of wit, and ready of discourse, who shew themselves ripe of judgment before their yeeres might seeme to yeeld it them: so are there among aged men on the other side some of shallow wit and little judgement; of whom the wisest men of al ages have esteemed, that to be old with a yong mans mind, is all one as to be yong in yeeres. For it is not grey haires or furrowes in the face, but prudence and wisedome that make men venerable when they are old: neither can there be any thing more unseemly, then an old man to live in such maner as if he began but then to live; which caused *Aristotle* to say, that it imported little whether a man were young of yeeres or of behaviour. Neverthelesse, because dayly experience teacheth us, that yeares commonly bring wisedome, by reason of the varietie of affaires that have passed thorough old mens hands, and which they have seene managed by other men: and that commonly youth hath neede of a guide and director, to take care of those things which himselfe cannot see or discerne. Therefore have lawes provided tutors for the ages before mentioned, untill they had attained the yeers by them limited, & thenceforth left men to their owne direction, unlesse in some particular cases accidentall, as when they be distraught of their wits, or else through extreme olde age they become children againe, as sometimes it falleth out. Knowledge then is the thing that maketh a man meete to governe himselfe; and the same being attained but by long studie and practise, wise men have therefore concluded, that youth cannot be prudent. For indeed the varietie of humane actions, by which, from many particular accidents, an universall rule must be gathered; because (as *Aristotle* sayth) the knowledge of universalities springeth from singularities, maketh knowledge so hard to be gotten, that many yeares are required thereunto. And from this reason is it also concluded, that humane felicitie cannot be attained in yong yeares, since by the definition thereof it is a perfect operation according to vertue in a perfect life: which perfection of life is not to be allowed but to many yeers. But the way unto it is made open by knowledge, and specially by the knowledge of a mans selfe. To which good education having prepared him and made him apt, when he is come to riper judgement by yeares, he may the better make choise of that way which shall leade him to the same, as the most perfect end and scope of all his actions. And this by considering wel of his own nature, which having annexed unto it a spark of divinitie, he shal not only as a meere earthly creature, but also as partaker of a more divine excellency, raise himself, & have perfect light to see the ready way which leadeth to felicitie. To this knowledge of himselfe, so necessary for the purchasing of humane felicitie, is Philosophie a singular helpe, as being called the science of truth, the mother of sciences, and the instructor of all things appertaining to happie life: and therefore should yong men apply themselves to the studie thereof with all carefulnesse, that thereby they may refine their mindes and their judgements, and find the knowledge of his wel-nigh divine nature, so much the more easily. And as this knowledge is of all other things most properly appertaining to humane wise-dome; so is the neglecting thereof the greatest and most harmefull folly of all others: for from the said knowledge (as from a foun-taine or well head) spring all vertues and goodnes; even as from the ignorance therof flow all vices and evils that are among men. But herein is one special regard to be had, which is, that self love cary not away the mind from the direct path to the same: for which cause *Plato* affirmed, that men ought earnestly to pray to God, that in seeking to know themselves, they might not be misled by their selfe love, or by the over-weening of themselves.

M. *Spenser* then said: If it be true that you say, by Philo-sophie we must learne to know our selves, how happened it, that the *Brachmani* men of so great fame, as you know, in *India*, would admit none to be their schollers in Philosophy, if they had not first learned to know them selves: as if they had concluded, that such knowledge came not from Philosophie, but appertained to some other skill or science.

Their opinion (said I) differeth not (as my author thinketh) from the opinion of the wise men of Greece. But that the said *Brachmani* herein shewed the selfe same thing that *Aristotle* teacheth, which is, that a man ought to make some triall of himselfe before he determine to follow any discipline, that he may discerne and judge whether there be in him any disposition wherby he may be apt to learne the same or no. And to the same effect in another place he affirmeth, that there must be a custome of wel-doing in them that will learne to be vertuous, which may frame in them an aptnesse to learne, by making them love what is honest and commendable, and to hate those things that are dishonest and reprochfull. For all men are not apt for all things: neither is it enough that the teacher be ready to instruct and skilfull, but the learner must also be apt of nature to apprehend and conceive the instructions that shall be given unto him. And this knowledge of himselfe, is fit for every man to have before he undertake the studie of Philosophie, to wit, that he enter into himselfe to trie whether he can well frame himself to endure the discipline of this mother of sciences, and the patience which is required in al those things besides, which appertaine to honestie and vertuous life. For he that will learne vertue in the schoole of Philosophie, must not bring a mind corrupted with false opinions, vices, wickednesse, disordinate appetites, ambitions, greedie desires of wealth, nor wanton lusts and longings, with such like, which will stop his eares that he shall not be able to heare the holy voice of Philosophie. Therefore *Epictetus* said very well, that they which were willing to study Philosophie, ought first to consider well whether their vessel be cleane and sweet, lest it should corrupt that which they meant to put into it. Declaring thereby withall, that learning put into a vicious mind is dangerous. But this maner of knowing a mans selfe, is not that which I spake of before, though it be that which the sayd Indian Philosophers meant, and is also very necessary and profitable. For to know a mans selfe perfectly, according to the former maner, is a matter of greater importance then so. Which made *Thales*, when he was asked what was the hardest thing for a man to learne, answer, that it was, to know himselfe. For this knowledge stayeth not at the consideration of this exteriour masse of our body, which represents itselfe unto our eyes, though even therein also may well be discerned the marvellous and artificiall handy-work of Gods divine Majestie, but penetrateth to the examination of the true inward man, which is the intellectuall soule, to which this body is given but for an instrument here in this life. And this knowledge is of so great importance, that man guided by the light of reason, knoweth that he is, as *Trismegistus* saith, a divine miracle, and therefore not made (as bruite beasts are) to the belly and to death, but to vertue and to eternall life, that thereby he may unite himselfe at the last with his Creator and maker of all things, when his soule shall be freed from these mortall bands and fetters of the flesh. Towards whom neverthelesse, it is his part to raise himselfe with the wings of his thoughts even whiles he is here in this world, soaring above mortall things, bending his mind to the contemplation of that divine nature, the most certaine roote of all goodnesse, the infallible truth, and the assured beginning and foundation of all vertues. And therefore said *Aristotle*, that the science of the soule was profitable to the knowledge of all truth. Whereunto may be added that which *Plato* and his followers have affirmed, to wit, that the soule knowing her self, knoweth also her maker; and disposeth her selfe not onely to obey him, but also to become like unto him: whereof in another place occasion of further speech will be ministred. Moreover, a man by knowing himselfe, becommeth in this life sage and prudent, and understandeth that he is made not to live onely, as other creatures are, but also to live well. For they that have not this knowledge, are like unto bruite beasts: and he seeth likewise, that nature, though she produceth man not learned, yet she hath framed us to vertue, and apt to knowledge. And that a man is placed as a meane creature betweene bruite beasts and those divine spirits above in heaven, having a disposition to decline (if he list) to the nature of those bruite beasts, and also to raise himselfe to a resemblance of God himselfe. Which things he weighing and considering, he reacheth not onely to the knowledge of himselfe, but of other men also. And by the guiding of Philosophie, to direct himselfe and others to the well governing of himselfe, of families, and Common-wealths, to the making of lawes and ordinances for the maintaining of vertue and beating downe of vice; and finally to set men in the way to their felicitie, by giving them to understand, that they onely are happie which be wise and vertuous, and meete to be Lords and rulers over other men, and over all things else created for the use of mankind. Of all which things when they shall consider man onely to be the end, marvelling at his excellencie, they are driven to acknowledge how much they are bound to the heavenly bountie and goodnesse, for creating him so noble a creature, and setting him so direct a course to everlasting joy and felicitie. Hence groweth a desire in them of what is good, beautifull, and honest, and of justice, and to make themselves like unto their maker: who (as the *Platonikes* say) is the centre, about which all soules capable of reason turne, even as the line turneth about the mathematicall point to make a circle: and so by good and vertuous operations to purchase in this life praise and commendation, and in the life to come eternal happinesse. These were the men whom the *Lacedemonians* accounted divine, and the *Platonikes* called the images of God.

Then said Captain *Carleil*, this your discourse, whereby you have shewed the importance and right meane of knowing our selves, hath bin very wise & fruitful, and fit to declare how we ought to frame our life in this world. But I make a doubt, whether all this that you have layed before us to be done, be in our power or no? for it seemeth strange, that, if it be in our power to give our selves to a commendable life, there be any (as we see there are many) so perverse, and of so crooked judgement, as to bend themselves to wickednesse and naughtie life, who, when they might be vertuous, would rather chuse to be vicious. And this maketh me oftentimes to thinke that the doing of good or evill is not in our power; but that either destinie (which as *Thales* was wont to say) ruled and mastred all things, or the starres with their influences doth draw us to do what we do.

To this demaund of yours, said I, you shal have an answer, such as mine author maketh, who, as a Philosopher naturally discoursing of the actions of the soule, delivereth his minde according to the sentence of all Philosophers. But because some part of your question toucheth a point now in controversie concerning Religion, it is good we have a safe conduct of my Lord Primate,[47] that his sence as a Philosopher may have free passage without danger of his censure.

That shall you have (said my Lord Primate) with a good will: for since we are here to discourse of Morall Philosophie, we wil for this time put Divinitie to silence, so farre forth as your author say not any thing so repugnant to the truth, as that it may breed any errour in the minds of the hearers.

Then (said I) the demaund of Captaine *Carleil* hath three severall points or articles: the one is, whether vertue and vertuous actions be in our power or no? Another, that it seemeth strange, if vice & vertue be in our power, that any man should be so senslesse as to apply himselfe to vice and forsake vertue. The last is, whether the good or evill we do, proceed from the influence of the heavens, or from necessitie of destinie, and not from our owne free election. And my author beginneth with the last, which he affirmeth to be most contrary to truth, and to the excellencie of mans nature, proceeding thence to the second, and lastly to the first. Therefore he saith, that whosoever holdeth mans will and election to be subject to the necessitie of destiny, destroyeth utterly (according to *Aristotles* saying) all that appertaineth to humane prudence, either in the care of himselfe or of his family, or in the ordering of lawes, and the universall government of Kingdomes and Common-weales, as well in peace as in warre: for if it were so, what need hath man to do any thing, but idly to attend what his destinie is to give him or to denie him, or to provide for any of those things whereof our humane life hath neede. What difference were there betweene the wise man and the foole, the carefull and the rechlesse, the diligent and the negligent? The punishment of malefactors, and the rewarding of wel-doers, shold be unjust and needlesse. For everything being done by the order of fatall disposition, and not by election, no man could either deserve praise, or incurre blame. Besides, nature should in vaine have given us the use of reason, to discourse or to consult, or the abilitie to will or chuse any thing; for whatsoever were appointed by destinie, should of necessitie come to passe; and if of necessitie, then neither prudence, counsell, nor election can have any place. And the use of free-will being so taken from us, we should be in worse state and condition then bruite beasts; for they guided by instinct of nature, bend themselves to those things whereunto their nature inclineth them: whereas we notwithstanding the use of reason, should be like bond-slaves, tied to what the necessitie of destinie should bind us unto. This was the cause why *Chrysippus* was worthily condemned among all the auncient Philosophers, for that he held destinie to be a sempiternal and unevitable necessitie and order of things which in maner of a chaine was linked orderly in it self, so as one succeeded another, and were fitly conjoyned together. By which description of destinie appeereth, that he meant to tie all things to necessitie. For albeit he affirmed withall, that our mind had some working in the matter, yet did he put necessitie to be so necessary, that there could no way be found, whereby our mind might come to have any part. For to say that our mind or will concurred, by willing or not willing whatsoever destinie drew us unto, was nought else but a taking away of free choice from our understanding or will, since our mind like a bond-slave was constrained to will, or not to will, as destinie did invite it, or rather force it. And like to this were the opinions of *Demetrius*, of *Parmenides*, and of *Heraclitus*, who subjected all things to necessitie, and deserved no lesse to be condemned then *Chrysippus* Prince of the Stoikes. Among which, some there were, who seeing many things to happen by chance or fortune; whereby it appeared that it could not be true, that things came by necessitie, lest they should denie a thing so manifest to sense, they supposed the beginnings and the endings of things to be of necessitie, but the meanes and circumstances they yeelded to be subject to the changes and alterations of fortune. And of this opinion was *Virgil* (as some thinke) in the conducting of *Aeneas* into *Italie*. For it should seeme that he departed his country to come into *Italie* by fatall disposition, that he might get *Lavinia* for his wife: but before he could arrive there, and winne her, he was mightily tossed and turmoyled by fortune; which neverthelesse could never crosse him so much, but that in the end he obtained his purpose, which by destiny was appointed for him. But howsoever *Virgil* thought in that point, which here need not to be disputed, sure I am, that he in the greatest part of his excellent Poeme, is rather a *Platonike* then a *Stoike*. Howbeit some *Platonikes* (as I thinke) were not farre different in opinion from the *Stoikes*: for they say, that fortune with all her force was not able to resist fatall destinie. Though *Plotinus* thought otherwise, and indeed much better, who answering them that would needs have the influence of starres to induce necessitie, prooved their reasons to be vaine onely by an ordinary thing in dayly experience: which is, that sundry persons borne under one self same constellation, are seene neverthelesse to have divers ends and divers successes, which they could not have, if those influences did worke their effects of necessitie. And as for *Epicures* opinion, which was, that the falling of his motes or *Atomi* should breed necessitie in our actions; he rather laughed at, then confuted. Yea he was further of opinion, that not onely humane prudence, and our free election, was able to resist the influences of the starres, but that also our complexion, our conversation and change of place might do the like: meaning that the good admonitions, and faithfull advice and counsell of friends, is sufficient to overcome destinie, and to free our mindes from the necessitie of fatall disposition. Wherefore though it be granted that there is a destinie, or that the starres and heavens, or the order of causes, have power over us to incline or dispose us more to one thing then to another; yet is it not to be allowed that they shall force us to follow the same inclination or disposition. For though the heavens be the universall principle or beginning of all things, and by that universalitie (as I may call it) the beginning of us also according to naturall Philosophie; yet is it not the onely cause of our being and of our nature: for to the making man, a man must concurre, and so restraine this universall cause to a more speciall. And as the heaven, or the order of higher causes, cannot ingender man without a man (speaking according to nature): so can they do nothing to bind the free election of man without his consent, who must voluntarily yeeld himselfe to accomplish that whereunto the heaven or the order of causes doth bend and incline him. And if we have power to master our complexion, so, as being naturally inclined to lust, we may by heed and diligence become continent; and being covetous, become liberall (though *Aristotle* say, that covetise is as incurable a disease of the mind, as the Dropsie or Ptisike is to the body): what a folly is it to beleeve that we cannot resist the inclinations of the stars, which are causes without us, and not the onely causes of our being; but have need of us, if they will bring forth their effects in us? The beginning of all our operation is undoubtedly in our selves: and all those things that have the beginning of their working in themselves, do worke freely and voluntarily. And consequently we may by our free choise and voluntarily give our selves to good or to evill, and master the inclination of the heavens, the starres, or destinie, which troubleth so much the braines of some, that in despite of nature they will needes make themselves bond being free: whom

Ptolomie doth fitly reprehend, by saying, that the wise man over-ruleth the starres. For well may the heavens or the stars, being corporall substances, have some power over our bodies, but over our mindes which are divine, simple, and spirituall substances, can they have none: for betweene the heavens & our minds is no such correspondence, that they may against our wils do ought at all in our minds which are wholy free from their influences, if any they have. And therefore do the best of the *Platonikes* say very wel, that man must oppose himselfe against his destinie, fighting to overcome the same with golden armes and weapons, to wit, vertues, which is (as *Plato* saith) the gold of the mind. For he that behaveth himselfe well, that is to say, ruleth wel his mind or soule, which is the true man indeed, as we have formerly shewed, shall never be abandoned to destinie or fortune: against which two powers mans counsell and wisedome resisteth in such sort, if he set himself resolutely thereunto, as it may wel appeere that he is Lord and master over his owne actions. Neither without cause did *Tully* say, that fatall destinie was but a name devised by old wives, who not knowing the causes of things, as soone as any thing fell out contrary to their expectation, straight imputed it to destinie; joyning thereunto such a necessitie, as it must needs (forsooth) force mans counsell and prudence. A thing most false, as hath bin declared. Is it not said in the Scripture, that God created man, and left him in the power of his owne counsell? How then doth *Menander* say, that men did many evils compelled by necessitie? I meane not by necessitie, as commonly we do, want or povertie, but by necessitie of destinie. We may then conclude, that our will and election is free, and that it is in our power to follow vice or vertue. Neverthelesse true it is that man may abuse this his libertie, and of a free man make himselfe bond if he will: and therefore do the *Platonikes* say, that a good and a wel-minded man doth all his actions freely; but that if he give himself to do evill, forsaking the light of reason, he becommeth a bruite beast, and looseth the divine gift of his libertie: for thenceforth doth he work no more freely of himself, but yeeldeth his minde, which ought to be the Lord of our libertie, slave to the two basest parts of the soule, and then reigneth no more the reasonable soule, but the brutish, which maketh him abandon the care of the minde, and onely to attend the pleasures of the body, as brute beasts doe.

Hitherto (said my Lord Primate) I find nothing to be mis-liked in your discourse, which (as a Philosopher) is declared according to morall reason. But, as a Christian, what sayth your author to Gods predestination? Is it not necessary, that what-soever God hath determined of us from the beginning in his fore-knowledge (being the most certaine and true knower of all things) shall come to passe?

This is (said I) no small question to be fully answered, and being also not very pertinent to the matter we have in hand (being meerely morall) my author medleth not with the par-ticular points of the same: onely hereof he saith, that *Euripides* had little reason to say, that God had care of greater things, but that he left the care and guiding of the lesser to fortune. For we are bound by holy writ to beleeve (and some of the auncient Philosophers have likewise so thought) that there moveth not a leafe upon a tree, nor falleth a haire from our heads, but by the will of God. Whereupon the holy Prophet *David* sayd, that God dwelleth on high, and beholdeth the things that are humble in heaven and in earth. And the *Peripatetikes* seemed to consent thereunto, when they sayd, that the heavenly providence fore-seeing that the particulars were not apt to preserve themselves eternally, had therfore ordained that they should be continued in their universalities, which are the severall kinds or *species*, containing under them the particulars, which of themselves are mortal and perishable, but are made perpetual in them through generation. He sayth also, that predestination is an ordinance or disposition of things in the mind of God from the beginning, of what shal be done by us in this life through grace. But he thinks not that it tieth our free wil, but that they go both together; that our well doing is acceptable and pleasing to God, and our evil deeds displeasing and offensive to his divine Majestie: and that for the good we shall receive reward, and punishment for the evill. The further discussing whereof appertaining rather to Divines then Morall Philosophers, he thinketh fit to referre unto them, and to beleeve that this is one of those secrets which God hath layed up in the treasury of his mind, whereunto no mortall eye or understanding can reach or penetrate, humbling our selves to his holy will, without searching into that which we cannot approch unto. And if *Socrates* in that time of darknesse and superstition of the heathen could exhort men to assure themselves, that God having created them, wold have no lesse care of them, then a good and just Prince would have of his subjects: how much more are we to beleeve that our heavenly Lord and God Almightie, who hath sent his onely begotten Sonne to redeeme us from the bondage of Sathan, doth dispose and ordaine of us as is best for us, and for the honor of his divine Majestie. For as they are to be commended that referre themselves humbly to whatsoever he hath determined of them, doing their best endevours to purchase his grace and favour: so are they to be misdoubted, who over-curiously will needes take upon them the judgment of Gods predestination or prescience. And that sentence cannot but be very good, which sayeth, that *he that made thee without thee, will not save thee without thee.* For were a man certaine to be damned, yet ought he not to do otherwise then well, because he is borne to vertue and not to vice: which the very heathen by the onely light of reason could well perceive. Besides, it is thoght, that al they, that are signed with the character of Christ in baptisme, may stedfastly beleeve that they are predestinated and chosen to salvation: not that our predestination giveth us a necessitie of wel doing, but because we having the grace of God to assist us, dispose our selves by the same grace to keep his commandements for our salvation, and for the honor and glory of his majestie: whereas by doing otherwise it is our owne wickednesse that excludeth us from that blisse. And further mine author saith not.

In good sooth (said sir *Robert Dillon*) this seemeth to me to be well and Christianlike spoken. For he that acknowledgeth not so great a gift from God, being a speciall marke or token by which we are distinguished from brute beasts, who wanting the use of reason, can have no free election, is not onely unthankfull, but doth foolishly thruste himselfe into the number of unreasonable creatures, while he will needs deprive himself of that he hath specially different from them. Neither doth the reverent regard to Gods providence impeach our free wil: which providence the *Platonikes* partly understanding, affirmed (as I have heard) that it did not alter or change the nature of things, but guided and directed destinie: imposing no necessitie of doing good or evill upon us. And if any it did impose, it should be onely to good, and never to evill. For what is divine must needes worke divinely, and divine working can produce none but good effects. Wherefore they concluded that our election was not constrained by Gods providence. This they confirmed by common experience. For (sayd they) if providence tie things to necessitie, then chance or fortune can have no place in the actions of men. But we see dayly many things maturely debated, which should by the naturall and ordinary course of causes have a determinate and certaine end, yet misse their effect whereunto they are ordained, and another produced which was never intended, which is the proper worke of fortune. I have also heard some Divines say, that it should seeme strange, if wise & prudent men in this world by their providence and foresight, seek evermore to bring perfection to those things which are under their governement, God contrariwise (who is the fountaine of all wisdome & prudence, and the true and absolute preserver and conserver of all things by him produced) should not give perfections and continuance through his providence to so singular a gift given unto man above all other creatures of the earth, but shold suffer it to perish, to bind us to servitude. And that if his providence should tie our free will to necessitie, he should do that which is contrary to his owne nature: for that therby he should take from us the reward of vertue, since doing well by necessitie, we could deserve neither praise nor recompence; he should also take from us all counsell and deliberation, which is needlesse and superfluous in all things, that of necessitie must come to passe: and lastly justice it selfe, whereby malefactors are punished, if constrained by necessitie they did wickedly, for then were their punishment unjust: which made S. *Augustine* say, that God would never damne a sinner, unlesse he found that he had sinned voluntarily. We may therefore (as I think) conclude, that being created by God, and endowed with so excellent a gift, as free choice and election, which, besides the place of Scripture above mentioned, is confirmed by another, where it is said, that God set before man life and death, good and evill, that he might take whether he list to chuse; he by his divine foresight doth rather give perfection thereunto, then take it from us. Yet the particular consideration and debating of this matter being fitter for Divines then for us, let us leave the scanning of it to them, and be content like men seeking by the rules of Morall Philosophie to find the ready way to humane felicitie in this life, to referre our selves in that point to the mercifull goodnesse of Almightie God. And therefore (I pray you) proceed to the rest of your discourse, and shew us the cause why so many give themselves rather to vice then to vertue, when they may do otherwise, which your author said he would declare in the second place.

So shall I (quoth I) and for the resolving of the same, you shal understand that *Plato* was of opinion, that no man willingly was wicked, because the habite of vice was not voluntarily received by any man. And for confirmation of this his opinion, this reason he made: as vertue (sayd he) is the health of the mind, so is vice the infirmitie of the same: and as the body receiveth willingly his health, and sicknesse against his will; even so the mind receiveth willingly vertue as his health, and vice unwillingly; knowing that thereby it becometh sicke and infected. But *Plotinus* assigned another reason, not needfull here to be rehearsed. Now *Aristotle* was of another mind, for he affirmed that man had free will by his owne choice and election.

How can man voluntarily embrace vice (said M. *Dormer*) which of all things is the worst, since the same author saith, that al men covet what is good, and since without vertue there can be no good.

These two sayings (said I) are not contradictory: for the most wicked man alive desireth what is good: and if vice should shew itselfe in his owne proper forme, he is so ugly and so horrible to behold, that every man would flie from him: therefore knowing how deservedly he should be hated and abhorred, if he were seene like himselfe, he presents himselfe under the shape of goodnesse, and hiding all his il favoured face, deceiveth the sensitive appetite; which being intised by the false image of goodnes, is so seduced, and through the corruption of his mind and judgement, by the ill habit, contracted from his child hood, he embraceth that which (if his judgement were sound) he wold never do. Wherfore *Plato* his meaning was (as it may be thought) that no man was willingly vicious, since, evill covering it selfe under the cloke of goodnesse, he was induced to do evill, thinking to do good: and so the opinions of both Philosophers concurre. But *Pythagoras* by the report of *Aristotle, lib. 8. Ethicor.* assigneth another cause, to wit, that ill doing is an infinite thing, and that by a thousand wayes men are led to wickednes and vicious actions, all easie to be taken: but to vertue there is but one onely way, and the same so environed and crossed with the bypaths that guide men to vice, as it must needs be hard to keepe it without entring into some of the by-wayes leading to vice and errour. For the eye that is not made cleere sighted by Philosophie, is not able to discerne that way from the rest.

It shold seeme (said M. *Dormer*) by this, that ignorance is the cause of well doing, and not mans choice or election: for where ignorance is, it may be said there is no election.

Not so (said I) if *Aristotle* be to be beleeved, who saith that ignorance so farre foorth as it concerneth mens actions, is of two sorts: the one is, when a man doth ill, not through ignorance, but ignorantly: the other is, when he doth it of meere ignorance, because he neither knoweth nor might know that such an action was evill. In the first case, are those that are hastie & cholerike, and drunkards: for though they knew before, that hastinesse and drunkennesse be evill, yet when the heate of choler, or the disordinate appetite of wine blindeth them, they erre ignorantly, but not of ignorance. In the latter are they that fall through meere ignorance, not knowing that what they do is evill. As if a Prince make a restraint or prohibition, that no man upon paine of death shall enter into his Forrest to hunt there, and a stranger not knowing this restraint, cometh thither with his hounds to hunt, as in former time haply he had done. This stranger breaketh the will of the Prince, and committeth a fault, but altogether through ignorance, because he had no knowledge of the prohibition. But if a hastie man knowing of the restraint, pursuing his enemy in his rage, or a drunken man, when wine hath made him not to discerne his way, entring into that forrest, have his dog following him, and the dog kill a Deere; his fault though it be ignorantly committed should not be through ignorance. And as the stranger, being sorie for his offence, and thereby shewing that he meant not to breake the Princes commaundement, were worthy pardon: even so the other were justly to be punished, since knowing the penaltie threatned to the offender, he would not bridle his furie, or abstaine from wine, but by following his passion or unruly appetite, incurre the danger of the same. And as the one may well be judged to have made a fault against his wil; so may the other be deemed to have wilfully broken the commandement. In which latter case of ignorance are all they that be vicious or wicked, who through the ill habite which they have made in vice, do any act contrary to law and the civill societie of men, for which they deserve to be adjudged wilfully evill, and by their owne free choice and election. For all men ought to know those things that generally are to be knowne, touching honest and civil conversation; and if they do not know them when they do il, it is because they chuse not to know that which is necessary for them to know. In which respect it is determined, that who so for want of knowing this generalitie will do amisse, should be esteemed wicked by his owne free wil and election. *Seneca* said very fitly, that such men did in the mids of the cleere light make darknes to themselves. And this is that ignorance which *Plato* calleth the defiling of the soul. Let us suppose that there may be one that knoweth not adultery to be sin or vice, and that in ignorance committeth adultery; shal we say he deserveth to be excused? God forbid: for he is cause of his owne ignorance, since it is in his power and in the power of all reasonable men to know what is fit and honest for vertuous life; and that the same is made knowne, as well by Gods law, as by the ordinances and customes of man, to all those that will not wittingly hood-winke themselves. Wherefore it is a wilfull sin committed by free election, and worthy punishment as a voluntary offence. And S. *Augustine* sayed not without cause, that all ignorance was not worthy pardon, but onely that of such men as had no meanes to attaine knowledge or learning: but they that have teachers to instruct them, and for want of studie and diligence abide in their ignorance, and so do evill, are not onely unworthy excuse, but deserve also sharpe punishment. So in another place he sayth, that no man is punished for that which naturally he knowes not: as the child for that he cannot speake, or because he cannot reade. But when he will not set his mind to learne as he ought, being of yeeres, and urged thereunto, he deserveth to be chastised, because it is in every mans power to be able to learne all that is necessary for him to know how to live well, and what things are to be embraced as good, and what to be eschewed as evill: and he that will not learne them, remaineth wilfully in his ignorance.

Yea but if I should chance (said Captaine *Dawtrey*) to be abroade with my bow and arrowes, and perceiving somewhat to stirre in a bush, should shoote thereat, supposing it to be a Deere or some other game, and should so kill my wife that were hidden there, as *Cephalus* did, should not my ignorance in that case excuse me?

This case (said I) appertaineth to the second part of ignorance, already spoken of, which is about the circumstances of the particular things, the ignorance whereof deserveth excuse, and so should this. But this ignorance should become wilfull wickednesse, if when you saw you had slaine your wife, intending to kill a Deere, you were not heartily sory therefore, but rather glad to be so rid of her: and so farre should you then be from excuse, that you should deserve to be severely punished for the fact. Much like to the case of *Cephalus* was that of *Adrastus*, but more miserable, in slaying of *Atys* the sonne of *Crœsus* King of *Lidia*. For *Crœsus* having given in charge to *Adrastus* his sonne, and they being one day gone to hunt a great wild Bore that did great harme in the countrey, accompanied with many yong gentlemen of *Lidia*, whiles the Bore was rushing forth, *Adrastus* threw a dart at him, and *Atys* comming by chance in the way, the dart hit him and slew him. Now though *Atys* were the only sonne of *Crœsus*, and were slaine by the hand of him that had him in charge; yet finding that it was done by meere mischance and through ignorance, and knowing how grievously *Adrastus* sorrowed for the same, he not onely freed him of any punishment therefore, but frankly pardoned him. And the repentance of the fact might have sufficed the doer; but he overcome with extreme griefe slew himselfe at the funerall of the dead young Prince, being unable to beare with a stout courage the anguish and vexation of minde that his mishappe did breed him. But this shewed *Adrastus* to be rather faint-hearted and weake of minde, then otherwise: for the purchasing of death to avoyde griefe or any other annoyance of the mind, is not the part of a valorous and couragious man, as the best among the ancient Philosophers have alwaies held. And because we know by the rule of Christ, that it is no matter disputable, it needeth not that thereof any further words be made.

You say well (said my Lord Primate) and I know that *Aristotle* is of minde, that it is a vile act for a man to kill himselfe to avoyde ignominie or afflictions. But to omit the judgement of the auncient Romanes, who held it the part of a stout heart, for a man to kill himselfe rather then to suffer shame or servitude, as we reade that *Cato* did, and *Cassius* and *Brutus*: yet it seemeth that *Plato*, whom your author determined to follow as well as *Aristotle*, maketh *Socrates* (in his dialogue intituled

Phaedon) to say, that a Philosopher ought not to kill himselfe, unlesse God lay a necessitie of doing it upon him. Out of which words it may well be gathered, he thought that not onely the common sort, but even Philosophers themselves, when necessitie constraineth them, might ridde themselves of their life.

That place (said I) is advisedly to be examined: for *Socrates* there meant not that any man willingly should lay violent hands upon himselfe; but if there be no remedy but that die he must, and that divers kindes of deaths are proposed unto him, he may chuse that kind which is lesse noysome to him or lesse grievous: as *Socrates* chose to die with the juice of hemlocks, and *Seneca* by the opening of his veines.

You may haply conster[48] that meaning out of that place (said my Lord Primate): but what will you say to that which is in his bookes of the Common-weale, where he writeth, that a man sicke of any grievous or long infirmitie, when he shall see himselfe out of hope to procure remedie, he should then make an end of his life.

To that place I say (quoth I) that it is to be considered how *Plato* sought to frame his Common-wealth in such sort as it should be rather divine then humane: and therefore as the citizens of the heavenly Common-wealth live in continuall happinesse and contentment, without feeling any annoyance or molestation at all: even so was his purpose, that the citizens of his Common-wealth should have no grievance, paine or molestation among them: but in an ordinary humane Common-wealth he would not have set downe any such precept.

You have salved that sore reasonable well also (sayed my Lord Primate) though there might be objections made against your answer. But how will another place of his be defended, which is in his booke of Lawes, where he sayth, that whosoever hath committed any offence in the highest degree, and findeth, that he hath not power to abstaine from the like eftsoones, ought to rid himselfe out of the world.

The answer to that (said I) is easie: for *Plato* his meaning therein is, that whosoever is wickedly given, and of so evill example as there is no hope of his amendment, should rather kill himselfe, then by living invite so many others to the like course of life: not unlike to the opinion alreadie recited, that it is better one die for a people, then that his life should be the occasion of the death of many. For *Plato* aymed evermore at the purging of all cities from such caterpillers; which appeereth manifestly by the pain he would have inflicted upon parricides. But that it was abhomination to him for a man to kill himselfe, he plainely sheweth in his ninth booke of Lawes, by the sentence he setteth downe against such men. Neverthelesse this indeed may be found in *Plato*, that vice was so odious unto him, that he would rather have a man to die, then to undertake any vile & vicious action, which might breed him perpetuall infamie. And *Aristotle* in this point agreeth with his master (though in many he delight to carpe him) that a man ought to chuse rather to die then commit any abhominable or grievous fact, or do that which might be for ever reprochful unto him. And *Plato* his expresse sence of this matter, is to be understood in the same dialogue which you first spake of, where *Socrates* is brought to say, that the Lord and Ruler of this whole world having sent us into this life, we are not to desire to leave it without his consent: and who so doth the contrary, offends nature, offendeth God. And this is the mystery of that precept of *Philolaus*, which forbiddeth a man to cleave wood in the high way: meaning that a man should not sever or devide the soule from the body, whiles he was in his way on this earthly pilgrimage; but should be content, that as God and nature had united and tied the soule to the bodie, so by them it might be unloosed againe: therefore the *Peripatetikes* also thought, that they which die a violent death, cannot be thought to have ended their dayes according to the course of time and nature. And with this my Lord Primate rested satisfied. I turned me to Captaine *Carleil*, and sayd: Now (sir) concerning your doubts proposed, you may have perceived, that whatsoever destinie be, neither it, nor the divine providence of Almightie God imposeth any necessitie upon us: that vertue and vice are in our power, vertue growing in us by the right use of our free choice, and vice by the abuse of the same, when through corruption of the judgement to do that is in apparance good, it chuseth the evill: and lastly what kind of ignorance is excusable, and which not.

Concerning my demaunds (sayd Captaine *Carleil*) I am resolved. But since I see our doings proceed from election, I would gladly know of you what maner of thing it is; for I cannot perceive whether it be a desire, or an anger, or an opinion, or what I should call it.

None of all these (said I) but rather a voluntary deliberation, following a mature and advised counsel: which counsell by *Plato* was termed a divine thing. For election is not made in a moment; but when a thing is proposed either to be accepted or refused, there must first be a counsell taken, respecting both the end of the action, and the meanes by which the same is to be compassed: so as there is required a time of consultation: and therefore it is said, that hast is enemie to counsell, and that oftentimes repentance followes them that resolve without discussing or debating of matters. Next unto counsell cometh judgement, and after judgement followeth election, and from election issueth the action or the effects that are resolved upon, and accepted as the best. And because fortune (though she be a cause rather by accident then of her selfe) hath no small part in most of our actions, the wisest men have said, that counsel is the eye of the mind, by helpe whereof, men of prudence see how to defend themselves from the blind strokes of fortune, and eschuing that which may hurt them, take hold of that which is profitable.

Why then (said my Lord Primate) it shold seeme that our counsell were wholy in our power. But *Xenophon* is of a contrary opinion: for he sayeth, that good counsell cometh from the Gods immortall, and that their counsels prosper who have them to be their friends, and theirs not, who have them to be their enemies.

To have God favourable unto us (said I) in all our doings, is not onely desirable, but that it may please him to grant his grace so to be, ought all men to crave by humble prayer at his hands. But that God is the author of our counsels otherwise then as an universall cause, is to be doubted: not that the singular gift of the mind, and the power thereof to deliberate and consult, commeth not from him; for the not acknowledging thereof, were not onely a grosse ignorance, but also an expresse impietie, & an unexcusable ingratitude. Howbeit since it hath pleased him to bestow upon us so great and liberal a gift as the mind, we may well beleeve that he will not take from us the free use therof. For to say that God were the imediate cause of our counsell, were as much as to take from us the use of reason, without which we are not any more men, as of late was sayd. And therfore besides *Aristotles* authoritie, grounded in that point upon good reason, we find in the Scripture, that after God had made man, and given him (by breathing upon him) the spirit of life, which is the soule of understanding, he left him in the hand of his owne counsell. Whereby it appeereth, that counsel commeth from our selves, and that election is the office of prudence, which is called the soule of the mind, and the *Platonikes* call the knowledge of good and evill: whereunto it seemed that *Tullie* agreed, when he said, that prudence was the science of things desirable, or to be eschued: which sentence S. *Augustine* reporteth. And *Fabius Maximus* said, that the Gods through prudence and our vertues, did grant us prosperous successes in our affaires: as if he should have said, that though God (as an universall cause) concurred to accomplish our deliberations; yet we were to endevour our selves, and to sharpen our wits to consult on the best meanes to compasse our good purposes, if we desire to have his favour, and not to sit idle, expecting what will fall out. And to end the discourse hereof, the auncient Philosophers of the best sort held, that the Gods seeing us employ our vertues and faculties of the mind (which hath a resemblance unto them) well and wisely, become our friends, and the rather grant us their helpe and favour. According to which opinion *Euripides* sayed, that the Gods did helpe them that were wise. But because we shall have occasion to speake more largely hereafter of Prudence, we will now returne to that which we left long sithens to speake of, by the interposing of the doubts moved: and that is the knowledge of our selves, as the thing that must guide us to that best and most perfect end; the inquiry wherof is the occasion of all this discourse. And because we are not of a simple nature, but compounded of severall qualities, and (as we may say) lives, according to that which in our first dayes discourse was declared: it is also necessary that these powers & faculties of the soule which are in us, and by which we participate of the nature of all things living, should have their ends and severall goods, as I may terme them: and that those ends should orderly answer ech to his severall power or facultie of the soule, though *Aristotle* thinke otherwise. These ends or goods are first profite, which respecteth the *vegetative* power: next, delight or pleasure, peculiar to the *sensitive* power: and lastly honestie, proper to the reasonable part or facultie of the soule. Wherefore *Zeno* may wel be thought to have bin astray, when he assigned one onely end or good to nature, and the same to be honesty. For albeit I cannot, nor meane to denie, but that honestie is not onely a good, but also the greatest good among all those that concurre to our felicitie; and without which, there can be no vertue: yet to say it is the onely good, I cannot be perswaded. For perusing every thing that hath life, common sense it self sheweth us, that ech kind of life hath his peculiar and severall end and good; and that honestie is the only proper good of creatures capable of reason, and not of other sensible creatures, or of plants and *vegetables*. And because it is a greater good, and containeth both the other, therefore is it more to be prised and valued then they. And man being the most perfect creature of the earth, is by nature framed to have a desire and an instinct unto them all, and to seeke to purchase them all three for the perfection of his felicitie in this life. Now forasmuch as all these three powers are in us, to the end we may enjoy the benefite that redoundeth from them, we cannot sever them one from another, if we meane to be happie in this life: neither yet ought we so to apply our selves to any one, or two of them lesse proper unto us, that therefore we forsake or neglect that other which is of most worth and proper to our nature; and that is honestie, which never can be severed from vertue. For that is it that giveth to us dignitie and excellency, not suffering us to do any thing unseemely, but stil directing us in all our actions, which proceed from reason. For he that stayeth himself only upon profit, or upon pleasure, or upon them both, sheweth plainly that he knoweth not himselfe: and therefore suffereth those things that are not proper to his nature, to master and over-rule him. And not knowing himselfe, he cannot use himselfe, nor take hold of that which is his proper good and end. Thus following (through the not knowing of himselfe) that which is good to other natures, he looseth his owne good, and falleth into evill, by the desire of profit, or disordinate appetite to pleasure. The consideration hereof perhaps caused some of the auncient Poets to faine, that men were turned into brute beasts, and into trees; to signifie under that fiction, that some proposing to themselves onely profite, some onely delight, without regard to reason and their owne proper good, had lost the excellent shape or forme of men, and were transformed into beasts or trees, having made the most excellent part of man, which is the mind and reasonable soule, subject to the basest and sensual parts and pleasures of the bodie. And this ignorance, concerning the knowledge of a mans selfe, is the cause that he cannot tell how to use himself. For these unreasonable affections do so darken the light of reason, that he is as a blind man, and giveth himselfe over to be guided, as one that hath lost the right way, to as blinde a guide as himselfe, and so wandreth astray which way soever his bad guide doth leade him. For he hath lost the knowledge of truth, which *Plato* sayeth, is the best guide of men to all goodnesse, and is comprehended by the mind onely, which (according to the saying of *Epicarmus*) doth only see & heare, all the rest of the parts of man being blind and deafe. They then which follow profite only, live the basest life of all, & may well be resembled to flies & gnats, the most imperfect among living creatures, or like to the shel-fishes that cleave to the rockes, as these men do to their pelfe; and so having proposed to themselves the basest end of all others, they may worthily be esteemed the basest sort of men.

Nay, in good faith sir (said Captaine *Dawtry*), not so, for I see them onely honored and esteemed that are rich; and I have knowne, and yet know some of very base and abject condition, who being become rich, are cherished and welcome in the best companies, & accepted among honorable personages: therefore (me thinketh) he spake advisedly that said,

> *Honour and friends by riches are acquired,*
> *But who is poore shall ech where be despised.*

And I remember I have read, that sometime there was a citizen in Rome, who was commonly held for a foole, and therefore in all companies his words were litle regarded, the rather because he was also poore; but after that by the death of a rich man to whom he was heire, he possessed wealth, he grew to be had in great estimation, even in the Senate, and his opinion evermore specially required in matters of greatest moment.

Yea marry (said M. *Dormer*) and *Aristotle* also affirmeth, that the end of the father of a families care is, the purchasing of riches; which being so, they are not so sleightly to be regarded, as your author sayes.

Did I not tell you (said I) that truth being gone, the true light and knowledge of things is taken out of the world; for it is she only that giveth us light to know, what and of what price all things are. And even as if the Sunne were taken away from the

141

earth, there would remaine nought but darknes and blindnesse among men: so truth being taken away, man is blinded from discerning any thing aright. This I say, because rich men onely for their wealth are esteemed worthy honour and dignity by such chiefly as want the light of truth, which is the vulgar sort, whose judgement is so corrupt and crooked, that they cannot discerne what true honor and dignity is. For they being weake minded and imperfect, admire showes and shadowes, being dazeled with the bright glistring of gold and precious stones, and cannot distinguish betweene things necessary and superfluous. Which ignorance of theirs, *Byas*, one of the seven sages of Greece, considering answered one of those base minded fellowes, who wold needes perswade him, that they were happie that could compasse great wealth: My friend (quoth he) much more happie are they that do not desire the same. The judgement of the wiser sort, hath ever bin farre different from this vulgar opinion. For they understand, that riches is none of those goods which alone make men happie; and that they do but go and come, as tides flow and ebbe, even at the pleasure of fortune, who giveth and taketh them as she list. And therefore they are no otherwise to be esteemed, then as they are necessary for the sustaining of life, nature being content with little, and the desire of having being infinite; never content with what it hath, but ever coveting what it hath not. Therefore right wise men have held that *Alexander* the Great was in truth poorer and needier then he that said

> *Let others hardly seeke to hoord up wealth*
> *For me I force not, though that povertie*
> *Chase from me idlenesse, and breed me health, &c.*

For that mans desires had their determinate stint, wheras *Alexanders* increased stil, the more he enlarged his dominions, being grieved that he had not conquered one world, because he had heard say, that *Democritus* was of opinion there were many. And although *Epicurus* in many things hath deserved blame, because he placed the highest good of man in pleasures proceeding from the senses; yet deserved he praise in that he said, that they to whom a little seemeth not enough, a great deale wil seem but a litle. Much to the like effect *Curius*, having conquered the Samnites, and for recompence of his great service the Romanes purposing to give him a far larger portion of the conquered land, then to the rest of the souldiers: he who had taught his desires to be brideled, and could cut short the superfluitie of his appetites, would in no wise take any more then a like share or portion, as was allotted to the rest of the souldiers, that were waxen olde in the warres, for their living and maintenance; saying, that he that could not content himselfe to live with that which sufficed others, could not be a good citizen. This worthy man made it appeere, that he indeede is to be accounted rich who desireth not to have much: and that in respect of what is needfull for mans life, every man may be rich; but in regard of our desires, every man is poore, and cannot be rich, because they be infinite. *Socrates* (according to the saying of *Byas* before rehearsed) said that it was far better not to desire any thing, then to compas what a man desireth. For it was not unknowne to that grave wise man, that from immoderate desires cometh greedinesse of the mind, whereby it is made unreasonable, and disposed to thinke a great deale to be but a little; whereas not to desire, maketh a little to seeme much. The way therefore to quiet the minde, is not to increase wealth, but to plucke from a mans desires, which otherwise will still increase as riches increaseth: for it is the honest and necessary use of riches that causeth them to be had in consideration among wise men, who esteeming them accordingly, are easily contented with a little; and where others admire those that have their coffers full of golde and pelfe, they little regard them, but despising superfluities, turne their minds to better thoughts, meete to make them purchase that felicitie which none of them can have, who amid great abundance of wealth & worldly riches, are voyd of vertue. For this respect did *Crates* the Philosopher (considering how the great care of gathering them withdrew the minde, which of it owne nature is excelse and high, from the knowledge of sublime matters, sinking it into the depth of base and vile cogitations) gave over his patrimony, which was in value neere fifteen hundred pounds, and betooke himselfe to those studies which he thought were aptest to set him the right course of getting (in steed of exterior riches) the true gold of the mind, which is vertue. And in truth happie is that man that can get store of that gold, by meanes whereof he may compasse his felicitie, which the other can never purchase, and are not to be coveted but for humane necessitie, as being of no value, or litle among wise men in respect of happines. For to say truly, what happines can there be in any thing that alike disquieteth as well them that have it, as them that have it not. Since he that wants it, by desiring it, keepeth his mind in continuall anguish and trouble; and he that hath it, is evermore tormented with feare of losse of it: and if he happen to loose it indeed, is miserably crucified for the losse thereof. Which thing made *Democritus* to say, that man was in his estimation so farre from being made happie by his riches, as he could not in truth account them to be to him any good at all. So *Solon* being with *Crœsus* King of *Persia*, who accounted himself of all men in the world the most happie, because of his excessive treasure; when the King had caused his treasury to be shewed unto him, seemed to make sleight estimation of the same: whereupon the King, as one dazeled with the glittering show of his gold, held him but for a foole. But foolish indeed was he himself, & not *Solon*, who knew very wel, that such things came to him by his great power and soveraignetie, not by his vertue, and therefore could they not make him happie. Neverthelesse *Crœsus* yet desirous to understand what *Solons* opinion was touching happines, asked him if he ever knew any man more happie then he: who answered him, yes; and among many, one named *Pellus* a citizen of *Athens*, who being a vertuous man, and having begotten children like himselfe, was dead in the field, fighting valiantly against the enemie in defence of his countrey, leaving after him an immortall fame of his valour. So much more did this wise man esteeme vertue then riches, that he thought so mightie a Monark with all his treasure not comparable to a meane citizen of *Athens* furnished with vertue. For he held them as needlesse and superfluous to him that had them without using them, as to them that did admire them and could not enjoy them. Let us therefore conclude, that plentie of wealth makes not any man happie: and that they who hunt after profit to become rich, are of al others the most base and ignoble, though the vulgar sort deeme them otherwise. And when *Aristotle* sayd, that the end of *Oeconomie* (for so he calleth the orderly distributing of things for houshold) was riches, he spake according to the common understanding and phrase: for in his Ethikes he sheweth plainely, that riches is but a certaine aboundance of necessary instruments for the use of a family. Whereby it may be understood, that for themselves they are not desirable, but as they are directed to a better end, which end is humane felicitie. As for the Senator you spake of, whom the whole Senate grew to esteeme when he was growne rich: you may be sure that it was not for nought that *Cicero* scoffed at them, when he asked one day in the assembly, whose that inheritance was, which was called Wisedome. And thus much may suffice for such as follow profite onely. Now for those that apply themselves wholy to their pleasures and delights, it is to be held, that they neither can be accounted happie, because forsaking their proper end and good, which is honestie, they bend themselves to the *sensitive* part onely which is common with them to brute beasts.

Here M. *Dormer* interrupting me, desired that I would stay a while to resolve him of one doubt, which my former words had bred in his mind, which was, that having said riches were of small account among wise men, and could not make men happie, it might seeme that nature had in vaine produced them.

That followeth not (said I) of any thing which I have spoken. For I have not said, that they were not necessary for the use of them: for common sence, experience, and the want of things behovefull to mans life, would say the contrary. Besides that, *Aristotle* in his tenth booke of Ethikes affirmeth, that not onely to the attaining of civill felicitie, but also for the contemplative life, these exterior goods are needfull, because a man may the better thereby contemplate when want distracteth not his minde: though among the *Platonikes*, some say the contrary; alledging that men are better disposed to contemplation without them, then with them. But thus much indeede I said, that they are not the true end or good of man, nor could yeeld him happinesse of themselves, or make him worthy honour. And that they, that bend their mindes onely to scrape and heape together mucke and pelfe, are of all others the basest and unworthiest: yet being used as they ought to be, for the behoofe and maintenance of mans life, and not as an end, or the proper good of man, I do not only not discommend them, but do also esteeme them in their quality so far forth as the infirmity of mans nature hath neede of them; whereof, since we shall have occasion to speake more hereafter, let us in Gods name proceed to speake of the life of them that have subjected their minds to that part of the soule which is wholy bent to sensualitie and delight. These men are like unto brute beasts wanting reason, and worse: for brute beasts following their naturall instinct and appetite, passe not the bonds of nature, and though they get no praise thereby, yet incurre they not any blame in that behalfe. But man, who setting reason aside,

145

chuseth vaine pleasures as his scope and end, and so plungeth his minde in them, that reason cannot performe her office and dutie, can in no wise escape from exceeding blame and reproch for the same. Of which sort of men, the *Platonikes* opinion was, that they were so far from being happie, as they were not to be reputed among the living, but the dead: not only in respect of the body, but of the soule likewise. For they held that the soule being drowned in delights, might wel be reckoned as dead, because beastly delight (like an ill weed) spreadeth it selfe in mans mind, till it overgrow all goodnesse, and so taketh away the use of reason, as it depriveth him of the qualitie proper to man, and draweth him into the pure qualitie of unreasonable creatures: which, how grievous and hatefull a thing it is, neede not be declared. *Aristotle* resembleth them to wilde young Stiers, that must be tamed with the yoke. But to shew you how this disordinate or tickling itch of delight proceedeth, in this sort it is: wheras man is composed of two principall parts, the body, and the soule or mind: the latter to rule and commaund, the former to obey and serve. They, which propose to them their delight and pleasure, onely take a cleane contrary course, making the body to commaund and rule, and the minde to serve and obey. And as in a houshold or family, al wold go to wrack, if the master or father of the family being prudent and carefull, should be constrained to obey his sonne or servant, who were foolish and negligent: even so must it of necessitie be in him, that by vice maketh his mind subject to the bodie, making to serve onely for the delighting thereof, and neglecting that which he should most earnestly study to maintaine and cherish; whence cometh (as *Socrates* saith) all evill and ruines among men. For from these disordinate pleasures, which spring from the senses of the body, through that power which the facultie of the soule ministreth unto them, do all wicked affections take their beginning, as angers, furies, fond loves, hatreds, ambitions, lustes, suspicions, jelousies, ill speaking, backbiting, false joyes, and true griefes; and finally the consuming of the body and goods, and the losse of honor and reputation. And oftentimes it is seene, that whiles a man spareth nothing so as he may purchase the fulfilling of his appetites, how unruly soever they be, he looseth by infirmitie or other unhappie accidents, his owne bodie, for whose pleasures he so earnestly travelled. For so it is written of *Epicurus*, who being growne ful of sicknes through

146

his disordinate life, died miserably tormented with pains & griefes: the like wherof we may daily see in many, if we consider their life and end. In respect hereof, some wise men have thought that pleasures are not in any wise to be accounted among the goods that are requisite for the attaining of humane felicitie: and *Antisthenes* so hated them, that he wished he might rather become mad, then to be over mastered by his sensuall delight. And in very deed they are no otherwise to be esteemed then mad men, who set their delights and pleasures before them as their end, not caring what they do, so as they may compasse the same. *Plato* therfore not without good cause said, that pleasure was the baite which allured men to all evil. And *Architas* the Tarentine was of opinion, that the pestilence was a lesser evill among men then pleasure of the bodie: from whence came trecheries, and betraying of countries, destructions of common-weales, murders, rapes, adulteries, and all other evils, even as from a spring or fountain. The cause whereof *Pythagoras* desiring to find out, said, that delight first crept into cities, then satietie, next violence, and lastly the ruine and overthrow of the Commonwealth. And to this opinion *Tullie* in his first booke of Lawes seemeth to leane, where he sayth, that this counterfetter of goodnesse, and mother of all evils (meaning pleasure) intruding her selfe into our senses, suffered us not to discerne those goods which are naturall and true goods indeed, and cary not with them such a scabbe and itch, which pleasure evermore hath about her; who finally is the roote of those principall passions, from which (as from the maine roote) all the rest do spring, as hope and feare, sorrow and gladnesse. For we receive not any pleasure, but that some molestation hath opened the way for it into our mindes: as no man taketh pleasure to eate untill the molestation of hunger call him thereunto, nor yet to drinke, if the annoyance of thirst go not before: to shew that the unnoblest and basest power of the minde must minister unto us the matter of those pleasures which we seek. And as we have said that molestation goeth before vaine and unruly delight, so doth displeasure and griefe follow, as if it should finally resolve into his first principle and beginning. The feare whereof diminisheth part of the hope a man might have to live stil contented, & disturbeth the joy which he feeleth in his unruly pleasures and delights. But those pleasures and delights accompany vertue, which are pleasures of such a kind as they never carry with them any displeasure or annoyance at all: wheras the other that are unruly, beginne with pleasure and end with bitter paine. And this moved *Aristotle* to say, that the right judgment of those pleasures is to be made at their farewell, not at their comming; for that they leave behind them evermore sadnes and repentance. So said *Theocritus*, that he that strove to fulfill his pleasures and delights, prepared to himself matter of perpetual griefe and sorow. There was a Sophist called *Ileus*, who though he had spent his youth wantonly in pleasures, yet he so called himselfe home when he was come to riper yeeres, that he never after suffered any vaine delights to tickle him, neither beauty of women, nor sweetnes of meates, nor any other such pleasures to draw him from a sober and temperate life. To which sobrietie and temperance of life *Licurgus* being desirous to draw the *Lacedemonians*, by his lawes he forbad them all those things that might turne their minds from manly thoughts, and make them soft and effeminate: for he said, that wanton pleasures were the flatterers of the mind. And as flatterers by their devices and arts, draw men that give eare unto them besides themselves, as hath bin already declared: so pleasures through their sweetnesse corrupt the senses, together with the mind to whom they are the ministers. And *Agesilaus* being once asked what good the lawes of *Lycurgus* had done to *Sparta*: Marry (sayd he) they have brought our men to despise those delights which might have made them to be no men. There are so many wise and grave sayings to this purpose, that to repeate them all, the day would be too short. It may therefore suffice what is already sayed, and confirmed by the consent of all the wise men in the world, to shew you manifestly, that the true & proper end of man is not to be atchieved by this sensual kind of life. And since that which is truly proper to any thing, cannot be common with any other (as to laugh is so proper to man, as no other creature can laugh but he) and pleasure is common to other creatures besides man, therefore it cannot in any wise be proper to him.

It cannot be gainsaid with any reason (said my Lord Primate) and therefore no doubt but every man ought to apply himselfe to follow that which is most proper to his owne nature; for that is his best: and pittie it is, and marvell eke, to see such numbers, that neither for love of vertue, nor feare of God, will frame themselves to a good and comendable course of life, but follow their vaine delights and pleasures insatiably.

Pittie indeed it is (said I) but no great marvell, because perfect judgements are rare; and many there be, who though they know the truth of things, yet suffer themselves to be caried away with apparances. For their delight proposing to them certain figures or images of what is good and faire, they are content to be deceived, and to become bondslaves to their senses, or rather charmed by them, as by some witch or inchantresse, and by them to be guided. But this notwithstanding I must advertise you, that I have not so absolutely spoken against pleasures, that you should therefore inferre that vertues should be without their pleasures also. For albeit pleasure be not vertue, nor yet mans true good, yet doth it follow vertue, even as the shadow followeth the bodie. And though vertues have difficulties and travels before they be gotten; yet when they are gotten, pleasure is the inseparable companion unto them; not such as keepeth company with lascivious and wanton affections, and is soone converted to griefe and repentance, but a delight that is permanent and stable: insomuch as some of very good judgement, have thought there is no pleasure worthy the name of delight, but that which proceedeth from vertue, and maketh our actions perfect. For this cause did *Aristotle* say, that most perfect was that delight which was comprehended by the most perfect part of the soule, which is the understanding. And this delight is so perfectly perfect in God, that he is far from any annoyance or molestation: for delight is not in God a passion, as in us our delights are, which never come to us without molestation, it being (as hath bin said) the begining of them. Therfore the pleasures of the mind are esteemed so much the more perfect, as the understanding is more perfect then the sense: which understanding delighteth onely in that pleasure that is accompanied with honestie, and this pleasure he esteemed to be so excellent, that he wished some new excellent name to be found for the same. But we having no other name to give it, call it by similitude with that name which is fit for the delightfullest thing that the senses can yeeld us: and therefore we call as well the imperfect delight of the senses, as that most perfect of the understanding, by the name of pleasure, though the one of them consist in extremes which is vicious, and the other in the meane where vertues have their place.

Here Captaine *Norreis* spake, saying; We have heard you

sundrie times say that vertues consist in the meane betweene two extremes, but how that meane is to be found, you have not yet declared to us: therefore (I pray you) let us be made acquainted with the way to compas the same, that we may learne to take hold of vertue, and not be deceived with the false semblance thereof to fall into vice.

This meane (said I) is found, when a man doth what he ought to do, when time serveth, in maner as he should, for such as becommeth him to do, and for causes honest and convenient. And whosoever setteth this rule to himselfe in all his actions, which being so conditioned, shall be farre off from the extremes, and neere unto vertue.

Yea (said Captain *Norreis*) this is soone said, but not so soone done: for it is not so easie a matter to hitte upon these conditions, but that a man may more easily misse them. But since by your words, neither delight alone, nor profit onely can worke humane felicitie, it should seeme (the qualitie and trade of the world considered) that it may well be gathered, that they which have them both linked together, are worthy to be esteemed happie: since plenty of wealth may yeeld them all their desires, and fulfill their delights. And this haply may be the cause why Kings and Princes are so accounted in this life.

Of the happinesse or unhappinesse of Princes, this is no place to treate (said I) neither appertaineth it to our matter: onely thus much I may remember by the way, that *Antigonus* affirmed it to be but a kind of pleasing servitude to be a King. And *Phalaris* the cruell tyrant considering wel his estate, said likewise, that if he had knowne before he made himself tyrant of his country, what trouble, care and danger followed rule and Segnorie, he wold rather have chosen any state of life then to be a King. Neverthelesse no sort of men place their felicitie more in pleasure then Princes do, when they have not due regard to their charge: for then they think that whatsoever may nourish their delight and pleasure, is lawfull for them to do. But miserable are the people over whom God hath set such to raigne, as put their pleasure or their profit only, before all respects, as the end of their governement: though Almightie God who is the King over Kings, oftentimes in his justice plagueth them, even with those things wherein they placed their greatest felicitie. *Dionysius* the yonger being borne in wealth and plentie, setting all his thoughts upon his pleasures, was therefore in the end driven out of his kingdome. For he thinking it lawfull for him to take all that he would have, even in his fathers life time began to defloure certain virgins of honest families: which thing his father understanding sharpely reprehended him for the same; and among other things told him, that howsoever himselfe had taken upon him by tyrannie the kingdome of Sicilie, yet he never had used any such violences. But his wanton sonne made him this answer: It may well be (quoth he) for you were not the sonne of a King. At which word the father grieving, replied unto him; Neither art thou like to leave thy sonne a King, unles thou change thy conditions. Which prognostication was verified, in that the sonne following his lewd course of life, shortly after his fathers death was chased out his kingdom by his subjects, and driven to get his living by keeping a schoole in Corinth: where on a time one seeing him live so poorely, asked him what he had learned of his schoole-master *Plato*, that he could no better behave himselfe in his royaltie; taxing him that for not applying himself to *Plato* his doctrine, he had bin the cause of his owne ruine. But his answer was better then his former cariage, for he said, that he had learned more then haply he could imagine. And what is that (quoth the other) I pray you teach it me. I have (said he) learned to beare this my adverse fortune patiently, & with a frank courage. And had he learned to observe that worthy sentence of *Agesilaus*, who was wont to say, that Kings and Princes ought to endevor to exceed other men in temperance & fortitude, and not in wantonnes & pleasures, he had never brought his high estate to so base a fortune as to keepe a schoole. But omitting to speake of Kings, I wil tel you that they are greatly deceived that think that profite joyned with delight may make men happie: for the more that profite and delight are knit together, the more doth wanton lust and unruly desires swell and increase, if they be not tempered by the rule of reason. Which made *Ovid* to say,

> From out the bowels of the earth is set
> That cursed pelfe, mens minds on ill to set.[49]

And *Plato* in his books of lawes saith, that a very rich man is seldome seene very good. Which saying you know our Saviour Christ confirmed, when he sayed, it was harder for a rich man to enter the kingdom of heaven, then a cable[48] to passe through a needles eye. And though *Aristotle* in one place sayth, that riches are necessary to make up a perfect humane felicitie: yet in another he calleth them but a foolish happinesse. Yea *Plato* affirmeth, that great riches are as harmeful in a citie as great povertie, by reason of the deliciousnes & wantonnes which they breed. For which reasons it may be very wel concluded, that neither wealth nor pleasure, nor yet they both together, ought to draw any man to propose them to himselfe for his end: but the more he hath of wealth, and useth it but for his pleasure, the further he goeth astray from his felicitie and his proper end. And that riches in a wanton lascivious mans possession, are like a sword in a mad mans hand. *Pythagoras* said, that as a horse cannot be ruled without a bit: so riches are hardly wel used without prudence, which wil in no wise dwell with them, who abandon themselves wholy to vaine delights. If to the vulgar sort therefore such men seeme happie, yet are they in very truth most miserable and unhappie. For these disordinate pleasures are intestine enemies, which never cease working til they overthrow a man, and breed him dishonour and shame: neither do they faile to bring him to an evill end, that sufferes them to master him, and useth his wealth to the pleasing of his appetites. As by *Dionysius* aforesayd may appeere, and also by *Sardanapalus*, who being a mightie Monarke, swimming in wealth and pleasures, and sparing nothing that might glut his lascivious appetites, grew so effeminate thereby, that as soone as he was assaulted by contrary fortune, he was driven to consume himselfe, his treasure, and all his filthy lustes at once in the fire. Which two examples among infinite moe that might be mentioned, shall for this time suffice to verifie that which hath bin said, to wit, that Gods judgements light for the most part upon such Princes, as, forgetting the great care and charge which is layd upon them, give themselves to care for nothing but their owne vaine appetites and delights. To whom *Antisthenes* spake, when he said, that riches were no goods if they were not accompanied with vertue that might instruct men how to use them well. And *Chilo* the *Lacedemonian* likewise, who was the first author of that grave sentence, *Magistratus virum indicat*, whereunto he added riches also, because they both together draw him the more easily to discover himselfe. *Socrates* wisely wished that he might have the grace to esteem no man rich but him that was given to the studie of wisedome and knowledge: for such (he said) had the true gold, which is vertue, a thing much more precious then all the golde in the whole world, and that which leadeth man the right way to his felicitie.

Then, said Captain *Norreis*, since by your discourse, all they are unhappie that tread the steps which leade to either of those two ends before mentioned of profite or pleasure; or to them both joined together: it must of force follow, that happy be they that direct their actions to that end which is proper to man, whereof I hope your next speech will be.

So must it (said I) for there remaineth nothing else to be treated of. And if mine author mistrusted his eloquence (as he doth) in a matter meete to be set forth so effectually as this; what may I say of my selfe, that am tied to declare to you in our language, inferior much to the *Italian*, al that he hath set downe touching the same: Sure it is, that if I were able to set before the eyes of your mindes a lively image of this excellent end, you wold be so delighted therewith that in regard thereof you would contemne and set light by all other pleasures in the world. But howsoever my utterance be, which I will do my best to fit as wel as I can to so high a subject, you shall heare what he in substance saith therupon; and I assure my self that the quality of the matter will easily supply whatsoever defect you may find in my phrase or maner of speech. You are therefore to understand, that as they whose judgements are corrupted, and minds informed with an il habite, to make them live after the maner before mentioned, do swarve from the nature of man so much, as they become like brute beasts or insensible plants voide of reason: even so are they among men, as divine creatures, who apply themselves to live according to reason. And such have aunciently bin called *Heroes*, because they approched in their actions neerer to God then others that lived not so. For they put all their endevours to adorne and set foorth that part of man which maketh him like unto the divine nature, or rather partaker of the same; teacheth him what is good, comely, honest, and honorable: and inviteth him continually to that which may conduct him to the highest and supreme good. This part is the minde, with the use of reason proceeding from it, as from a roote. But because two speciall offices appertaine to the use of reason (so farre foorth as serveth to this purpose) the one contemplation, and the other action. Touching the first, it raiseth us by the means of Arts and sciences (which purge the minde from base and corrupt affections) to the knowledge of

153

those things that are unchangeable, and still remaine the same, howsoever the heavens turne, time runne on, or fortune or any other cause rule things subject unto them. By means of which sciences, the minde climbing by degrees up to the eternall causes, considereth the order & maner wherewith things are knit together, & linked in a perpetual band. And thence it comprehendeth the forme of regiment, which the Creator and mover of all things useth in the maintaining and keeping them everlastingly in their severall offices and duties. And out of consideration hereof we learne, that he that directeth not his course of government by this rule, as neere as he can, to guide himselfe, his family, and the Common-wealth, can seldome or never attaine a good and happie end. Wherefore he draweth the celestiall governement to the use of humane and civill things, so farre as mans frailtie will permit. As *Socrates* did, who was said to have drawne Philosophie from heaven to the earth, to reforme the life and manners of men. Thus turning himselfe to the knowledge of his owne nature, and finding that he is composed of three severall natures, whereof ech hath her severall end, yet seeketh he to draw the ends of the two lesse perfect, to the end of that which is most perfect and proper to him. But finding that continuall contemplation of higher things, would be profitable onely to himself and to none other, in that he should thereby purchase no happinesse to any but to himselfe. And because he knoweth that he is not borne to himselfe alone, but to civill societie and conversation, and to the good of others as well as of himselfe, he therefore doth his endevour with all care and diligence so to cary himselfe in words and in deeds, as he might be a patterne and example to others of seemly and vertuous speeches and honest actions, and do them all the good he could in reducing them to a good and commendable forme of life. For the performance whereof, he perceiveth how requisite it is, that honestie and vertue be so united with profite and pleasure, that by a just and equall temper of them, both himselfe and others may attaine that end which is the *summum bonum*, and the thing wherupon all our discourse hath bin grounded. This end is not to be attained but by the meanes of morall vertues, which are the perfection of the minde, & setled habits in ruling the appetite which ariseth out of the unreasonable parts of the soule: for vertues are grounded in those parts which are without reason, but yet are apt to be ruled by reason. He therefore seeing morall

154

vertues are not gotten by knowing onely what they be, but through the long practise of many vertuous operations, whereby they fasten themselves so to the mind, as being converted once into an habite, it is very hard afterwards to lose the same: even as of vicious actions on the other side the like ensueth: therefore with all carefulnesse and diligence possible he laboreth to embrace the one, and to eschue the other; evermore striving to hold himselfe in the meane, and to avoide the approching of the extremes: to which, profite and delight under deceitful maskes of good, would entise and allure him.

I pray you (said Captain *Norreis*) tel us (since you say that vertue is in the mids betweene two extremes) whether that meane you speake of, wherin vertue sits, be so equally in the midst, as the extremes which be vicious, be alike distant from the same or no?

No (said I) they are not in that manner equidistant, for oftentimes vertue approcheth neerer to one of the extremes, then to the other. As for example, Fortitude, which consisteth in a meane betweene fearefulnesse and foole-hardinesse, hath yet a neerer resemblance to foole-hardinesse then to cowardise, and consequently is not alike distant from them both, and is in this manner to be understood, that albeit vertue consist in a meane between two extremes, whereof the one is a defect, and the other a superabundance, yet she is neither of them both, as by our example of Fortitude appeereth, which is neither foole-hardines, nor yet cowardise, but onely a commendable meane or temper betweene them both. And therfore *Aristotle* said right well that the meane of vertue betweene two extremes, was a *Geometricall* meane which hath a respect to proportion, and not an *Arithmeticall* meane which respecteth equall distance: so as you must understand that vertue is not called a meane betweene two extremes, because she participateth of either of them both, but because she is neither the one nor the other.

And why (said Captaine *Norreis*) is the *Geometricall* proportion rather to be observed therein, then the *Arithmeticall*?

Because (said I) though vertues are in the meane, yet do they bend oftentimes towards one of the extremes more then to the other, as hath bin said already: and by proportion *Geometricall* they are in the middest, which by *Arithmeticall* would not be so. For thereby they must be in the just middest, and equally distant from both the extremes. As for examples, let us suppose 6. to be the meane between 4. and 8; for 6. hath two more then 4, and so hath it two lesse then 8, and in respect of it selfe standeth just in the midst betweene 4. and 8, and equally distant from them both. And this is your *Arithmetical* meane. But the *Geometrical* proportion is after another maner. For suppose 2. and 8. to be the extremes, and 4. to be the mean: here you see that 2. & 4. have a double proportion, and so hath 4. and 8. the one to the other, and so 4. participateth of that double proportion as well with 8. as with 2, and yet is neerer to 2. then to 8; which it doth likewise in another respect: for if the two extremes be multiplied together, as 2. with 8. they make 16: and so much doth 4. likewise being multiplied in it self, for foure times 4. makes 16. And thus you see what difference is betweene *Geometricall* and *Arithmeticall* proportion. Now though every vertue have peculiar extremes betweene which it is placed: yet Philosophers say, that they consist all generally about matter of pleasure, or the contrary.

How can that be (said M. *Dormer*) when you have told us already, that vertue is not pleasure?

It is (said I) one thing to say vertue is pleasure, and an other to say that it consisteth in matter of pleasure or annoyance. And true it is that pleasure is not the matter of vertue, neither meant I so to say; but onely that vertue is busied about these two passions of pleasure and displeasure, whereof the fittest example may be taken from temperance. For as the temperate man embraceth the delight of the mind, so taketh he pleasure to abstaine from the unseemely delights of the body. And contrari-wise, the intemperate man is sad, because he hath them not.

Well (said M. *Dormer*) that matter is soone answered: but because I have heard the Stoikes were of opinion, that vertue was true felicitie, and that *Plotinus* said, that a man endued with vertue was sufficiently furnished for his felicitie, as being possessed of all the good that could be among men, I pray you what is your authors opinion in that point?

If I well remember (quoth I) it is a good while sithens I told you that mans felicitie is attained by vertue; but that vertue is his felicitie, that saith not mine author. And sure the opinion of *Aristotle* is better in that matter then that of the Stoikes. For reason itselfe telleth us that those things which are ordained to an end, cannot be the end itselfe to which they be ordained. And since vertues are ordained for the attaining of mans felicitie, which is (as hath bin sayd) a perfect action according to vertue in a perfect life. It is plaine, that vertue cannot be felicitie, though he that is vertuous approcheth neere to his felicitie.

You say true (sayd M. *Dormer*:) I remember you expounded the clause of a perfect life to be intended a long life, yet the same Stoikes held that a yong man might be happie: alledging felicitie was not to be measured by quantitie, but by qualitie; and that not length of time, but perfection onely is to be respected, which (they say) may be as well in a yong man as in an old. And they give the example of hunger and thirst: for suppose (say they) that two hungry or thirstie folke be called to eate or to drink, and the one to asswage his hunger or thirst be satisfied with a little, and the other require much meate or drink to be satiated, yet is he as well satisfied with the little whose nature requireth little, as he that requireth a great deale: even so (say they) in humane felicitie, the length of time or number of yeeres is not to be respected, but happinesse it selfe; and as happie is the young man who in a few yeeres hath attained his felicitie, as the olde man that hath bin many yeeres about it. For *Plotinus* saith, that the happie man cannot reckon upon the yeeres past of his felicitie, but onely on the present.

The Stoikes held strange opinions (sayd I) in many things. But if experience be needfull (as hath bin formerly sayd) and many actions, to make an habite in vertue, so as a man may by custome be brought to that passe as he shall not do any thing but according to vertue, then is length of life necessary for the attaining of vertue, which must first be gotten before a man can hope for any felicitie. Moreover, if Prudence be the very knot and band of all the morall vertues, and that the young man cannot be prudent, how can he then have perfect vertue? Wherfore the diffinition of humane felicitie to be a perfect operation according to vertue, hath need of this addition in a perfect life, which must be long and have a happie end. For though a man have runne through many yeeres in continuall prosperitie, and afterwards fall into grievous calamitie, though he cannot be thereby made miserable (which vice onely and not adversitie may bring him unto) yet may he not be rightly intitled happie. Youth therfore hath this defect in it, that albeit man be the subject of felicitie, yet a yong man cannot be properly and actually the subject thereof, and the child much lesse, because he is furder off from prudence, and because neither of them can have either perfect life or perfect vertue. And as for the opinion of *Plotinus*, he (as a *Platonike*) considered the soule simple and pure, freed from the other two powers that are rebellious to reason: and meant him onely to be happie, who separating the vertues of the mind from the senses, from worldly delights and concupiscences, did so interne himselfe with his thoughts in the contemplation of his Creator, as he despiseth riches, dignities, and honors, with all transitorie and fraile commodities: still looking to that good which is the highest and perfectest among all goods, which is God Omnipotent. And this he called the chiefe action of the understanding, and highest felicitie. And because he supposed that the mind should never depart from that action, he sayd that the time past was not to be accounted of in mans felicitie. By which it may appeere, that he spake not in that place of humane or civil felicitie, wherof our discourse is now according to *Aristotles* opinion, neither doth the authoritie of *Plotinus* help the Stoikes any whit at al, whose opinion is in that point to be rejected.

Since we are resolved (said Captain *Carleil*) that vertues are but the meane to purchase felicitie, and not felicitie it selfe, we would be glad to heare you declare how many they are, and of what qualitie, that we may know them, and make our selves happie by the purchase of them.

To answer you to this question (said I) according as I find the matter set downe by mine author, wold perhaps not satisfie you so fully as you would desire, or I could wish: for that (in my opinion) he hath treated of some of these morall vertues somewhat too briefly, and confusedly: I have therefore to helpe mine owne understanding had recourse to *Picolomini* when I came to this place, in whom having found a more plaine and easie method in the description of them, I have for the more perspicuitie of the translation, added somewhat taken from him, and (as well as I could) interlaced it with this discourse, where mine author seemed to me too brief, or too obscure. And if it may worke the same effect in you, that it hath done in me, to make you the better understand how many and of what qualitie those vertues are, I hope you will not mislike my attempt therein, but excuse me, though it be not so fully accomplished as I desire it were. There are then by the generall consent of all men foure principall vertues appertaining to civill life, which are, Fortitude, Temperance, Justice, and Prudence; from which foure are also derived (as branches from their trees) sundry others to make up the number of twelve, and they are these ensuing, Liberalitie, Magnificence, Magnanimitie, Mansuetude, Desire of honor, Veritie, Affability, and Urbanitie: of every of the which vertues, I will speake particularly, following chiefly mine author; but where need or occasion shall require, I wil for the cleerer understanding of the matter, supply out of *Picolomini* what I think is wanting. And to begin first with Fortitude. This vertue standeth in the meane betweene foole-hardinesse and cowardise; which two passions may justly be termed matter of Fortitude: and this vertue is exercised in things terrible and fearful, which are also difficult, causing griefe and paine, which the valiant man is willing to endure for vertues sake. For though his life be deere unto him, as it ought to be to every man of vertue, in respect of himself, of his friends, and of his countrey; and will not therefore upon small occasions expose himselfe to perill: yet when time and occasion require it, and that any honest cause call him thereunto, he will undertake cheerfully whatsoever dangerous enterprise, and with a stout courage, and readily performe the same. Neither shall labour or travel, hazard, nor death it selfe dismay him; but esteeming more his reputation then his life, he wil resolutely adventer[51] him self for honesties sake. But among all the actions of Fortitude, to fight for our countrey, and (if need be) to die for defence of the same, deserveth the greatest praise & commendation: as on the other side, to quarrel, & put a mans life in danger upon every trifling occasion, is not the part of a valiant man, but of a foole-hardy. *Cato* the elder therfore said very wel, that to know a valiant man, it imported much, to understand whether he made more account of his life or of his vertue, because not the aptnes to quarrell for every occasion, but the venturing his life for vertue & honestie maketh a man to be accounted valiant among wise men, who hold such men to be fools & miserable that thrust themselves rashly into quarels, as many do, through the corruption of our age, upon fanasticall points of honor, as if they were weary of their lives. Nevertheles there are some kindes of death, which a vertuous man abhorreth, as to die by tempest at sea, by thunder, by earthquake, and such other violent deaths where vertue can have no place. All which deaths, though they cannot dismay a vertuous mind, yet he cannot but be sory that he is brought to such an end, as affoordeth him no meanes to make shew of his valor. There be sundry vices which have a resemblance of this vertue: but because we have in our first dayes discourse spoken of them sufficiently, we shal not need at this time to say any more concerning the same. It is also to be considered, that this is a vertue as wel of the body as of the mind: for to the exercise of fortitude, a man must have a strong body, & of a good complexion, his lims wel framed, and thereto a stout and a constant mind fitly coupled, that it may rule and guide the body prudently. For (as *Isocrates* sayd to *Demonicus*) unlesse strength of body be matched with wisedom, it is doubtles harmfull to him that hath it. The mind must be so disposed & armed against fortune, that she be froward or favorable, it may stand alwayes invincible against all misfortunes and adversities, and yet not raise it selfe for prosperous successes. For it is as true a token of a base mind to be proud & insolent in prosperitie, as to be daunted and faint-hearted in adversitie and affliction. Amid which afflictions, that part of Fortitude which is called patience hath place, of which *Plato* hath written largely, and among other things this he sayth, that the valiant man hath gotten such a habit in his mind of Fortitude, that amid pleasures or amid calamities, he is alwayes the same man; resisting the assaults of fortune with the vertue of his minde. But the Christian writers have much more extolled this vertue then any other; yet *Aristotle* toucheth it, where he sayth, that the vertue of Fortitude is cleerly discerned by the voluntary enduring of grievous accidents, which in effect is that same habite which we call patience. *Alexander Mamea* (as *Herodian* reporteth) was wont to say, that valiant men, and modest or temperate men, ought to wish for prosperous estate: but that if things fall out contrary to their desire, they are to beare them with an invincible courage. And *Plotinus* defining the sayd vertue, sayd that it was a habite of the mind, which was not subject to passions: as in another place he describeth the valiant man to be he, that is not moved from the vertuous habit of his mind, neither by pleasing or delightfull accidents, nor yet by grievous or displeasant; yea he so abhorred that a man should be mastered by happie or unhappie accidents, that he sticked not to affirme, that from this basenes of mind proceeded that opinion

160

which wold take from us our free election. For their cowardise, who suffer themselves to be overcome by such passions, perswades them that such things happen of necessitie, and through the immutable order of things: and so they make themselves wittingly slaves where they were free, wanting either will or power to use that libertie of their mind, either in the one fortune or in the other. For who so is armed with true fortitude, outward things whatsoever they be, neither give nor take ought from them. But they that cannot temper themselves in prosperitie, nor beare adversitie stoutly, make it apparant that fortune mastreth them. Whereunto S. *Ambrose* alluding, saith to *Simplician*, that vertuous men become neither greater nor meaner by the change of mortall successes, because by this vertue they overcome both fortunes. Such a man was *Socrates*, whose wife sayd of him, that whatsoever had befallen him, he never came home but with one and the selfe same countenance, never altered or changed. To the same effect *Seneca* sayd, that a wel disposed minde holdeth evermore one course howsoever the world fare; whether fortune bestow her gifts plentifully upon him, or frowardly take them away. For the valiant man never grieveth at any thing that happeneth in this life to other men, Fortitude being a sure shield for humane weaknesse, which maketh all the darts of fortune how sharpe soever they be, to turne point againe, without once so much as rasing, much lesse entring thereinto. There is nothing in the world that ought to be more deere to a man then his children, who are his true and lively images, and after a sort the ministers of his immortalitie: wherefore the losse of them (especially when they are vertuous) should of all other things be most grievous unto him. Neverthelesse *Anaxagoras* when newes was brought to him that his onely sonne was dead, answered the messenger, It is no new thing that thou tellest me, for I having begotten him, know right wel that he was mortall. So well had Philosophie taught him to beare the freakes of fortune, and armed his minde in such sort, as it could not be surprised with any sudden passion. Our very birth hath death fastened unto it: therefore the Poet sayd right well:

> *Whiles borne we are we die, so that our ending*
> *From our first being taketh his beginning.*

And to conclude touching this vertue, we must have such an habit thereof in our mindes, and so accompany the same with

Prudence, as Fortune either good or bad may not prevaile against us; never thinking our victorie over her assured, until we have cleane daunted and beaten her downe. *Carneades* in this behalfe advised wel, that in time of prosperitie we should forethinke some adversities, and suppose them to be already fallen upon us, whereby we might be the better prepared in minde to beare them if they came indeed. And *Zeno* when he received advertisement that a shippe wherein he had great wealth was wracked and cast away, shewed himselfe farre from being grieved thereat: for he thanked fortune, that by taking againe those goods which she had given him, he had gotten so good an occasion to forsake the care of inriching himselfe temporally, & to betake himselfe wholly to the study of Philosophie.

Next followeth the vertue of Temperance, whose subject is that power of the soule whence cometh the *concupiscible* appetite; and she is exercised specially about the senses of tasting and feeling, but chiefly about the wanton lusts of the flesh: for though the tast ill used, be a cause of intemperance, yet is it by the meane of the sense of feeling. In which respect it may be said, that the disordinate lust of the body that maketh men intemperate, is in the sense of feeling, not over all the body, but onely in those parts which serve for those delights. And they being most mightie, are by temperance to be restrained with the bridle of modestie, and kept within due termes. For which cause *Plato* called her the gardien or safe keeper of all humane vertues. For she with sober and advised language telleth us, that nothing is comely that is not honest, nor nothing honest that is not comely: far from the disordinate appetites perswasion, which sayth, whatsoever pleaseth is lawful, and that all is lawful that pleaseth. But Temperance with her wholesome advertisements withdraweth us from all that is unfitting or undecent, if we give eare unto her. Which undecency or unfittingnes cometh neither from the senses of seeing, nor yet of hearing or smelling. For men by delighting beyond measure in the objects of those senses, are not called Intemperate, but runne into other lesser defects, not needful here to be spoken of. But Intemperance groweth principally (as we have said) out of the tast and the feeling, two senses that make us most like unto brute beasts, if we suffer our selves to be led by them, following our delights as they do: for they corrupt mans prudence, put his mind astray, & take away from him the light of reason, which

162

from other creatures they cannot take. I remember that among the Grecians it was reported, how under the images of *Anacarsis* a most continent Philosopher was ever written, that temperance was to be used in the tongue, in the belly, & in the privie parts, thereby giving us to understand in which senses principally Temperance should be used. And though all other creatures have their exterior senses as well as man, yet none take delight in them, but accidentally. For the hound delighteth not in the sent of the hare, but insomuch as he hopeth to feede upon her: nor the wolfe delighteth in the bleating of a Lambe, but as he intendeth to devoure it: neither doth the sight of a bullock please the Lion for any respect, but that he expecteth to slake his hunger on the carcasse of it. All their principall delight is in the tast and in the feeling: and because they have no light of reason, but are guided onely by naturall instinct, therefore they are not called temperate or intemperate, as having no free choice, which proceedeth from reason onely. But men who have the gift of the mind from God, and are capable by their judgement to discerne and chuse what is good, and to eschue what is evill, unles they be misled by their appetite, deserve, when they chuse that which is just and reasonable, to be called temperate. And to such men *Plotinus* was wont to say, that delight of the senses was given for a refreshing and lightning of the heavy burthen of cares and troubles, which this mortall life bringeth upon us. Shewing thereby that such delights are not in themselves evil, but onely when they be ill used. Which thing *Aristotle* before him signified, when he sayd, that every man was not to be called intemperate, that sought for some pleasure; but that to such only, as hunted after dishonest and unlawfull delights, that name was to be applied: for honest delights for recreation of the mind are not to be disallowed; joyning therein with *Anacarsis*, who sayd, that the continuance of travell, without intermission, was a thing impossible: wherefore it was requisite for men sometime to sport themselves, that they might returne the fresher to their honest labours. Whence *Ovid* tooke his verses, saying,

> *Long cannot last the labour that doth want*
> *An interchangeable repose some-while :*
> *For it restores the forces languishant,*
> *And doth refresh the members spent with toile.*[52]

And *Cicero* the father and light of Romane eloquence, sayth, that games and sports were permitted for the refreshing of the mind, even as meate and drinke for the restoring of the body; especially after the attending of grave and weightie affaires. But such as have made an ill habit, and suffered their judgements to be corrupted, making choice of dishonest delights to follow their senses onely, are rightly called intemperate, because they procure onely the pleasures of the body, without regard of the mind. And they are so much worse then incontinent men: as these feele yet sometimes a remorse of their ill actions, and thereby correct themselves; whereas the other persevere in their ill choise (if we may properly cal that a choise which proceedeth from a corrupted judgement) and care not to amend themselves; and are like to a man full of dropsie: for their viciousnesse is as hopelesse of recovery, as is the dropsie when it is ful growne within the body. And therfore they may well be accounted of a lost life, who have contracted so ill an habit, that they still keepe reason subject to their passions & appetites, which is called by *Plotinus* the infirmity of the mind. But where Temperance ruleth & bridleth the inordinate delights, it is not so: for this vertue which is the meane in all actions, and a seemlinesse in all things appertaining to civill life, doth increase mans praise and commendations, multiplieth honor upon him, lengtheneth his life, and lightneth the burthen of all his troubles: finally it so fashioneth a man, as whether he be alone or in company, whether he be in publike or in privat, he never undertaketh any thing but that which carieth withall reputation, dignitie & honor. For it withholdeth him from all that is unseemly, and leadeth him to all that is honest and commendable. Neither is this vertue exercised only in things appertaining to the appetite, but (as *Aristotle* saith) she is the conserver of prudence: and by *Plato* his opinion, she stretcheth her power to those actions that appertaine to Fortitude also. For she teacheth man to know the meane of fearfulnes in cases of danger apparant, & in what measure paine or trouble is to be endured. *Pythagoras* said she was the mean of al things: and therfore as the beauty of the body is a meet & seemly disposition of the members, breeding grateful sweetnes, and being tempered with fresh colours, draweth the eyes of men to behold it with wonder & delight: even so this vertue causeth al the actions of a temperate man with her bright shining light to be admired and extolled; for she is called by *Pythagoras* the rule of

164

al decency & comelines. Of her hath youth more need (according to *Aristotle*) then old age, because young men are much more stirred with concupiscence and unruly affections then old men. And the Philosophers have assigned her for companions, shame-fastnes (which holdeth men from doing any filthy act) honestie, abstinence, continency (which bridleth the concupiscible passions that they over-rule not the will) mansuetude or mildnes (which tempereth the fury of anger) modestie (which is the rule of decent motions of the body) and to be short, al those gifts of the mind which accompany seemlines and decency, of which we shal particularly say somewhat as briefly as we may. And because this vertue stretcheth her branches so far, *Plato* said it was hard to define her, and more hard to use her: the one because she is hardly discerned from other vertues: the other, because we bring with us from our mothers womb the desire of delight, wherby we are norished, grow, & draw out the line of our life: for which cause *Aristotle* said, that it was harder for a man to resist the pleasures of the body, then pain.

Next followes the excellent vertue of Liberality, which is busied about giving and receiving conveniently, and is placed between two extremes; the one Avarice, which taketh more or giveth lesse then is meet: the other Prodigalitie, which gives more then is convenient: and he that can cary himself even between these two extremes, may justly be called a liberall man; giving where, when, to such persons, and in such sort as is fit, for respect of honestie. Unto liberality is joyned magnificence, which is a vertue concerning riches also; which the magnificall man useth in great things, and such as are to have long continuance, & are done in respect of vertue, as sumptuous buildings, rich furnitures, and the like: therfore a poore man cannot actually attaine to be either magnificent or liberal. The liberall man is not magnificent, because magnificence is more then liberalitie: but the magnificent man is liberal.

Arme in arme with Magnificence goeth Magnanimity, waited upon by Mansuetude, desire of honor, veritie, affability & urbanity. Al which vertues appertain to civil conversation, & are very profitable, breeding decency, honesty, dignitie & honour. And though honour be reckoned in the number of those things that are called exterior goods yet is it highly to be prised among all other, because it is the certaine token of vertuous life, and is the due reward of vertue. For vertue hath two sorts of rewards: the one that is outward, and that is honour (which cometh from others that honor vertue, and is not in the vertuous man himselfe): the other inward, which is felicitie, the true and perfectest end of all our vertuous actions whiles we are alive. And man having all these vertuous habits in him, gotten by continuall wel doing, which consisteth in particulars: he hath also need of the conversation of other men, lest the occasion of doing vertuously shold faile him. For though a man have never so perfect a knowledge of al the vertues, unles he put them in action, he can never be happie. And specially therfore is friendship necessary for him, which either is a vertue, or fast linked to vertue, and groweth out of the love which men beare, first to their parents and kinsmen, next to their citizens or countreymen, and lastly to strangers. For as concerning civill felicitie, man cannot, nor ought not to be alone: in which respect conversation and friendship are necessary for the accomplishment of the same. Some therefore have sayd, that it were as hurtfull to take the bright shining beames of the Sunne from the world, as to deprive men of the benefite of friendship: since without friends, a man is so farre from being happie, as it may be said, he cannot live, or be at all. This friendship is a communion and knitting together of minds, which neither length of time, distance of place, great prosperitie, nor great adversitie, ne yet any other grievous accident may sever or separate. And *Plotinus*, though all his drift were to raise man from all base affects of the mind, and to settle him in contemplation, yet he thought friendship necessary no lesse for the mind then for the body. *Aristotle* sayd, that he that lived alone could be none other then either a God or a brute beast. Solitarinesse then is evill for all sorts of men, but most of all for yong men, who wanting experience in themselves, have great neede of the good instructions and admonitions of others. Therefore *Crates* the Philosopher seeing a yong man alone, went unto him, & asked of him what he was doing so all alone: and the young man answering, that he was discoursing with himselfe: take heed (said *Crates* then) that thou talk not with an il man. Considering wisely, that a man void of prudence (as yong men commonly are) is like to busie his head with ill thoughts, which will provoke him to ill deeds also. Conversation therfore and friendship are necessary for the accomplishment of civill felicitie, which without love cannot be. And that friendship is firme and durable which groweth out of vertue, and from similitude of behaviour and conditions. *Plato* saith, that beauty beareth the greatest sway in friendship, but that is the beauty of the mind, which vertue brings forth: but if to the beauty of the mind, that of the body also be joyned, they both do the sooner and the faster tie together the minds of vertuous men. For the exterior beauty of the body prepareth the way to the knowledge of the other inward of the mind, which (as hath bin sayd) is indeed the true man: but he that loveth but the body, loveth not the man, but that which nature hath given him for an instrument. And if this beauty of the bodie happen to draw any man to love a foule or dishonest mind, that love cannot be termed rightly friendship, but a filthy and loathsome conjunction of two bodies, too much frequented by yong men with naughtie women, who are not onely unworthy any love, but ought of all men to be eschued as abhominable, and driven out of all well ordered Common-weales. This friendship tieth (though with divers respects) children to their parents, kinred to kinred, the husband to the wife, and the minds of men of valour & vertue fast together, as a thing agreeable to all the qualities which our soule containeth: but this friendship betweene men of valour and courage, springeth from that faculty of the mind, whence cometh reasonable anger, the heate whereof stirreth & inflameth the mindes of such men to valour and fortitude. And though this friendship be good and commendable, yet is that more firme & permanent which groweth out of the that part of the mind which is garnished with reason and vertuous habits: for it bindeth mens minds so fast together, and breedeth so firme a consent in them, that they become as one; in so much as it seemeth that one mind dwelleth in two bodies to guide and rule them. Which made *Zeno* say that his friend was another himself. Now albeit we see dayly friendships to be broken off upon sleight occasions, yet is that not to be imputed to any imperfection in the nature of friendship.

It is marvel (said Captain *Carleil*) that friends should so easily break the bonds of friendship, if they were so fast knit as you have sayd: the cause whereof were worth the knowing.

That shall I declare unto you (said I:) Many apparances of friendship there are, which be as farre from true friendship, as the painted image of a man is from a man indeed: for some are friends for profit, some for pleasure, and some for other respects:

which respects failing, love also quaileth; and so the foundation of friendship being gone, it must needs fall to the ground. Others first love, and after beginne to judge of the person: and when they find themselves deceived in their expectation whatsoever it were, they untie the knot of friendship faster then they hasted to knit the same before. But if judgement leade the daunce, as it ought to do, and that a man chuse to love another, because he esteemeth him worthy for his vertues to be beloved; such friendship is sure and firme, never to be dissolved, nay not so much as a mislike can grow betweene such friends. For *Aristotle* holdeth, that discord cannot possibly dwell together with friendship. All other friendships are subject to quarrels & dissentions, but especially that which is grounded upon profit: wheras those friends whom vertue coupleth together, as they have but one wil, so have they all things common, according to the lawes of *Pythagoras*. Which lawes *Plato* allowed, and *Aristotle* likewise, though in the communion of goods he were contrary to *Plato*, affirming that where all things were common, it was not possible that the commonwealth could stand. The stedfastnesse of friendship therefore consisteth in the communion and equalitie of minds, betweene which neither anger, dissention, nor ingratitude can grow; for true friends provoke not one another with contention, anger or unthankfulnesse. And in regard hereof, the opinion of *Plato* was, that pleasantnes and cheerfulnesse was fitter among friends then gravitie or severitie.

But I pray you (sayd Captaine *Norreis*) tell us whether this friendship you speake of may be between many or no?

Sir (answered I) a man cannot in truth be friend to many at once, in this degree of friendship which we are treating of. For since the worker of this fast friendship, is the likenes of minds and conditions. As there is a variety of faces infinite, insomuch as it is a very rare thing to find two altogether like the one to the other: so falleth it out likewise in minds: and the saying is, that one mind ruleth two bodies, and not mo; according to which saying, friendship cannot be in perfection betweene many. The reason wherof may be, that love and true affection being the most excellent thing among the effects of friendship, and things excellent being rare, therfore true friendship is so rare, as not onely in our age, but also in all ages past, we find scarce two or three couples of friends to be recorded. Neither can a man indeed devide his love into many shares, without impairing it; nor give like helpe, use like conversation, or do other friendly offices toward many, which are needfull, and required betweene two fast friends, such as we speake of.

I cannot tell (sayd sir *Robert Dillon*) why you make friendship so rare a matter, when dayly example sheweth us, that there are many men who have many friends. Let us consider privatly or publikely our owne acquaintances, and we shall see so many kind offices of friendship stirring, as it may be thought, the auncient times brought forth men more savage & unfit for amity; or else that our times are happier in that point then theirs. I remember yet that I have read of *Epaminondas*, how he was wont to say, that a man shold not come home from the pallace untill he had purchased some friends. The like is written of *Scipio* the yonger, who affirmed that the firmest and most profitable possession that a man could have in this world, was the having of many friends. Also the Emperour *Trajan* was accustomed to say, that he accounted that day lost wherein he had not gotten one friend.

All this (said I) is true: but many are friends in name, who when they be put to trial prove nothing so. And therfore was it said, that there were many apparances & sorts of friendship, which properly are not to be esteemed true friendship, but are rather to be termed civil benevolence, or publike friendship; being a certaine generall love, which the nature of man, and the communion of countries breedeth of it selfe. And this love maketh one man courteous, gracious, and affable to another, if he degenerate not from his owne nature which hath framed him sociable; it maketh him apt to help, and ready to defend, and to use all the offices of humanitie and benevolence that become him towards all men: but specially towards such as either countrey, neighbourhood, likenesse of exercises or delights, of such like things have united and knit together. All which breed rather an accidentall then a sound and true friendship. For among many such, few will be found that will expose themselves to perils or dangers for their friends, or in respect of their friends safetie will set light by their goods, yea their owne lives, as these few recorded in auncient writings have done. This made *Demetrius Falareus* to say, that true friends went willingly to be partakers of their friends prosperity if they were called therunto: but that

169

if adversitie or misfortune did befal them, they taried not then to be called, but ran of themselves to offer their helpe and comfort. And *Anacarsis* esteemed one good friend worth many common & ordinary, such as we dayly see called friends, either for countries sake, or because they keepe company together in travell by land or sea, or traffike, or serve together in the warres, or such like occasions: all which are in truth but shadowes rather of friendship, then friendship indeed. A friend is not so easily to be discerned, but that a man must (as the proverbe saith) eate a bushell of salt with him before he account him a true friend. Wherupon followeth, that there can be no perfect friendship, but after long experience and conversation. *Plato* respecting this, said, that friendship was an habit gotten by love long time growne: and in another place, that it was an inveterate love, which is all one; to wit, that it must be purchased, and confirmed by long tract of time. Nevertheles though love be the meane to knit friendship, yet is it not friendship it selfe, but the roote rather of the same. And as without the root nothing can prosper nor grow: so without love no friendship can prosper. Thus then you may understand, that true friendship is not gotten by publike meetings, walkings or trading, nor in one day or two; and that all sorts of benevolence or mutuall offices of courtesie and civilitie, or every shew of love maketh not up a friendship. For once againe I will tell you that friendship is so excellent a thing as it cannot be in perfection, but onely betweene two good and vertuous men of like commendable life and behaviour. That it is the greatest externall good that can be purchased in this life, and that it is the same which *Aristotle* said was more needfull then justice, and therefore highly to be prised of the man that laboured for civill happinesse. Who although he have all those exteriour goods which appertaine to civil life, as wealth, health, children, and such like, without which *Aristotle* holdeth that no man can be perfectly happie in this world, yet if he want friends, he lacketh a principal instrument for his felicitie; not only in respect of the many benefits which friends bring with them, but chiefly for the delight of his own vertuous operations, and the exercise of the like with them, when they shall be induced by him to vertuous actions: which breedeth an unspeakable contentment. Besides that, solitarinesse bereaveth a man of the sweetest part of his life that is the conversation among friends, increasing the contentation[53] of a happie man, as he is to be a civill man: for of that other solitarinesse which appertaineth to contemplation, this place serveth not to speake. Wee may therefore right well conclude, that without friendship a man cannot have his civill felicitie accomplished. But if I should say all that might be said concerning friendship, I should be too long; neither would I have said so much thereof, had it not bin to shew you, how solitarinesse cannot serve the turne of him that would be happie in this life. Wherfore companie being necessary to felicitie, will minister unto the happie man occasions to use his liberalitie: for sweete and pleasing conversation, and to supply the wants & necessities of friends, is the true & comfortable sauce to friendship. It will make him to shew the greatnes of his courage in great things, guided alwayes by judgement and reason, and to direct all his actions to the mark of honour, a thing esteemed (as we have said) among all others the greatest externall good: not that he shal set honor for his end (for that he knoweth would be unfitting) but honorable and vertuous actions, contenting himselfe that honor be the reward of them, and vertue be the hire for her selfe. For to her, others will give honour as to a divine thing, wheresoever they shall see her. But Magnanimitie is not a vertue fit for every man, but for such onely as are furnished with all other vertues, and among vertuous men are esteemed in the highest degree. And he that is not such a man, and will yet make a shew of Magnanimitie, will be but laughed at and scorned, because vice and Magnanimitie, for the contrarietie that is betweene them, cannot dwell together in any wise; the one deserving all honour, and the other all reproch & blame. For Magnanimitie produceth effects agreeable to all the rest of the vertues, which is the cause that so singular a gift of the mind is not attained but with great difficultie: but the more travell is taken in getting it, the greater is the praise to him that hath purchased the same. He that is adorned with this vertue, joyeth when great honours fall upon him, he little esteemeth any perill, when honestie inviteth him thereunto, and not anger, nor fury, nor desire of revenge, nor onely respect of honour. In matter of riches he always observeth a due temper as wel as the liberall man, whom he excelleth in this, that the Magnanimous man exerciseth his vertue in high matters that beare with them dignitie and importance; whereas the liberall man is busied in things of lesse moment. He hath also a due regard concerning honours, in the purchase whereof he is not injurious or threatning, nor puffed up with pride or ambition, but knowing right well that who so offereth injury to another, cannot be rightly called Magnanimous, he abstaineth from doing any: and if any man have offered him injurie, he holdeth it for the greatest and honorablest revenge to forgive, though he have the partie in his power, & may satisfie himselfe; and thinketh that the greatest displeasure he can worke to his enemy, is to shew himselfe evermore garnished with vertue. Moreover, he is alwayes higher then his fortune, be it never so great, and be she never so contrary she cannot overthrow him. He will never refuse to spend his life (though it be deere unto him, knowing his owne worth) for the defence of his countrey, of his friends, of his parents, of his religion, or for Gods cause, with whom he is continually in thought, though he be bodily here below on earth conversant among men, never busied in base conceits or imaginations. His reputation is so deere unto him, as he wil sooner loose his life, then spot it by any vile act: wherefore if he be in the field with his armes for any the causes before said, he never turneth his backe to flie, but fighteth with a firme resolution, either to overcome or die. He is much more ready to bestow a good turne or benefite then to receive it; holding that it is more honorable for a man to part with his goods, then to take at any other mans hand: nevertheles if he chance to receive any profite or commoditie by any other, he layeth it up carefully in his remembrance, and never thinketh himself out of debt until he hath requited it double at the least. A propertie well becomming a divine mind rather then an humane: for of al others Ingratitude is the vilest & abhominablest vice, which among the Persians was severely punished. A vice that may be accounted not onely contrary to honestie, but also a cruell beastlinesse. The Comike Poet saith, that wicked is the man that knoweth how to receive a benefit, but not to recompence the same. Which sentence is in effect also in *Euripides*, who sayth, that he who forgetteth benefits received, can never be reputed of an honest or generous mind. Our Christian writers have said, that it is enemie to grace, enemie to our salvation, to our life, & all civill societie. And accordingly *Seneca* was of opinion, that no vice was more contrary to humanitie, or did sooner dissolve the unitie of mens minds then ingratitude, more abhominable before God, or more

172

odious to al vertuous & honest minds. But among ungrateful wretches, he that sheweth ingratitude towards those that have instructed him in learning and vertue, opening to him the gate by which he must enter to attain to his felicitie, is the most beastly of all others: for that to them he ought to have more regard then to his owne father, from whom though he hath his being, yet from the other he hath his well being, and is made fit and capable of dignitie and honour by the meane of vertue. And as gratitude or thankfulnes is the ornament of all other vertues, from which proceedeth the love between the child and the parent, betweene the scholer and his master, the charitie towards our countrey, the honor toward God, the friendship betweene men, and the reverence towards our superiours: so no doubt ingratitude cannot be but directly contrary to all these, and therefore the foulest of al other vices; from which all the evils in the world proceed, to the perpetuall infamie of him that is unthankful. Neither is it to be wondred, that such men (like infernall furies) cast behind them Religion, pietie, love, faith, all goodnes, justice, and humanitie it selfe, seeking like ravenous wolves to live and feed upon the bloud of other men. Not onely from private houses therefore, but from Cities and Common-weales, ought this pestiferous generation to be carefully banished, as an infection among people, & the ruine of al conversation, lest their contagion spred that same evil over all the rest. *Pythagoras*, who was the first that ever was called a Philosopher (which is as much as to say, a lover of wisedome, and consequently of truth) did forbid all men to lodge an unthankfull man under his roofe. And because the Swallow (as *Plutarke* saith) betokeneth ingratitude, he would not have them to be sufffered to nestle in a house. And to say truly, such men are worse then the most savage and cruell beasts of the field: for of the gratitude of some of them, even the fiercest, many most notable examples have bin recorded; namely this: One *Elpi* a dweller in the Ile of *Samos*, who traded into Afrike, comming with his ship on that coast, went a shore, where he met a Lion, in whose teeth a bone of some beast stucke in such sort as he could not close his mouth, or make any shift to eate: *Elpi* pittying the beast, who seemed to crave at his hands releefe, tooke out the bone, and so delivered him of that mischiefe. But this thankfull Lion failed not every day after so long as his ship lay there at rode[54] to bring him duly his share of what prey

173

soever he tooke, which was sufficient to feed him and all his
company. Yea even among serpents we reade examples of thankfulnesse: for it is written, that a certaine child brought up a
young serpent, and fed it familiarly a long time; but when it
was growne great, one day following the instinct of nature, it
left the child and went to the woods. It happened that some
while after that child being become now meete to travell, passing
thorough a wood was assaulted by robbers, who having taken
him were purposed to have slaine him: but he with pittifull
voice intreating and crying to them that they should spare his
life, the same serpent (who by chance was then neere at hand)
heard his crie, and knowing his voice, came suddenly out with
such fury upon the theeves, that they were glad to take their
heeles, and to leave the yong man there to save themselves, who
by the thankfulnesse of the serpent was thus saved. But because
you may haply make doubt of these histories, supposing them to
be old and fabulous, give me leave (besides mine author) to recite
unto you a strange example of gratitude in a beast, which I have
understood from a person of such credite, as I dare avouch it for
a truth, since himselfe affirmed that he knew the gentleman in
the west country of England, to whom the thing happened even
of late yeeres. This gentleman had a mastiffe, which he made
much account of because he was very faire and hardie, and therefore cherished him so as his neighbours tooke knowledge of his
affection to the dogge: in respect whereof, though they received
harme from him (for I must tel you he had a qualitie to worry
sheepe by night) yet sought they no redresse, but by complaint
to the master, who in no case could be induced to beleeve that
his dogge had that qualitie, so cunning was he to take his times
and to hide his fault. Howbeit upon the renewing of complaints
he caused a muzzle to be made, and every night to be put on his
dogs head; supposing thereby to be not onely assured himself, but
to satisfie his neighbours also, that it was not he that committed
those outrages. But for all this, neither the harme nor the complaints were stopped; for this dog had gotten the knack with his
feet to pull off his muzzle, and then going abroad to do his feate,
at his returne he would thrust his head into the muzzle againe,
in such sort as any man would have freed him of any such fact.
Yet no other dogge being neere to do the like but he, and still
the harme being freshly done, his master once resolved to watch

his dogge a whole night to satisfie himselfe and his neighbours of the truth: which thing he did so discreetly, as he discovered his dogs subtiltie, and saw him unmuzzle himselfe, go abroade, and returne so cleaned as no spot of bloud could be discerned about him, and thrusting his head into his muzzle to lie him downe as if he had bin free from any such offence. The gentleman thus resolved of his dogges conditions, went to bed, and slept the rest of the night; and the next morning coming downe, he found his dogge lying in the hall, and looking somewhat angerly upon him, he spoke these words, Ah thou sheepbiter, thou sheepbiter, thou must be hanged; and so indeed had purposed with himselfe to have had him executed. But whiles he was busied in some household affaires, the dog stole out of doores and ran away; so as when his master gave order how he should be hanged, he was no where to be found. And these circumstances of the tale I have the rather related, that you may wonder at the understanding of this beast. Now for his gratitude, thus it fell out: Some two yeeres after or lesse that he was thus runne away to escape hanging, it was the gentlemans chance upon some occasions to travell on foote through the countrey, and in a certaine wood fit for such purposes, he met two tinkers that set upon him suddenly to rob him: these two tinkers had with them a mastiffe that caried their packes, as many in England do; which dog when in the fight (for the gentleman defended himselfe manfully) he had knowne either by his voice or otherwise his old master, he ranged himselfe to his partie, and set upon his latter masters so fiercely, that they lost their courages, and being wounded ran away: and then the gentleman also refigured his old servant, by whose meanes he was delivered from so great a danger; and so tooke home his dog again, who had in the meane time forgone his naughtie qualitie, and was ever after much made of by his master as he right well deserved. How shamefull a thing is it therefore to man, that brute beasts should give him examples of gratitude; and he contrariwise, on whom God hath bestowed so great a gift as reason to discerne the good from the bad, should rather follow the example of the worst sort of beasts in doing ill, then of such as by naturall instinct shew him the way to goodnesse? For the ungratefull man is of the nature of the wolfe, of whom it is written, that being suckled when it was yong by an Ewe; when it grew great, in recompence of his nourishment he devoured her: declaring that the wickednes of the unthankfull person cannot be overcome by any benefits, be they never so great. But of this abhominable vice we have said enough, and more then needed, but that I was willing to give you to understand, how farre it ought to be from him that is vertuous, and would be raysed to the reputation of a magnanimous man: of whom returning to speake, thus much is to be added, that he useth himselfe and all his abilitie evermore with greatnesse of courage, spending when occasion serveth magnifically, in workes worthy admiration, and in helping of others honorably. Towards all men he is courteous, gentle, and affable, never giving occasion of offence or mislike in his conversation: such due regard he hath to place, time, persons, and other circumstances, so as he never doth any thing unseemely or unworthy himselfe. And so he tempereth pleasantnesse with gravitie, benignitie with dignitie, that to the humble he never seemeth proud, nor to the great ones never base or demisse:[55] but valewing himselfe neither more nor lesse then he is worth, insisteth still upon truth, discovering himselfe modestly and decently as he is indeed a man of vertue, and with grave, yet gentle speeches giving satisfaction to all persons of what degree soever. And finally in all his actions and behavior he taketh great heed that he commit not any thing whereby he may have cause to die his cheeke with the purple blush; but evermore deserve of all men praise and commendation.

If I should not interrupt, or prolong your discourse too much, I would be glad (said Captaine *Norreis*) to learne what is the cause that shamefastnesse maketh the red colour come into a mans face, and that feare doth make him pale?

The reason is (said I) because shamefastnes springeth in us for some thing that we thinke blame-worthy: and the minde finding that what is to be reprehended in us, commeth from abroade, it seeketh to hide the fault committed, and to avoide the reproch thereof, by setting that colour on our face as a maske to defend us withall. And albeit that shamefastnesse or blushing seeme to be a certaine still confession of the fault, yet it carieth with it such a grace, as passeth not without commendation, specially in youth, as hath bin said. But feare which proceedeth from imagination of some evill to come, and is at hand, maketh the mind which conceiveth it to startle, and looking about for meanes of defence, it calleth al the bloud into the innermost parts, specially to the heart, as the chiefe fort or castle; whereby the exterior parts being abandoned and deprived of heate, and of that colour which it had from the bloud and the spirits, there remaineth nothing but palenesse. And hereof it commeth to passe, that we see such men as are surprised with feare, to be not only pale, but to tremble also, as if their members would shake off from their bodies: even as the leaves fall from the tree as soone as the cold wether causeth the sappe to be called from the branches to the roote, for the preservation of the vertue vegetative. But such feare is unseemly, and a token of a cowardly mind, and is seldom seene in men of valour. For they are never so suddenly overtaken by any humane accident, but that they are armed, and know that their vertue is to be made knowne in fearfull and terrible occasions, which are the very matter and subject of their glory. Neither doth fortune with her smiling, so assure them, but that they look for her frowning countenance to follow: and therefore in prosperity prepare themselves for adversity; whereby when others fal under her strokes, they not only feare her not, but couragiously fight against her, & overcome her. Yet you must understand that every sort of feare is not reprochfull: for that feare which withholdeth men from doing evill, or things that may breed them shame, is worthy commendation: which made *Xenophon* to say that he was most fearful to do any thing that was dishonest. And much more commendable is that feare which groweth from the reverence and respect we beare to God, to our parents, and our superiours: for that leades a man to goodnes, whereas the other bringeth a man to all evill and wickednesse. And now having satisfied your demaund, let me briefly runne through the rest of the vertues before mentioned in their order. Next therefore to Magnanimitie cometh the goodly vertue of Mansuetude,[56] being a meane betweene wrathfulnesse with desire of revenge, stirred up in the irascible appetite in respect of some injury done or supposed to be done, and coldnesse or lacke of feeling of wrongs when they are offered: which coldnesse or insensibilitie of wrongs, is by this vertue kindled or stirred up to feele and mislike the injuries which unruly persons do oftentimes offer to men of vertue. For as it is necessary upon many occasions to be angry, not with intention to offend others, but for the defence of a mans selfe, and of those to whom he is tyed, and specially of his reputation, lest by being too dull and carelesse in regarding injuries done unto him, he become apt to be ridden and depressed by every ruffling companion: so to be either too sudden or outragious in anger, and thereby to be incited to do any act contrary to reason, cannot in any sort agree with vertue, or become a gentleman. For to speak of that bearing which is undertaken for Christian humilitie, or feare of offending God, appertaineth not to this place. This vertue then of Mansuetude, is she that holdeth the reines in her hand, to bridle the vehemency of anger, shewing when, where, with whom, for what cause, how farre foorth, and how long it is fit and convenient to be angry; and likewise to let them loose, and to spurre forward the mind that is restie[57] or slow in apprehending the just causes of wrath, with regard of like circumstances: directing the particular actions of the vertuous man in such cases according to reason; to whom she, as all other the vertues, is to have a continuall eye and regard in every thing.

Desire of Honor succeedeth next, and is a vertue that is busied about the same subject with Magnanimitie. For as the magnanimous man respecteth onely great and excessive honors: so doth this vertue teach the meane in purchasing of smaller honours or dignities, such as civill men of all sorts are to be employed in. For as there are some that seeke by all meanes possible to catch at every shew of honor, at every office or degree that is to be gotten, and spare not to undergo any indignity, or to try any base or unlawfull meanes to compasse the same, heaving and shoving like men in a throng to come to be formost, though they deserve to be far behind: so are there others so scrupulous and so addicted to their ease and quiet, that they cannot endure to take upon them any paines, or any place that may bring them either trouble or hazard; absolutely refusing in that respect, and despising al dignities and offices, together with the honor they might purchase by the same. The first sort of men are called ambitious: the other insensible and carelesse of their reputation. Betweene which two extremes this vertue hath her place, to keepe the first from seeking, not by vertue, but by corruption, deceit, or other unfit meanes to compasse honors, dignities, or authoritie, as many do, slandering and backbiting such as are competitors with them; or else most basely flattering, and with cappe and knee crouching to those that they thinke may yeeld them helpe, or favour them in their purchase, which they seeke and beg to supply their owne unworthinesse: and to quicken the other, whose mindes have no care of their credit & reputation, but live in base companies, and estrange themselves from all civill conversation, like brute and savage beasts. And in this respect is she worthy high estimation, and necessary for all them that esteeme true honour (as they ought) to be the most excellent good among exteriour things: who neverthelesse temper themselves from ambition, so as they are not drawne to commit any vile or base act for the atchieving of the same, but strive evermore by vertue to purchase their honor & reputation. Neither is this vertue all one with Magnanimitie, because it requireth not so excellent an habit as doth Magnanimitie, though they both be busied about the same subject: for between them is the like difference as is betweene Magnificence and Liberalitie, whereof we have already spoken.

Veritie is the vertue which followeth in order, by which a man in all his conversation, in all his actions, and in al his words sheweth himselfe sincere and ful of truth, making his words and deeds alwayes to agree, so as he never sayeth one thing for another, but still affirmeth those things that are, and denieth those that are not. The two extremes of this vertue, are on the one side dissimulation or jesting, called in Greeke *Ironia*, and on the other side boasting. For some there are that seeke by this vice to purchase reputation and credit, or profit; or else even for foolish delight give themselves to vanting[58] and telling such strange things of themselves, as though they be incredible, yet wil they needs have men forsooth to beleeve them. Others for the same respects dissemble the good parts that haply are in them, & seeme willing to make men beleeve that their good qualities are not so great as they are; with a counterfeit modestie faining alwayes to abase themselves in such sort as men may easily discover them to be plaine hypocrites, and that under pretence of humilitie they labour to set pride on horsebacke: yea some even of meriment, or by long custome of lying, thinke it sport sufficient never to tell any thing but exorbitant and strange lies, insomuch as in fine, though they wittingly speak no truth, yet themselves fal to beleeving what they say to be most true. Betweene these two vices sitteth this bright-shining vertue of Truth (as she is a morall vertue) by which men use the benefit of their speech to that true use for which it is bestowed upon them by God, and purchase to themselves not onely honour and praise, but also trust and credit with all men, so as their words are observed as oracles: whereas of the others, no man maketh more account then of the sound of bels, or of old wives tales. This is that excellent vertue that is of all others the best fitting a Gentleman, and maketh him respected and welcom in all companies: which made *Pythagoras* to say, that next unto God, truth in man was most to be reverenced: whose contrary likewise is of all other things the most unfitting, the very destroier of humane conversation the mother of scandals, and the deadly enemy of friendship: the odiousnesse whereof may be discerned by this, that albeit we stick not sometimes to confesse our faults, though they be very great, to our friends, yet we are ashamed to let them know that we have told a lie.

The vertue of Affabilitie which succeedeth, is a certaine meane, by which men seeke to live and converse with others, so as they may purchase the favor and good liking of all men, not forgetting their owne gravitie and reputation. And because there are some that thinke with pleasing speeches and pleasant conceits to be welcom into all companies, they give themselves to flatter, to commend and extoll every man, to sooth all that they heare spoken, and still to smile or laugh in every mans face; purchasing thereby in the end to be esteemed but as ridiculous sycophants or base flatterers: and others, holding a contrary course, never speake word that may be gratefull or pleasing to any man, supposing thereby to be held for grave and wise men, evermore opposing themselves to what others say, dispraising al mens doings, and finally with frowning countenance making themselves odious in all companies. Therefore is this excellent vertue set as a meane to direct men how to use their words and behaviour in honest and civill conversation, that they may be gratefull. For thereby they know how to distinguish the degrees and qualities of persons, of times, of places, and by discreete cariage to make themselves welcome every where, without touch of flattery. And Affabilitie resembleth very much friendship in the particular actions therof, both having a purpose to please, & never to displease. But betweene them there is this difference, that friendship doth all things with a speciall fervent affection interchangeably borne; whereas Affabilitie respecteth not the mutual affection, but only a desire to be generally acceptable and pleasing to all good men, to every one in their severall degrees and qualities, and without regard of the conditions before specified. In the exercise of which vertue, among other observations, this is one principall, never to let passe a word out of the mouth before it be considered and examined whether it may offend any man or no. For many men through lack of this consideration have let slip words that they would afterwards have redeemed at a high rate, but could not; whence arise oftentimes great mischiefes, as dayly experience sheweth us. Lastly, as the body hath need of rest after travell, so hath the mind (overwearied with study or affaires) need of recreation, that it may return the fresher to be busied again. And this recreation is best found in certaine pastimes or sports, used by gentlemen when they meete to be merry together, wherein no basenesse or unseemlinesse is seene: and therefore are these sports properly called, recreations of the mind. But because in such meetings where men come to passe the time together, they faile in their conversation two wayes by excesse, the one contrary to the other; therefore is the meane which teacheth the tempering of those excesses, called the vertue of Urbanitie, a Latine name, which in English we cannot better, and therefore must give it passe to be denizened among us. The one excesse of too much, is, when men seeke in such assemblies or meetings onely to make the company laugh, and so they laugh, care not whether the occasion be given of any wanton speech or scurrilitie, or over-bitter taunting, without respect of persons, and if they may breake a jest upon any man, either present or absent, they will not for-beare it to shew their wit, though it be never so much to the shame and ignominie of the partie; yea and they will laugh thereat themselves so exceedingly, that they will make others of force to laugh at their laughter, though they mislike their speech. And such men may be justly termed jesters, or knavish fooles, specially if to their words they adde gestures and countenances undecent for civill men, not sparing also ribald speeches even in the presence of sober and modest gentlewomen. A thing that among honest and vertuous men is most odious, whose conversation ought to be farre from uncleannesse or malice. Opposite to these are certaine persons, who in all companies never let fall any wittie speech themselves, or any merry conceit; nor yet when they heare them proceed from others, will once affoord to grace them with so much as a smile: but rather bend the browes thereat, or seeme not to know or to conceive any delight therein, behaving themselves like rude clownes which want capacitie to comprehend the substance of a pithy & pleasant speech. These *Aristotle* calleth harsh and rustike fellowes. Now betweene this rusticity and this foolish jesting is this vertue of Urbanitie the meane, which the Greeks call *Eutrapelia*, and teacheth a man to frame all his speeches in assemblies and meetings where he chaunceth to be for the reviving or recreating of his spirits, so as they may be sharpe and wittie, and yet not bitter or overbiting to offend, nor yet to taxe or reprove any man so, as he may have just cause to complaine: though (to say truth) a discreet or wittie jest cannot be much worth, or move men to laugh, unles it have a certaine deceit or offence intended towards some body, who neverthelesse must not be so pricked, as he may have cause to be grieved thereat, but rather be merry at the conceit. For since words and gestures are the true tokens commonly of the qualitie of the mind, he, that in his conversation causeth not the sweetnes of his mind and the candor of his noblest part to shine through all his actions, words and gestures, cannot be esteemed a man of worth and vertue. He must continually have great regard to the time, place, persons, and other circumstances, according to which he is so to order his pleasant conceits and merry jests, not onely to move meriment and laughter, but that withall he may keepe his gravitie & dignitie, and eschue above all things licentious & wanton speeches, which in no wise become a man that is desirous to beare up his reputation & credit as a civill man. And thus having given you a tast of every of the vertues assigned to wait upon Magnanimity somewhat more amply then mine author, who hath (in my opinion) a little too briefly touched them in the description of a magnanimous man: I will now returne to his discourse again, by which I am come to treate of Justice; the efficacie and power wherof is such, that some sages have held her only to be vertue, as if she should containe in her al other vertues: and that the rest that are severally named should be but as parts of her, diversly intituled in respect of the divers objects, about which they are exercised. It is therefore to be considered, that this vertue is to be taken two waies; the one when she is generally considered, and then is she alone al the vertues: in which respect *Agesilaus* was wont to say, that where Justice was, there needed no Fortitude. And *Antisthenes* and *Plato* likewise were of opinion, that he that was just needed no lawes, because this vertue was sufficient to keep him within the compasse of living wel and vertuously. The other way is, when she is taken for one of the foure principall vertues, and so is she a habit, whereby is knowne what is just, and the same is accordingly desired and done. This is that incorrupted virgin, which the auncients so termed, because she is such a friend to bashfulnes and modesty, by which men are made worthy reverence, by which they learne the measure of distributions and commutations, giving recompence to vertue as much as it deserveth, not by equality of number, but by equality of measure: to much vertue great reward, to meane vertue meaner recompence: and this is the Geometrical proportion which *Aristotle* speaks of. For where much desert is, though much be given, and lesse, where lesse is deserved, and the rewards compared together be unequall; yet as they have severally deserved, they are equally rewarded. With some example we shall make the thing more plaine. Suppose her be two vessels, the one greater then the other, and that you fill them both with wine or other liquor, the lesser shall nevertheles be as well full as the greater: and if they both had speech and understanding, neither could the one complaine for having too much, nor the other too little, both being full according to their capacitie, and so receiving his due. In this sort doth Justice distribute to every one that which is his due. She produceth lawes, by which vertue is rewarded, and vice punished. She correcteth faults and errours according to their equalitie. She setteth us in the direct way that leadeth to felicitie. She teacheth rulers and magistrates to commaund, and subjects to obey: and therefore she is the true rule which sheweth the inferiour powers and faculties of the soule how to obey Reason as their Queene and mistris. Which commaund of Reason, *Plotinus* esteemed to be so important to be exercised over the passions, as he esteemed them only to be worthily called wise men, who subjected their passions in such sort to reason, that they should never arise to oppose themselves against her. She instructeth man to rule, not onely himselfe, but his wife, his children, and his family also. She preserveth and maintaineth States and Common-weales, by setting an even course of cariage betweene Princes and their subjects. She maketh men understand, how the doing of injury is contrary to the nature of man, who is borne to be mild, benigne & gentle; and not to be (as wild beasts are) furious, fierce and cruel: for such they are that hurt others wittingly. And when injuries happen to be done, she distinguisheth them, she seeketh to make them equall, or to diminish them, or to take them cleane away: evermore teaching us this lesson, that it is better to receive an injury then to do it. It is she that maketh those things that are severally produced for the good of sundry nations, common to all, by the meane of commutation, of buying and selling, and having invented coine, hath set it to be a law, or rather a judge in cases of inequalitie, to see that every man have his due and no more. Finally she tempereth with equitie (which may be termed a kind of clemency joyned to justice) things severely established by law, to the end that exact justice may not prove to be exact wrong. And where as lawes not tempered by discreet Judges, are like tyrants over men: this equitie was held by *Plato* to be of such importance, that when the *Arcadians* sent unto him, desiring him to set them downe lawes to be ruled by, he understanding that they were a people not capable of equitie, refused flatly to make them any lawes at all. *Agesilaus* said, that to be too just, was not onely farre from humanitie, but even crueltie it self. And *Trajan* the Emperor wished Princes to link equitie & justice together, saying, that dominions were otherwise inhumanely governed. The Ægyptians also to shew that lawes are to be administred with equitie, expressed justice in their *Hieroglifikes* by a left hand open, meaning, that as the left hand is slower and weaker then the right: so that justice ought to be advisedly administred, and not with force or fury. And the opinion of some was, that the axes and rods which were accustomably borne before the Romane Consuls, were bound about with bands; to declare, that as there must be a time to unbind the axes before they could be used to the death of any man: so ought there to be a time to deliberate for them that execute the law; wherein they may consider whether that which the rigor of law commaundeth may not without impeachment of Justice be tempered and reduced to benignitie and equitie. To conclude, Justice is she that maintaineth common utilitie, that giveth the rule, the order, the measure and manner of all things both publike and private, the band of humane conversation and friendship. She it is that maketh man resemble God, and so farre extendeth her power in the conjunction of mens minds, that she not onely knitteth honest men together in civill societie, but even wicked men and theeves, whose companies could not continue, if among their injustices Justice had not some place. She is of so rare goodnesse and sinceritie, that she maketh man, not onely to abstaine from taking anothers goods, but also from coveting the same.

Indeed (said M. *Dormer*) if Justice be such a vertue as you have described, me thinke that we have smal need of other vertues; for she comprehendeth them all within her selfe.

So doth she (answered I) if she be generally considered as before hath bin said. But if we call her to the company of the other vertues, as here we place her, she hath as much need of them as they of her, if she shall produce those effects which we have spoken of. For as one vice draweth another after it, as do the linkes of a chaine the one the other: even so are the vertues much more happily linked together in such sort as they cannot be severed. But though a man be endued with them all, yet is he called a just man, a valiant, a prudent, or a temperate man, according as he inclineth more to this then to that, or in his actions maketh more shew of the one then of the other: for our naturall imperfection wil not suffer any one man to excel in them all; which made me say a while sithens, that it is so hard a thing to be magnanimous, since the vertue of Magnanimity must be grounded upon all the rest. But to excell in justice, is a thing most glorious; for it is said of her, that neither the morning starre nor the evening star shineth as she doth. And *Hesiodus* called her the daughter of *Jupiter*. Wherupon *Plato* supposing, that who so embraced Justice contracted parentage with *Jupiter* the King of Gods and men, accounted the just man had gotten a place very neere unto God.

Verily (said M. *Dormer*) and not without cause. For it behoveth him that will be just to be voide of all vice, and furnished with all other vertues. And therefore me thinketh, he that said Justice might wel be without Prudence, considered ill what belonged to Justice. For Prudence is most necessary to discerne what is just from what is unjust; and a good judgment therin can no man have that wanteth Prudence: without which judgment, Justice can never rule wel those things that are under her government. And as *Agesilaus* said of Fortitude, so thinke I of Justice, that if she be not guided by Prudence (which is aptly called the eie of the mind) she works more harme then good.

You thinke truly (said I) and of this vertue the course of our author draweth me to treate, & to declare of what importance she is to humane things, and how beneficial. But let me first put you in mind that hitherto hath bin spoken but of those vertues which have their foundation in the unreasonable parts of the mind: of which mind they are the habits, consisting in the meane betwixt two extremes, and busied about the affects & actions of men. Likewise hath bin declared how the affects come from the powers or appetites of the soule, to wit, the concupiscible and the irascible, and how all commendable actions proceed from election, before which Counsell must go. And albeit we made mention there of Prudence, yet it was then referred to a fitter place to talke thereof more largely, when the drift of our discourse should bring us thither. Now therefore being come to that place which is proper to her, I am to speake of therof. But before I proceed any further, you must understand that there be two sorts of vertues: for some are morall, concerning manners, of which we have discoursed hitherto, and shewed how they are grounded in those parts of the mind that are devoide of reason. Others are of the mind or understanding, in which respect they are called Intellective; and of them henceforth must be our speech. But you must remember, that though it was said, that those morall vertues were founded in those parts of the mind wanting reason, yet were they guided by the light of reason. And this light of reason (as much as concerneth mens actions) is nothing else but Prudence, which is a vertue of the understanding, and the rule and measure of all the morall vertues concerning our actions and affects: even as sapience or wisedome is the guide and governesse of speculation. And forsomuch as reason is capable of two intellective vertues, whereof the one is active, and the other speculative, this latter intendeth alwaies the knowledge of truth: & the first is busied about the knowledge of what is good. Which good, when it is come to the height of his perfection in our actions, is the end of them; and then have we attained that furthest and absolute terme or bound, unto which we have directed all our civill actions. Hereupon *Plotinus* said, that there were in us two principles or originall causes of doing; whereof the one is the mind, which cals us to contemplation: the other is reason, guiding us to civill actions; and from her doth that which is good & faire never depart. And though it may be objected, that both these intellective vertues are exercised in or about the knowledge of truth, as indeed they be; yet is it to be advertised,[59] that it is in divers respects that they be so exercised. For that part which is exercised in contemplation, is busied about truth simply; that is to say, about those things that never change, and are alwayes the same; as God first of all; then all the universall things which nature hath produced: about which Prudence hath nothing to do to busie her selfe, because they are not subject to mans counsell, nor to his election: and of such things properly is truth the subject: which truth (as *Plato* said) is the guide to lead men to al goodnes. But Prudence worketh properly about such things as are subject to change; and may be & not be; may be done or not done; and (when al is said) are fortunable: of which there is no certaine and infallible truth, as is of things eternall. Nevertheles Prudence in this inconstancie of things sensible, seeketh alwayes to apply it self to that which is most likely to happen, and doth seeme most probable to the discourse of reason. And this also is that truth about which she discourseth, seeking still to chuse that which is or seemeth to her best and most faire. Without Prudence can no vertuous operation be brought to passe. For she onely foreseeth and knoweth what is convenient and seemely: and withholdeth a man at all times from vice or any voluntary wicked action: so that he that is not honest cannot be prudent. It is neither art nor science, but an habit of the mind, never severed from reason, in the discoursing of those things about which man is to use reason, for private or publike benefit. So as it may well be said, that in respect of the subject it is all one with that science which is called Civil: but in respect of the reason of the one & of the other, they be different. For Prudence is in the prudent man principally for his privat good and profit, and next for the publike weale: but the civil or politike man considereth that which is profitable to the Common-wealth. And though both be busied about the benefit of mankind according to reason, yet so farre forth as the prudent man respecteth his privat good, it is called in him Prudence. But when it is applied to the universal commoditie of the Commonweal, it is called the civil facultie or science. Which facultie without prudence wil be of smal effect in government: the rule wherof it fetcheth from Temperance, which is called the preserver of Prudence. Nevertheles the prudent man may at

187

once provide both for his private affaires & for the publike, though his office be rather to command others to execute things then to do himself. And albeit in that point *Socrates* was deceived, saying that Prudence was all the vertues together, yet is she so inseparable a companion unto them all, as if she be taken from them, they remaine of smal valew or effect. The office of this vertue, is to consider what is profitable, and to apprehend it: and likewise to eschew all that is hurtful. And to discourse of things sensible and usuall, thereby to shew what is fit to be chosen, and what to be forsaken. In regard wherof *Plato* said that Prudence guided us to happines of life, and imprudence made us miserable and unhappie: affirming that she onely directed us to do all our affaires wel, yea & to know our selves. Among the representations of vertues, Prudence is commonly set with a looking-glas in her hand: which by all likelihood is done to give us to understand, that as the glasse being cleere sheweth a man his face; so Prudence wel used shewes to him himself, making him to know what he is, and to what end created. The knowledge wherof works in him, that as he travels to attain for himself profit & goodnes; so acknowledging himselfe to be borne for the good also of others, endevoreth to direct the affaires also of his parents, friends and Common-weale to the same end of profit & goodnes. Now although it hath bin said, that Prudence is a science of good and evil, yet is it to be understood that she is not properly termed a science; but is (as was said even now) so far from it, that she is busied about things casual which may happen and not happen, wherof there can be no certaine science: wheras Science laboreth about things certaine & eternal. Prudence considereth what is profitable & good; Science searcheth out truth simply. And as these two be different the one from the other: so is there difference between the wise man & the prudent. For the wise man being stil busied about the causes of things, and the marvellous effects which they produce by the meanes of Gods goodnes, is as it were out of the world, litle respecting any profit, which the prudent hath still regard unto. For the wise man hath his mind alwaies raised to the contemplation of sublime things, whereby these baser of the earth seeme to him worthy no estimation, the rather because he knoweth right well that nature hath need of very little to sustaine her. And although *Plato* say that those men are called wise, who by the light of reason, know what is profitable, not onely for themselves and particular persons, but generally for the commonweale, he there useth the name of a wise man according to the common maner of speech, and not properly. But that you may the better understand my authors meaning, you must give me leave to enlarge a litle the ground of this his distinction. You are therfore to consider, that there be three several things in us, to wit, sense and feeling, understanding and appetite. Of which the first is the beginning of no action properly, because it is common to us with brute beasts, who are not said to do any action, for that they want judgement and election. The appetite, so farre forth as it is obedient to reason, either followeth or eschueth things presented thereunto: and in this part Counsell hath place and election, as hath bin formerly said: which election is the inducement to action, for thereby we worke either good or evil; and it is provoked by the appetite, though reason brideling the concupiscible desire be the minister of good election. But the understanding stretcheth furder then so. For it travels about things eternal, necessary, and so true as they never change, nor can be any other then as by nature they have bin framed. But it is busied about this truth two manner of wayes; for either it seeketh the knowledge of principles, from whence true conclusions are drawne; or else of principles that be the origine of things. If we consider the understanding according to the first manner, it breedeth science in us, which commeth from the knowledge of true principles, which are the grounds of true conclusions. And in this sort do we know all things naturall and corporall, yet eternall and immutable, as causes naturall, nature her selfe, time, place, the elements, heaven, the first mover, so farre forth as he is applied to a moveable body (for so far forth as he is a simple substance, unmoveable, indivisible, free from all change: and as he is alone by him selfe infinite, neither body, nor vertue contained in a bodie, the first of all things naturally moved, yea before the matter it selfe, & al other the properties attributed to that simple, pure and divine nature, it is a thing not appertaining to the naturall Philosopher to treate of him) and generally all other things natural. But taking the understanding according to the second way, it raiseth us up to the knowledge of that divine power, from which all things great and small, mortall and immortall, have their beginning: and this knowledge is called wisedome: which, together with vertue, we attaine by the meanes of Philosophie, the onely school-mistris of humane and divine learning, and the true guide to commendable life and vertuous actions, being indeed the greatest gift that God giveth to man in this transitory life. Now as these vertues before specified direct us to that perfectest end that man in this world can attaine unto by his vertuous deeds: so doth this habit, called wisedome, conduct him to a farre more excellent end then this civill or politike end. And if that which vertue guideth us unto, be worthy to be called perfect in this world, this other (which wisedome leadeth us unto) may well be termed most perfect: because this divine habit addresseth us to the knowledge of the most pure, simple, and excellentest nature, which is God eternall and immortall, the fountaine of all goodnesse, and infallible truth, the onely and absolute rest and quiet of our soules & minds. For which cause *Plato* said, that humane things, if they were compared to divine, were unworthy the employing any study in them, as being of no price or estimation at all: for they are rather shadowes of things then things indeed, evermore fleeting and slippery, as dayly experience teacheth us. But being as we are among men, and set to live and converse with them civilly, the civill man must not give himself to contemplation, to stay upon it as wisedome would perswade him, untill he have first employed his wit and prudence to the good and profit as well of others as of himselfe. Giving them to understand, how man is the perfection of all creatures under heaven, and placed as the center betweene things divine and mortall: and shewing to them how great is the perfection of mans mind, make them know how unworthy & unfit it is for a man to suffer those parts that he hath common with brute beasts to master and over-rule those by which he is made not much inferiour to divine creatures: and causing them to lift up their minds to this consideration, instruct them so to dispose and rule through vertuous habits those parts which of themselves are rebellious to reason, as they may be forced to obey her no otherwise then their Queene and mistris: and through Fortitude, Temperance, Justice, and Prudence, with the rest of the vertues that spring from them, frame their behaviour, and direct all their actions to that end which we have intituled by the name of civill felicitie, to wit, that perfect action or operation according to vertue in a perfect life, whereof hath formerly bin largely discoursed. Which felicitie once attained, is of that nature, that no man which is possessed thereof can become miserable or unhappie. For vice only can reduce man to be miserable, and that is evermore banished from felicitie, whose conversation is onely with vertue: to whom she is so fast linked and tied in the mind of man, that he hath no power to dissolve or sever the same. And this felicitie is not only a degree, but even the very foundation of that other, which we may attaine by the meane of wisedome. For after we have once setled and grounded our selves in the morall vertues, and done well in respect of our selves, and also holpen others as much as we could, we may then raise our thoughts to a higher consideration, and examining more inwardly our owne estate, find that this most excellent gift of understanding hath bin given us to a further end and purpose then this humane felicitie: and therfore bend all our wits to a better use of our selves, which is to take the way of that other felicitie, so to place our selves, not onely above the ordinary ranke of men, but even to approch (as neere as our frailtie will permit) to God himselfe, the last end of all our thoughts and actions. From this perfect knowledge of our selves we ascend by degrees to such a height, as leaving all worldly cares, we apply al our studies to the searching of divine things, to the end that by attaining the understanding and knowledge of our maker, and the Creator of all things, we may plainely discerne that whatsoever is here among us on earth, is but smoke and dust: and that to be even glutted with all the good that this life can affoord, is but a possession of smoke, and a shadow of the true good which is above. And so knowing that the mind is the true man, given unto us of speciall grace to guide the body, we may turne our selves to that happinesse which maketh us immortal, by raising the mind to the height of that heavenly felicitie: the sweetnesse and delight whereof, is so much greater then that of humane felicitie, (though without this the other cannot be) as the habit of that excellent power of the vertue intellective, is employed about a more noble object, then that which the vertue active doth intend. For it is evermore busied about things eternall and universall, and about the contemplation of the most high and gracious God. Of this excellent degree of felicitie hath *Aristotle* spoken in his first and tenth books of Ethikes, declaring how it ought to be the finall end of all our operations, and hath attributed this excellent kind of faculty to those men only who are properly called Sages or wise men: because they, by the meanes of actions and of sciences, finding that these mortall things are not able to bring a man to full and perfect happinesse, do so raise themselves from these baser cogitations, as they apply their mind and understanding wholy to the knowledge of divine essences. And such men (saith he) as have attained that degree, are rather to be esteemed divine then humane. For whiles they live in contemplation, they are not like men living among men, composed of body and soule, but as divine creatures freed from mortall affections arising from the body, and bent onely to that which may purchase the never-ending felicitie of the soule; which according to *Plato* and *Aristotle*, is the true man. And to this opinion did our Saviour Christ (who is the infallible veritie) give authoritie and confirmation, when he said, that we ought to have such care of that soule which is in us according to the image of God, that we should esteeme nothing (how great or precious soever the world esteemed it) at so high a rate, as for the purchasing thereof we should hurt or loose the same: for his words are, *What availeth it a man to gaine all the world and loose his owne soule?*[60] By this opinion of these two Philosophers, we may plainly understand, that even in that darknesse of auncient superstition, God had yet given such light of reason to the mindes of men to illumine them withall, that they saw how through sciences and wisedome they were to seeke the way that should leade them to their perfect felicitie, that is, to God Almightie himselfe, who is such an end as no other end can be supposed beyond him; but to him all other ends are directed, as to the true and most happie terme, bound or limit of all vertues and vertuous actions, and of civill felicitie it selfe. But because that divine part of the Intellective soule which is in us, is to have consideration not onely of our present state of life, but also to that eternitie, wherein our immortall mindes, made to the likenesse of God, are to live with him eternally. Therfore did *Aristotle* fitly teach, that men ought to bend and frame their minds wholy to that true and absolute end: for that the minde being divine, it is his proper office to seeke to unite it selfe to his first principle or beginning, which is God. Neither hath his divine Majestie of his aboundant grace bestowed the vertue intellective upon man to any other end, then that he might know it to be his speciall dutie to raise himselfe to him, as to the author

192

and free giver of all goodnesse: and as he hath bestowed on him a soule made to his own likenes, so he should therewith bend his endevour to be like him in all his actions, as farre as the corruption contracted by the communion of the bodie will permit. Which thing the *Platonikes* considering, have spoken much more largely thereof then *Aristotle*, following therein the steps of their master. But some will say, that *Aristotle* spake the lesse thereof, thinking that the soule of man, even concerning the understanding, was not immortall; because it seemeth to them, that when the soule hath no more the senses of the bodie to serve her as instruments whereby she understandeth and knoweth, she should no longer live. For since nature cannot suffer any thing to be idle in the world, and the soule wanting the bodie can have no operation, therefore they thinke it is to be concluded, that with the bodie she must needs fall and die: for that if she should happen to remaine after she were separated from the bodie, yet she should not have any operation, insomuch as having the understanding for her proper operation, and seeing she cannot understand but by the ministery of the senses, from which she can have no helpe when she is loosed from the bodie, it followeth that she hath no operation, and then must she be idle in nature, which is in no sort to be allowed. But my author (as afore is said) doth thinke, that these men mistake *Aristotle*, not considering that he, speaking as a natural Philosopher of the soule, was not to treate thereof but naturally; and in so doing, was to restraine himselfe within the bounds of nature: according to which, he is not to consider any forme separate from the matter, from which we (as all other natural things) have our bodies. This *Aristotle* considering and knowing, that as a natural Philosopher he was not to speake of the Intellective soule, said, that understanding being separated from the other powers of the minde, as a thing eternall, severed from the corruptible part, it appertained not to him to treate thereof in that place, where he spake of the soule as she was the actor of the bodie, and used it as her instrument. For he saw wel inough, that though the understanding tooke beginning with the bodie, because it was the forme thereof; yet was it not the actor of the body, so as it should use any member thereof as an instrument: but was onely a forme that was to exercise all the other powers of the other soules. For it is likewise *Aristotles* opinion, that where the understanding is in things corruptible, there

193

hath it also the faculties of all the other soules within it selfe. Which thing he shewed more cleerely in his first booke *de Partibus Animalium*, saying, that to speake of the Intellective soule all that might be sayd, was not the office of a naturall Philosopher. And this for two reasons. The one is, that the Intellective soule is no actor of the bodie, because she hath in her no part of motion, either of her selfe, or accidentally. For she neither increaseth nor diminisheth the bodie, she nourisheth it not, nor maintaineth it; for these are functions appertaining to the vegetative soule; shee chaungeth it not, nor mooveth it from place to place; for that is the office of the sensitive soule: and these be the motions which the bodie can have from the soule (saving generation and corruption, which are changes made in an instant): therefore inasmuch as she is intellective, she is not subject to the consideration of the naturall Philosopher. The other reason is, for that the naturall Philosopher considereth not the substances separated from the matter, and therefore his office is not to consider the excellencie of the Intellective soule, which is not the actor of the bodie, though she be the forme thereof. And therefore *Aristotle* telleth us in his second booke of Physikes, that the terme or bound of the naturall Philosophers consideration, is the Intellective soule. For albeit he may consider the soule so farre as she moveth and is not moved; as he may also the first mover: yet doth he not consider her essence, nor the essence of the first mover: for this appertaineth to the Metaphysike, who considereth of the substances separated and immortall. And hence commeth it that *Aristotle* treating in his booke of Physikes of nature, as she is the beginning of all movings and of rest; when he is come to the first mover who is immoveable, yet moveth all that is moved in the world, proceeded not any further to shew his nature: understanding right well, that the naturall Philosophers office was not, to consider any thing that is simply immoveable, as well in respect of the whole, as of the parts, as the first mover is. But let us (without questioning further thereupon) hold this for certaine, not onely by that which Christian Religion teacheth us, but also by that which *Aristotle* hath held, that our soules are immortall. For if it were otherwise, we should be of all other creatures that nature produceth the most unhappie: and in vaine should that desire of immortalitie (which all men have) be given unto us. Besides that, man, as man, that is to say, as a creature intellective, should not have that end which is ordained for him, which is contemplative felicitie. Neither is it to the purpose to say, that such felicitie is not attained by morall vertues, but by wisedome only, or that there be but few so wise as to seek this excellent felicitie, and infinite the number of those that thinke but little upon it: for all men are borne apt unto it, if they will apply their minds unto the same. And though among all generations of men there should be but three or foure that bent their endevour to attaine it, they onely were sufficient to prove our intention, because it is most certaine, that the number of foolish men is infinite, who not knowing themselves, cannot tell how to use themselves, & direct their endevours to that which is the proper end of man. Of whom it is said, *People on whom night commeth before Sunne-set*. A wicked generation, whose whole life-time flieth from them unprofitably, in such sort, as they can scarce perceive that they have lived. For although there be infinitely more such in this world then of quicke and elevated spirits, yet ought not we to endure, that their negligence, who know not themselves to be men, should prejudice the mindes of such as know what they are, and raise their thoughts carefully to divine things. And therefore leaving their opinions that will needs say, that *Aristotle* impiously and madly hath held the contrary, it shall be best to proceed in our discourse of the felicitie that is to be attained by contemplation.

I pray you (said Captaine *Carleil*) since there is a contrarietie of opinions among Philosophers, concerning the immortalitie of the soule, and that the knowledge therof appertaineth to the better understanding of this contemplative felicitie, let us heare, if your author give any furder light thereunto, since such good fellowes seeke to cast so darke a mist before our eyes, under the cloke of *Aristotles* opinion. For albeit you spake somewhat of it yesterday, so farre as concerned our maner of learning according to *Aristotle*, yet was it but by the way, and not as it concerned this felicitie: and if such a matter as this were twise repeated, it could not but be profitable to us, though it be somewhat troublesome to you.

Whereupon I said: that which my author was not willing to undertake, you presse me unto, as if you were the same persons, and had the same sence that those introduced by him had: and therefore since you also will have it so, I am content to close up this your feast with this last dish; notwithstanding that the evening draw on, and that to speake thereof at large would aske a long time. But knitting up, as well as I can, a great volume in a little roome, I will deliver unto you that which the shortnesse of our time wil permit, and pray with mine author his divine Majestie, who hath given us an immortall soule, that he wil vouchsafe us his grace to say so much and no more of this matter, as may be to his glory, and to all our comforts. Know ye then that these men, that out of *Aristotles* writings gather our intellective soule to be mortall, take for their foundation and ground this; that the soule is the actor of the bodie, and useth it but after the maner before mentioned. And to maintaine this their opinion, they wrest divers places of his untruly, and contrary to the mind of this great Philosopher, as shall be declared unto you. True it is, that while the intellective soule is the forme of the body, she hath some need of him to understand. For without the fantasie[61] we can understand nothing in this life, since from the senses the formes of all things are represented unto us, as yesterday was declared. And this did *Aristotle* meane to teach us, when contrary to the opinion of some former Philosophers he said, that sense and understanding was not all one, although there be some similitude betweene them. And because the essences of things are knowne by their operations, according to *Aristotle*; and that the intellective soule understandeth (which is a spiritual operation;) it followeth that simply of her owne nature she is all spirit, and therefore immortall, for else to understand, would not be her propertie. Whereunto also *Aristotle* agreeth, in saying, that some parts of the soule are not conjoyned to the bodie, and therfore are separable: and that the understanding and the contemplative power was another kind of soule, and not drawne from the power of matter, as the other two are, whose operations were ordained for the Intellective soule, insomuch as she is the forme of the bodie: which sheweth plainely that she is eternall and immortall. And in the twelfth of his Metaphysikes, making a doubt, whether any forme remaine after the extinguishing of the matter, he sayd doubtfully of the other two, that not every soule, but the Intellective onely remained. And here is to be noted, that his opinion was not (though some would have it so) that the fantasie was the forme of the bodie, for that dieth with the bodie, as shall be shewed hereafter: but he considered the understanding it selfe, as a soule, and as the

196

forme of the bodie; and not as a separable intelligence, the lowest of all others, and common to all men, as *Theophrastus* and *Themistius* (though diversly) have thought. Neither yet that it was God Almightie, as *Alexander* supposeth: for God is not the forme of our bodies, nor hath any man ever doubted whether God were immortall. So as our understanding is neither God, nor yet a separate intelligence, common to all men, like those that governe an universal spheare, as they above mentioned have thought, & as some of our Christians have dreamed; who being raised to Ecclesiasticall dignitie, have chosen rather to follow the Greeks vanity and the Arabians, then favour the religious and true interpreters of *Aristotles* mind. Whereas they ought rather to have rooted such opinions out of mens mindes, as apt to draw them to perdition, and not to maske them with the vizard of naturall Philosophers: as if things naturall, that may seeme contrary to Christianitie, were to be set before men in writing, to be confirmed by naturall reasons apparant at least, though not true, to perswade their mindes amisse. But *Johannes Gramaticus* among the Greekes hath declared *Aristotles* mind aright; and so hath he that is called the Angelicall Doctour in sundry places as a most excellent spirit and a religious man, whatsoever *Scotus* write against him. And what better testimonie neede we have of the vanitie of these mens interpretations, then *Aristotle* himselfe? who most effectually sheweth the same, where he sayth, that the waxing old of man proceedeth not from the Intellective soule, but from the bodie wherein she is (which neverthelesse is to be understood as she is the forme thereof:) and in so saying, declareth, that every man hath his Intellective soule: which soule is a meane betwixt separated substances and corporall; and therefore partly she communicateth with the bodie to informe the same, and partly she useth (as proper to her) the vertue of the separated substances (as much as her nature may beare) in the use of understanding. And since it is cleere, that in nature the most perfect things containe the lesse perfect, I cannot conceive from whence proceedeth the frensie of these men, that will rather draw the soule Intellective to be mortall then immortall; seeing that to understand is the most singular operation that the soule hath, and to whom the powers of the other soules are referred, as to the better end, and obey as hand-maides to their mistresse, in such as propose to themselves to live like men. Neither doth the

197

reason alledged by some serve, who say, that because there is great imperfection in the Intellective soule in comparison of the separate intelligences, it sheweth the same to be mortall. For if this reason were true, they might as well by the same conclude, that the separate intelligences were also mortall. For since *Aristotle* sayth, that onely the first intelligence (who in his phrase is the first mover) is perfect; and that all the other compared to him are unperfect, (imperfection being in these mens fancie the cause of mortalnesse) it must follow, that as imperfect, they should be mortall: which is as contrary to *Aristotles* mind, as any thing can be. Wherefore we must not say, that imperfection in the intellective soule (in respect of the intelligences separated) causeth the same to die with the bodie, since her office dependeth not on the bodie: but it is onely to be sayd, that she ceaseth to informe the bodie through the defect thereof, & not of her self; who being freed from the bodie, remaineth neverthelesse perfect in her being. For albeit she have some respect to the bodie whiles she informeth the same, yet hath she not her absolute being from it. And therefore sayd *Aristotle*, that the vertue of the sense is not equall to the vertue of the understanding; for that a mightie or strong Sensible, weakeneth, and oftentimes corrupteth the sense; whereas from an excellent Intelligible, the understanding gathereth greater vertue: which thing could not be sayd, if the understanding were as these people suppose, a separate intelligence, wherof the particulars did participate. Wherefore we must needs say he meant of the understanding of every particular man, as of the forme of this man, and that man: for he spake of the understanding of particular men, and not of intelligences, as those men have belike dreamed. And this sheweth (howsoever any thinke the contrary) that as well the Agent understanding and the possible also (whereof this is ordained as matter to that, and both necessary to understand) are essential parts of the soule, and not two separate intelligences, as *Themistius* would have them. The reason likewise which some alledge, is not good, when they argue, that the soule being the forme of the bodie, should ever have a desire, after she were separated from the same, to reunite her selfe againe thereunto: but the bodie being rotten and corrupted, her desire in that behalfe should be vaine. For I say, that since the soule hath informed the body, she hath done as much as to her appertained, neither is she to desire any further (to speake naturally) then she hath accomplished: and therefore she remaineth as a separate intelligence. Which hath made the Peripatetikes to affirme, that the soule separated from the bodie, is not the same that she was, when she was in the bodie; because that joyned to the bodie she was the forme thereof, but separated she can no more be so. But this difficultie, which naturall Philosophers have not knowne how to resolve as they ought, our blessed Saviour the Sonne of God hath fully resolved, by rising againe the third day (not to say any thing of others raised by him) and promising to us the like resurrection.

This (said my Lord Primate) all true Christians beleeve: but since we are debating of *Aristotles* opinions, where he saith, that the passible understanding dieth, and some of his Interpreters say, that it is the possible understanding, how shall we make this to agree with the immortalitie of the soule?

Well inough (sayd I:) for they that so interpret him deceive themselves: for there is as great difference (as *Aristotle* himselfe teacheth) betweene the passible soule and the possible soule, as betweene that which is eternall and that which is corruptible. The passible understanding according to *Aristotle* is the fantasie, or the imaginative or cogitative power, call it how you please, the which *Averroes* sayd was taken at large, but not properly for the understanding; and as an inward sense depending upon the bodie, receiveth the sensible kindes from the common sense, and presenteth them to the possible understanding, which is the place of the intelligible kindes or formes, as *Aristotle* in sundrie places declareth. And who so shall well consider *Themistius*, where he speaketh of the multiplication of the understanding, shall finde that he supposed it not as our Christian writers doe, but tooke the vertue fantastike for the understanding, multiplied in particular persons. And therefore she being mingled with the bodie, faileth also with the same: and this is that interiour thing which *Aristotle* saith is corrupted, whereby the understanding loseth his vertue (as shall be shewed) which happeneth not to the possible understanding, because it is an essentiall part of the Intellective soule, not mingled with the bodie, and free from any passion, as a divine substance. Of which bodie she useth no part for her instrument to understand, though she have neede of the fantasie to receive the Intelligible formes whiles she is the forme of the bodie. And this necessitie, which the understanding hath of the

199

fantasie to understand, sheweth the contrarie of that which these fellowes inferre, who hold the understanding to be mortall in that respect. For by this it appeareth, that the understanding proceedeth not from the power of the matter: for if so it were, it should have no neede of the fantasie, but should it selfe be the fantasie: and therefore *Aristotle* right well perceiving that our understanding was not fantasie, nor used anie part of the body for an instrument, sayd, that the understanding came from abroad, as shall be declared. It is therefore no good consequence to say, that because the possible soule dieth, therefore the possible soule likewise is mortall.

Yea but (said M. *Spenser*) we have from *Aristotle*, that the possible understanding suffreth in the act of understanding; and to suffer importeth corruption; by which reason it should be mortall as is the passible.

Neither is that reason (quoth I) sufficient: for although the name of suffering agree with the possible understanding, and with the passible (leaving the difference betweene *Alexander* and *Aristotle* in that point) the reason and manner in them is different. For the suffering of the possible understanding tendeth to the destruction thereof, whereas the suffering of the possible is to the greater perfection of the same. And for this cause *Aristotle* telleth us, that the suffering of the senses, and that of the understanding are not both of one nature: because the first breedes destruction, and the latter perfection; and that therefore an excellent Intelligible giveth perfection to the understanding, whereas an excellent Sensible corrupteth the sense. But not having any other word meete to expresse this suffering of the understanding, whiles it is in that act, we use the same that agreeth to the passible, though the reason of them both be verie diverse. The possible understanding (as hath bene sayd alreadie) being the place of the Intelligible formes, standeth in respect of the Agent understanding, as the matter in respect of the forme: for the first is but in power (for which respect *Averroes* called it the materiall understanding:) and this later is in act. And this Agent understanding, by illumining the formes which are in him as blind (even as colours are in things before they be made apparent to the eye by the illumination of light) understandeth the kinds of things, and understanding them understandeth it selfe. For in spirituall things, that which understandeth and that which is understood, become all one thing: and turning it selfe about the universall kinds, understandeth withall, things particular. And this is that which the possible understanding suffereth from the Agent, receiving thereby that perfection which you have heard.

Why (said Maister *Spenser*) doth it not seeme, that *Aristotle* when he saith, that after death we have no memorie, that he meant that this our understanding was mortall? For if it were not so, man should not lose the remembrance of things done in this life.

Nay (answered I) what a sillie part had it bene of *Aristotle* rather, if he had thought the intellective soule to be mortall, to say that we remembred nothing after this life, when nothing of us should have remained? And therefore it may serve to prove the immortalitie of the soule, and not the corruption, as you surmise (onely for arguments sake) that truth may be sifted out. But our not remembring then, commeth from the corruptible part, which is the vertue of the fantasie: which being a power of the sensitive soule, that keepeth in store the remembrance of materiall things, that vertue which should represent them failing in us, we cannot remember them after death. For the memorie is no part of the understanding, but of the sensitive soule: and therefore *Aristotle* said, that memorie came from sense, insomuch as creatures wanting reason have memorie, though they have not rememorating as man hath: for thereto is discourse required; which according to *Aristotle* is nothing else but an action of the understanding in the vertue imaginative. Which thing neither in those creatures devoid of reason, nor yet in separated intelligences can have place, because those want discourse, and these are pure acts (as Philosophers call them.)

Doth not *Aristotle* (sayd my Lord Primate) in his Ethikes say, that the contentments and the troubles of those which live, appertaine unto the dead, and breede them griefe or delight? And how is it then that he should say, we have no memorie after this life?

Aristotle in that place (sayd I) spake in reproofe of *Solon*, who had sayd, that no man could be accounted happie till after his death: and meant there to shew, that although it were graunted that man had memorie after his death, of things done in this life, yet could he not be happie when he was dead, by reason of the strange accidents which this life bringeth foorth: and therefore he said not simply that we remember; but that supposing we did, yet could we not be happie when we were dead, so making good his opinion against *Solon* by naturall reason.

Yet (sayd Maister *Spenser*) let me aske you this question; if the understanding be immortall, and multiplied still to the number of all the men, that have bene, are, and shall be, how can it stand with that which *Aristotle* telleth us of multiplication, which (saith he) proceedeth from the matter; and things materiall are always corruptible?

Marrie (Sir said I) this is to be understood of materiall things, and not of Intelligible and spirituall, such as is the understanding. And that the understanding might remaine after the matter were gone, as the forme of the bodie, he hath (as before is said) declared in his Metaphysikes, affirming the Intellective soule to be perpetuall, though it be separated from the bodie, whose forme it was.

But how cometh it to passe (replied Maister *Spenser*) that the soule being immortall and impassible, yet by experience we see dayly, that she is troubled with Lethargies, Phrensies, Melancholie, drunkennesse, and such other passions, by which we see her overcome, and to be debarred from her office and function.

These (quoth I) are passions of the vertue cogitative, fantastike, or imaginative, called by *Aristotle* (as I have said alreadie) the passible understanding; and not of the Intellective soule. Which passible understanding being an inward sense, and therefore tyed to the bodie, feeleth the passions of the same; whereby it is offended, and cannot performe his office towards the other, but runneth into such inconveniences by reason of his infirmity, and for want of reasons direction. And whereas *Hippocrates* saith that they that being sicke in minde, and touched with anie corporall disease, have little or no feeling of paine; it sheweth plainely that it is as I have said. For if you marke it well, this word *feele* explaneth the whole, since feeling is a propertie of the Sensitive soule, and the understanding feeleth not. And in like manner are the words of *Aristotle* to be understood, where he saith, that such whose flesh is soft are apt to learne, and they that are melancholy to be wise. For that the Sensitive vertue taketh more easily the formes or kindes of things in such subjects according to their nature, and representeth them to the understanding, from whence knowledge and understanding proceedeth, as yesterday was sayd. And this happeneth not onely in these passions, but also in all other alterations, as of gladnesse, of sorow, of hope and of feare, with such like which appertaine not to the understanding, to which (sayd *Aristotle*) who would ascribe such affects, might as well say that the understanding layed bricke to build, or cast a loome to weave.

Why, (sayd M. *Spenser*) doth your author meane (as some have not sticked even in our dayes to affirme) that there are in us two severall soules, the one sensitive and mortall, and the other Intellective and Divine?

Nothing lesse (said I) for that I hold were manifest heresie as well in Philosophie as in Christianitie. For *Aristotle* teacheth us, that the Vegetative and Sensitive soule, or their powers, were in the soule Intellective, as the triangle is in the square: which could not be if the sensitive were separated from the Intellective. And speaking of the varietie of soules, and of their powers, he sayth, that the Sensitive could not be without the Vegetative, but that this latter might well be without the former: and that all the other vertues of all the three soules are in those creatures that have reason and understanding. It cannot therefore be sayd (according to *Aristotle*) that the Sensitive soule in man is severed from the Intellective. And because man participateth (as hath bene sayd) of all the three faculties of the soules, I see not why these fellowes that mention two, speake not of all three as well, seeing that in man are the operations of all three. For if they say that it sufficeth to speake of the Sensitive, by which man is a living creature, and containeth the Vegetative; why should they not as well say, that the Intellective alone includeth both the other? and then is there no need of severing at all. By which it may appeere, that this frantike opinion gathered from the Assirians, is not onely contrary to *Aristotle*, but to reason it selfe. For *Aristotle* saith, that all things have their being from their formes; and that in naturall things, the more perfect containe the lesse perfect, when the lesser is ordained for the more: and that therefore onely the Intellective soule which containeth within it the natures of both the others, is the onely and true forme of man, malgre[62] all such dolts as would have man to be (by reason of divers formes) both a brute and a reasonable creature, who seeke to set men astray from the right way with such fanaticall devices. Let us therefore conclude with *Aristotle*, that both the passible and the possible understandings are vertues of the Intellective soule, insomuch as she is the particular and proper forme of every man, and that as a humane soule she is everlasting, impassible, not mingled with the bodie, but severed from the same, simple and divine, not drawne from any power of matter, but infused into us from abroade, not ingendred by seede: which being once freed from the bodie (because nature admitteth nothing that is idle) is altogether bent and intent to contemplation, being then (as Philosophers call it) *actus purus*, a pure understanding, not needing the bodie either as an object, or as a subject. In consideration whereof *Aristotle* sayd, that man through contemplation became divine; and that the true man (which both he and his divine master agreed to be the minde) did enjoy thereby (not as a mortall man living in the world, but as a divine creature) that high felicitie, to which, civill felicitie was ordained; and attained to wisedome & science, after the exercise of the morall vertues, as meanes to guide and conduct him to the same. And not impertinently have the Platonikes (following their master in that point) sayd, that nature had given us sense, not because we should stay thereupon, but to the end that thereby might grow in us imagination, from imagination discourse, from discourse intelligence, and from intelligence gladnesse unspeakable, which might raise us (as divine, and freed from the bands of the flesh) to the knowledge of God, who is the beginning and the end of all goodnesse, towards whom we ought with all endevour to lift up our minds, as to our chiefe and most perfect good: for he onely is our *summum bonum*. For to them it seemed that the man whom contemplation had raised to such a degree of felicitie, became all wholy understanding by that light which God imparteth to the spirits that are so purged through the exercise of morall vertues; which vertues are termed by *Plato* the purgers of the mind: stirring up therein a most ardent desire to forsake this mortall bodie, and to unite it selfe with him. And this is that contemplation of death which the Philosophie of *Plato* calleth us unto. For he that is come to this degree of perfection, is as dead to the world and worldly pleasures, because he considereth that God is the center of al perfections, & that about

204

him al our thoughts & desires are to be turned & employed. Such doth God draw unto himselfe, and afterwards maketh them partakers of his joyes everlasting: giving them in the meane while a most sweet tast even in this life of that other life most happie, and those exceeding delights, beyond which no desire can extend, nor yet reach unto the same. So as being full of this excellent felicitie, they thinke every minute of an houre to be a long time that debarreth them from issuing out of this mortall prison, to returne into their heavenly countrey; where, with that vertue which is proper to the soule alone, they may among the blessed spirits enjoy their maker: whose Majestie and power all the parts of the world declare, the heavens, the earth, the sea, the day, the night: whereat the infernall spirits tremble and shake; even as good men on earth bow downe and worship the same with continuall himnes and praises; and in heaven no lesse, all the orders and blessed companie of Saints and Angels do the like world without end.

This (loe) is as much as mine author hath discoursed upon this subject, which I have Englished for my exercise in both languages, and have at your intreaties communicated unto you: I will not say, being betrayed by M. *Spenser*, but surely cunningly thrust in, to take up this taske, whereby he might shift himselfe from that trouble. But howsoever it be, if it have liked you as it is, I shall thinke my time well spent, both in the translating of it at the first, and in the relating of it upon this occasion in this manner. For as I sayd before I began, that I would not tye my selfe to the strict lawes of an interpreter: so have I in some places omitted here and there haply some sentences (without which this our Discourse might be complete enough, because they are rather points of subtiller investigation then our speech required, though the Author therein perhaps aymed at the commendation of a great reader or absolute Philosopher:) and in the descriptions of some of the morall vertues, added somewhat out of others. And what hath beene sayd concerning civill felicitie by him, and delivered in substance by me, I thinke you will allow to be sufficient. Since therefore my taske is done, and that it groweth late, with this onely petition, that you will be content to beare with the roughnesse of my speech in reporting that unto you, which in his language our Author hath eloquently set downe, I end.

Here all the companie arose, and giving me great thankes, seemed to rest very well satisfied, as well with the manner as with the matter, at the least so of their courtesie they protested. And taking their leaves departed towards the Citie.

FINIS.

NOTES TO THE TEXT

1. Probably from Horace's *Ars Poetica*, 128–130.

2. *qui nobis haec otia fecit.* who has given us this leisure (Vergil, *Eclogues*, I, 6).

3. *instar multorum Judicum.* a substitute for many judges.

4. *geason.* uncommon.

5. *denizened.* v. denizen. To admit an alien to residence and rights of citizenship.

6. *foreslow.* To delay, impede.

7. *disple.* To discipline.

8. *Ellebore.* obs. Hellebore. A name once given to species of *Helleborus* and *Veratrum*, reputed as specifics for mental disease.

9. *Gravior . . . difficile.* For it is a more serious fault to desert clear principles than not to undertake them; for it is not difficult to undertake great things, but to persevere in them. (Probably from Cicero.)

10. *Posuêre in montibus urbem.* placed their city on the mountain (Vergil, *Aeneid*, VII, 53). *Gravior est culpa &c.* is the same phrase as on p. 12. *Habitabant vallibus imis.* they lived in the deepest valleys (Vergil, *Aeneid*, III, 110).

11. Plutarch, *Life of Aemilius Paulus*, V. Plutarch gives this anecdote of the divorce as anonymous; he quotes it only in connection with Aemilius.

12. *Virtutis laus, actio.* The praise for virtue, action (Cicero, *De Officiis*, II, 19; Cicero has *virtutis laus omnis in actione consistit*). *Non nobis . . . vendicant.* We have not been born for ourselves, our country, parents, and friends each claim a share for themselves (probably also from Cicero's *De Officiis*).

13. *Ne Hercules quidem contra duos.* Not even Hercules [could prevail] against two.

14. *controllers.* censorious critics.

15. *furbush.* furzen bush (?) *furze* is the popular name of the *ulex europaeus*, a spiny evergreen shrub with yellow flowers, growing abundantly on waste lands throughout Europe. This meaning of *furbush* seems to fit the context in Bryskett: " . . . he that shooteth at a starre, aimeth higher than he that shooteth at a furbush. . . ."

16. *marches.* boundaries, frontiers, borders.

17. *dandiprats.* small, insignificant, or contemptuous fellows, derived from perhaps the *dandiprat,* a small sixteenth century coin, worth three halfpence.

18. *venter.* v. vent, to let loose, wreak one's anger on a person or thing.

19. Virgil, *Aeneid,* V, 344–5. And the virtue that is more pleasing when found in a fair form.

20. Phocylides. *Elegaic Poems,* xiii.

$$\chi\rho\eta \ \pi\alpha\iota\delta' \ \check{\epsilon}\tau' \ \acute{\epsilon}\acute{o}\nu\tau\alpha$$
$$\kappa\alpha\lambda\alpha \ \delta\iota\delta\alpha\sigma\kappa\acute{\epsilon}\mu\epsilon\nu \ \check{\epsilon}\rho\tau\alpha.$$

[We should learn noble deeds when we are yet children.]

21. *over-curstly.* too strictly, i.e. overly severe as contrasted to over-fondly, too affectionate.

22. *wrawling.* making noise proper to cats at rutting time (from *caterwauling*).

23. *sithes and howes.* scythes and hoes.

24. *file.* defile.

25. *wan.* won.

26. *trucheman.* a truchman or interpreter, from medieval Latin *turchemanus,* Fr. *trucheman.*

27. *banket.* banquet. The context suggests here an obsolete meaning of banquet as a course of sweetmeats, fruit, and wine; a dessert.

28. *rerebanket.* literally a rear-banquet. See O.E.D. *reresupper*: a supper (usually of a sumptuous nature) following upon the usual evening meal, and thus coming very late at night.

29. *adhuc sub judice lis est.* The dispute is still before the judge (Horace, *Ars Poetica,* 78). *corpori omnino saluberrimum.* most healthful by far for the body. *coloris, odoris, and saporis.* color, bouquet, and flavor.

30. There may be a sly joke here: Bryskett was clerk of customs in wines, " a taster for the Queenes advantage."

31. *Ne quid nimis.* nothing in excess.

32. Horace, *Ars Poetica,* 161–165:

> imberbis iuvenis, tandem custode remoto,
> gaudet equis canibusque et aprici gramine Campi,
> cereus in vitium flecti, monitoribus asper,
> utilium tardus provisor, prodigus aeris,
> sublimis cupidusque et amata relinquere pernix.

[The beardless youth, freed at last from his tutor, finds joy in horses and hounds and the grass of the sunny Campus, soft as wax for moulding to evil, peevish with his counsellors, slow to make needful provision, lavish of money, spirited, of strong desires, but swift to change his fancies.]

33. Possibly Cicero, *Tusculanae Disputationes*.

34. *skim*. scum.

35. *coccle*. cockle, the English name of the bivalve molluscs.

36. *treatie*, treatment.

37. *Theodota*. Theodora.

38. Petrarch, *Rime Sparse*, CCCXXVII, lines 11–13:
> Dormit' ài, bella Donna, un breve sonno:
> or se' svegliata fra li spirti eletti,
> ove nel suo fattor l' alma s' interna; . . .

39. *delights*. Bryskett probably uses the plural here as an Englishing of *delices* (sensual or worldly pleasure). Spenser often uses the word this way.

40. Horace, *Epistles*, I, xvi, 52:
> oderunt peccare boni virtutis amore.
> tu nihil admittes in te formidine poenae:

41. Petrarch, *Rime Sparse*, LXVII, lines 9–11:
> Solo ov'io era, tra boschetti e colli,
> vergogna ebbi di me, ch' al cor gentile
> basta ben tanto, ed altro spron non volli.

42. *Lansknight and the Switzer*. *Lansknecht* or Lanceknights were one of a class of mercenary soldiers in the German and other armies of the sixteenth and seventeenth centuries; a rare use of the singular for the Swiss guards.

43. *meares*, mear(e), variant of *mare, mere*. a boundary.

44. *cesse*. Irish term: to impose soldiers upon a community, to be supported at a fixed rate.

45. *coynie*, derives from Irish *connemh*, billeting; *coynye, coignye* (v. tr.), to billet upon (also Irish).

46. *pupillage*. literally, pupil age; the condition of being a minor or ward; nonage, minority.

47. It is good . . . Primate. Bryskett inserted this original phrase.

48. *conster*. construe (formerly spelled and pronounced *conster*); to give the sense or meaning of, to interpret.

49. Ovid, *Metamorphoses*, I, 137–140:
> nec tantum segetes alimentaque debita dives
> poscebatur humus, sed itum est in viscera terrae,
> quasque recondiderat Stygiisque admoverat umbris,
> effodiuntur opes, inritamenta malorum.

[Not only did men demand of the bounteous fields the crops and sustenance they owed, but they delved as well into the very bowels of the earth; and the wealth which the creator had hidden away and buried deep amidst the very Stygian shades, was brought to light, wealth that pricks men on to crime.]

50. *cable*. a misprint for *camel*.

51. *adventer,* adventure, risk, venture.

52. Ovid, *Heroides*, IV, 89–90:

> quod caret alterna requie, durabile non est;
> haec reparat vires fessaque membra novat.

[That which lacks its alternations of repose will not endure; this is what repairs the strength and renews the wearied limbs.]

53. *contentation*. satisfaction, satisfied condition.

54. *at rode*. road: a sheltered piece of water near the shore where the vessel may lie at anchor in safety; a roadstead.

55. *demisse*. humble.

56. *Mansuetude,* gentleness, meekness (derived from Latin *mansuetus, mansuescere,* to tame).

57. *restie,* restive.

58. *vanting*. boasting, bragging (from *vaunt*).

59. *advertised*. to be generally known.

60. Mark, 8:36.

61. *fantasie*. Bryskett, on p. 199 states that "The possible understanding according to *Aristotle* is the fantasie, or the imaginative or cogitative power, call it how you please. . . ."

62. *malgre*. (*maugre, mauger, maulgre*) in spite of, despite; or *malgre* — as Spenser used it — a curse upon . . .

APPENDIX

This specimen is representative of the whole of the translated section in the *Discourse*; it consists of the first eleven sentences made by Bryskett in the opening of his translation of Giraldi in the first day's dialogue (see pp. 26–27 above). Bryskett follows his source fairly closely, even to the point of reproducing as far as it is possible in English Giraldi's syntax and punctuation; for instance the first four English sentences are almost grammatically parallel to Giraldi's structure. The omission of Giraldi's phrase in the sixth sentence, " & che sia opinione . . . pigliano non," is not an oversight. Here Bryskett may seem to be dodging the issue of the mother's role in the child's conception as raised by Giraldi, but Bryskett had an eye for tightening up his material by omitting to translate phrases or sentences whose sense was or would be presented elsewhere; this particular issue is discussed at the end of the third day's dialogue. Such omissions, however, are few. Instead, the accuracy of Bryskett's translation is notable in an age when paraphrase was generally looser, frequent omission and — at the other extreme — clumsy circumlocutions and doubling of phrases were acceptable. The quality of Bryskett's English is, then, quite high. He occasionally slips into making an opaque sentence (such as the long, too involved seventh sentence below), but even then one might recognize that the cause was Bryskett's attempt to follow Giraldi closely.

1. Il fine in tutte le cose, che occorrono nel mondo, è il primo considerato da coloro, che fare le deono, quantunque poscia egli sia l'vltimo, che si esseguisca. 2. Et come egli hà nome di effetto, poi che à quel termine è condotto, al quale di condurlo haúea conceputo nell' animo, chi a fare, ò ad operare si era dato, così è egli cagione, che moue tutte le altre à produrlo in effeto. 3. Et, però nel molere trattare del fine, che voi chiesto me hauete, & che hora è il primo, che à ragionar ci moue, bisogna ricorrere à principii, che possono essere cagione di condurte l'huomo à questo fine. 4. Et me sarebbe mestiero, prima che più oltre io procedesi, parlare della generatione de gli huomini. Imperoche, come le sementi producono frutti loro conue-neuoli, & proprii, cosi auiene souente anco ne gli huomini, Perche quali sono il padre, & la madre, tali sono, per lo più, i figliuoli, /5. & mi bisognerebbe, oltre a questo, mostrare, che è da hauere da chi uuole essere lodeuolmente padre spetial cura non solo à lui, (il quale

211

uoglio io presupporre di tutto quello ornato, che à gentil animo, et à bel corpo appertiene), Ma alla madre, /6. Perche, anchora, ch'ella habbia il seme dal padre, & che sia opinione di alcuni, che il seme della madre non concorra alla generatione (opinione contraria ad Hippocrate, & al suo diuino interprete, & parimente è Platone) pigliano non. dimeno (quando anco ciò uere fosse) i conceputi fanciulli il nutrimento nel uentre della Madre, infino al tempo del parto, Onde auiene spesse uolte, che si ueggono ne figlouoli i vitii delle madri. 7. Et, che per ciò dee multo benè auertine ciasouno, che prendere uuol moglie, di non la pigliare ignobile, nè vitiosa, nè lasciua, nè defore nè manca, Non sciancata, non balbetante, ò uero, che habbia altri simili defetti, Ma nobile, virtuosa, pudica, di aspetto grato, & di bella, grande, & compita statura di corpo, & di grata, & spedita fauella, accioche da padre, & da madre nobili, uirtuosi, modesti, & di compito corpo, & di diceuole proportione, naschino anco figliuoli di tali qualità ornati. 8. Et quindi è auenuto, che si dice in prouerbio, quali tu uuoi i figliuoli, tal prenditi la moglie, /9. Et cio fu cagione, ch'hauendo Archidamo, Re de Lacedomonii, presaper moglie una donna picciola, egli fù condannato da suoi cittadini, perche dueano, ch'egli hauea presa una moglie, che loro parturirebbe no Re, ma huomiccuoli, /10. Parendo loro, che gran parte della maestà regale fosse nella forma del corpo, ne senze cagio, /11. Perche si ritroua scritto, che una bella apparenza d'huomo, è la prima cessa degna d'impero.

1. The end in all things that men do in this world, is the first that is considered, though afterwards it be the last to be put in execution. 2. And as, when it is brought to perfection, it beareth the name of effect, so is it the cause that moveth all other to bring it to effect. 3. And therefore to treat of that end, which is now the motion inducing us to discourse hereupon, we must come to the first principles which may be the causes to bring a man to this end. 4. In which respect it were needful for me first to speake of the generation of man, since as all seeds bring forth their fruit like to themselves; so falleth it out for the most part in men: for such as are the father and the mother, such are most commonly the children. 5. I should likewise declare how he that wil be a commendable father, ought to have a special care, not of himselfe onely (for him we wil suppose to be a man endewed with all the ornaments required for a wel composed body and mind) but of the mother also. 6. For albeit she receive the seed of generation from the man; yet howsoever it be, the children when they be once conceived, take their nourishment from the mother, and in her wombe, until the time of their birth: whereby we see the children very often to retaine the vices of the mother. 7. Also that in regard hereof, every

212

man that intendeth to take a wife, ought to be very carefull in the choice of her; so that she may not be base of parentage, vitious, wanton, deformed, lame, or otherwise imperfect or defective: but well borne, vertuous, chaste, of tall and comely of shape and proportion, like children may betweene them be brought forth. 8. For from wise men hath proceeded that warning to men, that such wives they should chuse as they wished to have their children. 9. And *Arcidamus* King of *Sparta*, was condemned by his citizens to pay a fine, for having taken to wife a woman of very low stature; because (they said) she is like to bring us forth no kings, but dandiprats. 10. Thereby declaring how they accounted no small part of the majestie of a king, to consist in the comely presence and stature of his body; and not without cause. 11. For it is written, that the goodly shew and appearance of a man, is the first thing worthy soveraigntie.

A SELECT BIBLIOGRAPHY OF LODOWICK BRYSKETT

Primary texts

STC 3958. *A discourse of civill life; containing the ethike part of morall philosophie.* 4°. (R. Field?) f. E. Blount, 1606. Ent. to E. Blount, 10 mr. L. O. NY.

STC 3959. (Anr issue with imprint) f. W. Aspley, 1606. L. H. HD.

Primary sources

Piccolomini, Alessandro; Abp. (1508–1578). *Della Instituzione morale.* libri XII. Venetia, 1560.

Giraldi Cintio, Giovanni Battista (1504–1573). *De gli hecatommithi.* Monte Regale, Lionardo Tarrentino, 1565. 2 vols. (" Tre dialoghi della vita civile " are in Vol. II, 1–224.)

Guazzo, Stefano. *La Civil Conversazione.* Brescia, 1574.

Secondary works

The Complete Works of Spenser in Verse and Prose, ed. A. B. Grosart and others. 9 vols. London, 1882–84. Vol. I contains an appendix summary of Bryskett's *Discourse,* 500–508.

A Dictionary of National Biography, ed. Sir Leslie Stephen and Sir Sidney Lee. 63 vols. London, 1885–1900. Article on " Bryskett, Lodowick or Lewis " (fl. 1571–1611) signed by " S. L."

Mustard, W. P. " Lodowick Bryskett and Bernardo Tasso," *American Journal of Philology,* XXXV (1914), 192–199.

Erskine, John. " The Virtue of Friendship in the *Faerie Queene,*" *PMLA,* XXX (New Series, XXIII, 1915), 831–850.

Crane, Thomas Frederick. *Italian Social Customs of the Sixteenth Century and Their Influence on the Literatures of Europe* (Cornell Studies in English, Vol. V). New Haven, 1920.

Plomer, Henry R., and Tom Peete Cross. *The Life and Correspondence of Lodowick Bryskett* (Modern Philology Monographs of the University of Chicago). Chicago, Illinois, 1927.

Jenkins, Raymond. " Spenser and the Clerkship in Munster," *PMLA,* XLVII (1932), 109–121.

Jones, Deborah. " Lodowick Bryskett and His Family " in *Thomas Lodge and Other Elizabethans,* ed. Charles J. Sisson. Cambridge, Mass., 1933, 243–362; rptd. New York, 1966.

Judson, Alexander C. *The Life of Edmund Spenser.* Baltimore, 1945. (Published with the *Variorum Spenser.*)

Draper, J. W. " Shakespeare and the *Conversazione,*" *Italica,* XXIII (1946), 7–17.

Judson, Alexander C. "Spenser and the Munster Officials," *Studies in Philology*, XLIV (1947), 157–173.

The Works of Edmund Spenser: A Variorum Edition, ed. Edwin Greenlaw and others. Baltimore, 1949. Vol. IX: *Spenser's Prose Works*, ed. Rudolf Gottfried, contains Spenser's *A View of the Present State of Ireland*.

Lievsay, John. *Stefano Guazzo and the English Renaissance (1575–1675)*. Chapel Hill, 1961.

Quinn, David Beers. *The Elizabethans and the Irish*. Ithaca, 1966.